Women and Distance Education

By focusing on women in distance education, Christine von Prümmer examines the often neglected area of gender issues throughout the distance education world. A wide variety of evidence from different countries supports the conclusion that open and distance learning has the potential to provide equal opportunities in higher and continuing education and that these are often being missed.

Women and Distance Education:

- is concerned with how women manage further education courses without giving up careers or family commitments;
- provides a wealth of empirical data and material, much of which is the author's own work;
- examines the differences in the learning styles and communication patterns of women and men;
- brings a broad international perspective to the research data and analysis;
- covers issues of minority women, considering class and gender;
- considers how the www and the electronic campus impacts equality in distance learning.

The author believes that it is up to distance education policy-makers to provide a framework for women students that will limit the risks and maximise the opportunities. This book, which draws on fascinating case study material, will offer vital information for these policy-makers and will be relevant for the whole distance education community.

Christine von Prümmer is a Senior Researcher at the German FernUniversität, a Distance Teaching University. She has experience of evaluating distance education systems and has carried out cross-national comparative research on the situation of women and men in distance education.

Routledge Studies in Distance Education
General editors: Desmond Keegan and Alan Tait

Distance Education
Theoretical Principles of Distance Education
Edited by Desmond Keegan

Distance Education: New Perspectives
Edited by Keith Harry, Magnus John and Desmond Keegan

Collaboration in Distance Education
Edited by Louise Moran and Ian Mugridge

Otto Peters on Distance Education
Edited by Desmond Keegan

Theory and Practice in Distance Education
Börje Holmberg

Technology, Open Learning and Distance Education
A.W. (Tony) Bates

Open and Distance Learning Today
Edited by Fred Lockwood

Foundations of Distance Education, 3rd edition
Desmond Keegan

Opening Education
Terry Evans and Daryl Nation

Staff Development in Open and Flexible Learning
Edited by Colin Latchem and Fred Lockwood

Globalising Education: Trends and Applications
Robin Mason

Women and Distance Education

Challenges and opportunities

Christine von Prümmer

London and New York

First published 2000
by RoutledgeFalmer
11 New Fetter Lane, London EC4P 4EE

Simultaneously published in the USA and Canada
by RoutledgeFalmer
29 West 35th Street, New York, NY 10001

RoutledgeFalmer is an imprint of the Taylor & Francis Group

Typeset in 10/12pt Times by Graphicraft Limited, Hong Kong
Printed and bound in Great Britain by TJ International Ltd,
Padstow, Cornwall

British Library Cataloguing in Publication Data
A catalogue record for this book is available
from the British Library

Library of Congress Cataloging in Publication Data
Prümmer, Christine von, 1946–
    Women and distance education: challenges and
opportunities / Christine von Prümmer.
        p. cm. — (Routledge studies in distance education)
    Includes bibliographical references and index.
    1. Women—Education (Higher)—Germany—Case studies.
    2. Distance education—Germany—Case studies.
    3. Fernuniversitèt-Gesamthochschule-Hagen. I. Title.
    II. Series.

LC2106 .P78 2000
378.1'75—dc21
                                              00-020211

ISBN 0-415-23258-9

Contents

Illustrations

Figures

Tables

Foreword

It is both a pleasure and a real privilege to be invited to write the foreword to *Women and Distance Education* by Christine von Prümmer. Dr von Prümmer's work in evaluation and institutional research at the FeU in Hagen, Germany, over more than twenty years, has made a central contribution to the understanding of gender and education, and of women in distance education (DE) more specifically. Elements of the work have been presented at a number of conferences and in journal articles, and are here set out in full for the first time. Why is it so important?

First of all, this work is important in the ways in which it addresses a core concept in open and distance learning, that is openness itself. Dr von Prümmer has been amongst the first to ask, within the discipline of educational research, about the openness of distance learning, with its home-based and part-time learning opportunities. She addresses the rhetoric of distance learning, and compels her readers to ask, with her, open for whom exactly? The questions she directs to her own institution concerning the low number of women students raise issues which cannot be ignored about the gendered nature of curriculum and of teaching and learning infrastructures. Where institutions are gender-blind, exclusion is accompanied by its legitimation. What after all can be the problem? Dr von Prümmer's work answers that question, and answers it with meticulous research and not with rhetoric or prejudice.

The work that is done here for women has great importance for all humanity. It establishes the heterogeneity of learners, and opens the path for others to examine ethnicity, social class, the social geography of rural and urban learners, the context of students with special needs: the necessity, in other words, of considering who learners are if we are to aim conscientiously to meet their needs. Thus the feminism which drives this work supports all the minorities who make up the majority of our learners, and cannot be dismissed or diminished as a separatist or divisive paradigm.

This is not to say, however, that research of this kind has not met such opposition. It has been sustained through a network of women researchers and practitioners, who for a significant period met as the Womens'

International Network (WIN) within the ICDE. I am also pleased to say that the Cambridge International Conference on Open and Distance Learning has also on a number of occasions provided a venue for such networking and support.

In conclusion, I would first like to commend this book to readers primarily for what it tells them: and that means reading it! Second, it stands as an example of the importance of researching difficult issues, and refusing to accept the ideology that open and distance learning has elaborated for itself over the last twenty years, and which powerful institutions defend so energetically. This means reflecting on the issues of education and equity which inspire this book, which were the founding values of modern open and distance learning, and on that basis planning further work.

Alan Tait
School of Education
Open University, UK

Preface

When I started work at the West German FernUniversität (FeU) over twenty
years ago I was enthusiastic about this 'new' way of providing opportunities
for higher education to people who had no other way to obtain a university
degree or to pursue their personal development through individual courses
of study. I was thinking of people with disabilities unable to go to regular
universities, of people abroad, of people living in areas which were far from
university towns, and of people who were prevented by their life circumstances from attending classes. The catch-phrase was 'second chance'
education for disadvantaged groups, and I was excited about the chance
of contributing to this cause through my work as the course evaluator
who was to be directly involved in improving the quality of the teaching
material.

The FernUniversität was founded in 1974 and teaching started in October
1975. In 1978 it was still a new institution bent on proving its academic
standing as one of Germany's universities and on providing tertiary education which was second-chance without the stigma of being second-best. The
focus was on *Studieren neben dem Beruf*, i.e. on distance students who were
studying while working in a job, and all efforts were directed toward creating a distance teaching system which would provide the best possible conditions for people who were part-time students while being in full-time
employment. The vast majority – over 80% – of the students enrolled in
courses at the FeU in the first years were men, many of whom wanted to
obtain a university degree in order to further their career prospects, or at
least secure their jobs or occupational positions.

At the time, there was little concern with the under-representation of
women which was seen as a result of the limited range of subjects available
for study. Apart from its Department of Education and Social Sciences, the
FeU offered degrees in subject areas which were traditionally male oriented:
computer science, mathematics, electrical engineering, and economics, all
with strong mathematical elements. The latter included both economics and
business studies, and it attracted more than half of the total student intake
each academic year. The Department of Education and Social Sciences,

which offered a degree programme leading to the teaching certificate for secondary-school teachers and an M.A. in the major subject of education, was the only department with a sizeable proportion of women students, a fact which seemed to confirm the assumption that it was 'natural' that less than one-fifth of FeU students were women.

It was not until 1980 that gender issues were raised at the FeU, yet even then nobody questioned the underlying premise that distance education with its flexible hours and absence of attendance requirements was exceptionally well suited for housebound mothers of young children. This seemed to be confirmed by the fact that other distance education institutions had a much higher percentage of women students, presumably because of the kinds of degree programmes they offered. This was certainly true at the Canadian Athabasca University where I spent a few months in 1983, and where two-thirds of the students were women, a totally different situation from that of our own institution.

While I was in Canada, I had the opportunity of studying certain aspects of the situation of women distance students, and I heard about the new Women's International Network (WIN) which was formed during the 1982 world conference in Vancouver. My Canadian colleagues also took me to see both the theatre and the film version of *Educating Rita*, the story of an Open University student which provided me with the first inkling of other factors which might influence the opportunities for women to become distance students in the first place, and to then complete a degree course successfully.

Back in Germany I decided to find out more about the real reasons behind the under-representation of women. The first step was a statistical analysis of the enrolment data of FeU students in order to determine the validity of the 'male bias in degree programmes' argument. As it turned out, there were fewer women in each of the subject areas at the FeU than in comparable subjects at other German universities. It became clear that other factors must be at work hampering women's access to the degree programmes offered in the distance teaching mode. In order to investigate these factors I designed a research project looking into the situation of women and men studying at a distance, with special emphasis on the study motivation and learning environment of women and men and on possible gender differences concerning the compatibility of distance studies with occupational and family responsibilities.

It was extremely fortunate that in Gill Kirkup of the Open University in Britain (OU UK) I met a colleague interested in doing a parallel study of OU UK students and that the joint data analysis yielded such rich information. In comparing the findings from the two surveys we could identify processes and gender patterns which might have been difficult to discover by looking at each set of respondents separately. As far as I know, our research was the first internationally comparative project which gathered empirical evidence on women and men in two distance teaching universities, allowing for cross-cultural and cross-institutional analyses. Apart from being a wonderful working relationship, our collaboration cannot be valued too highly with regard to the insights it provided, and continues to provide, about women in distance education.

There was one set of questions in the German survey which was not replicated in the British one, namely questions on the parental and family background of the mature students studying at a distance. The idea of looking at 'distance education as a social chance for women' had first been voiced by Helga Körnig, a government official involved in setting up the FeU, in her contribution to the International Council for Distance Education (ICDE) conference in Melbourne in 1985. When it became clear that this issue could not be pursued in the course of institutional research at the FernUniversität due to a lack of time and pressing other research topics, I decided to use the data as the basis for a doctoral dissertation on the opportunities the FeU offers women from a working-class background who did not have the chance to complete secondary school and enter a university in the usual way. This analysis, very briefly, showed that women with working-class parents have been educationally disadvantaged and use their distance education as a chance to get an academic degree, thus achieving upward occupational and social mobility through better qualifications. At the same time they minimise the existential risk by retaining their current job which, although possibly boring or unsatisfactory, provides them with a secure income while they prepare for a new career or for promotion.

The present book draws on the joint research and interpretation of the work I undertook with Gill Kirkup in England, and with my colleague Ute Rossié at the FeU, and also on the work I did for my dissertation. In addition, I have included findings from more recent research on current issues, such as computer access and communication in distance education. I do not attempt to present a comprehensive picture of distance education or a tour through the relevant literature. Rather, I concentrate on facets of distance education which affect women, and I am confident that a knowledge of the factors at work will be helpful in overcoming obstacles which women encounter in their distance studies.

I am no longer as naïve as I was twenty years ago concerning the automatic benefits of DE for women, but I am still excited about the possibilities it can offer to women who take this chance to achieve formal qualifications or personal development through distance education. As a sociologist and a feminist I am concerned with helping to make the distance education system more 'women-friendly' and their chances of success more realistic. As a woman working in a distance teaching university (DTU) I feel connected to the women who study and work in open and distance learning (ODL) institutions and who join forces, for instance in WIN, to take the risk of making these institutions better places to be.

Abbreviations

AK Wiss *Arbeitskreis Wissenschaftlerinnen von NRW*, a network of feminist academics in the state/province of NRW*.

AKAD *Akademikergesellschaft für Erwachsenenfortbildung*, Society for Continuing and Adult Education. A private distance education institution teaching up to university level certificates and continuing education.

AMTEC Association for Media and Technology in Education in Canada.

AU Athabasca University, a distance teaching university in Athabasca (until 1984 located in Edmonton), Alberta, Canada.

BA Bachelor of Arts

BMBF *Bundesministerium für Bildung und Forschung*, formerly the *Bundesministerium für Bildung, Wissenschaft, Forschung und Technologie*, the Federal Ministry of Education, Science and Technology (formerly BMBW).

BMBW *Bundesministerium für Bildung und Wissenschaft*, the Federal Ministry of Education and Science (later bmbf*).

btx Videotex, early form of electronic communication, used for a period at the FeU* for administering computer-marked assignments.

CNNML Canadian Network for New Media Learning.

DE Distance education.

DGB *Deutscher Gewerkschaftsbund*.

DIFF *Deutsches Institut für Fernstudienforschung*, The German Institute for Research into DE*.

DTU Distance teaching university.

FeU *FernUniversität–Gesamthochschule in Hagen*, Germany, the only university-level DE* provider in Germany (until unification, in West Germany; East Germany, by contrast, had a decentralised system of dual-mode universities teaching both on-campus and extra-mural students); the FeU is a state university in NRW*.

HRK	*Hochschulrektorenkonferenz*: Standing Conference of Vice Chancellors/Presidents of Universities in Germany.
ICDE	International Council for Distance Education.
ICTs	Information and communication technologies.
ISDN	Integrated Services Digital Network
LVU	*Lernraum Virtuelle Universität*: Virtual University Learning Environment.
M.A.	*Magister Artium*: Master of Arts, degree conferred after a minimum of nine semesters of academic study at a German university.
NRW	*Nordrhein-Westfalen* (North-Rhine Westphalia), as far as population size goes the largest of the states/provinces of the German Federal Republic and traditionally a working-class area. Includes the *Ruhrgebiet*, the heavily industrialised coal and steel belt.
ODL	Open and distance learning.
OU UK	The Open University at Milton Keynes, in the UK.
PC	Personal computer.
SPD	Social Democratic Party of Germany.
SPSS	Statistical Package for the Social Sciences (software product).
UNED	*Universidad Nacional de Educacion a Distancia* in Madrid, Spain.
WIN	Women's International Network, an association of women distance educators and researchers.
www	World-wide web.
ZFE	*Zentrum für Fernstudienentwicklung*: Centre for the Development of Distance Education at the FeU*.
ZIFF	*Zentrales Institut für Fernstudienforschung*: Central Institute for Research in Distance Education at the FeU*.
Ø	Arithmetic mean.
Δ	Difference between two percentage points, used in group comparisons.

Note: * These terms are explained elsewhere in the list of abbreviations and glossary.

Glossary of German terms

Please note that throughout the book all translations from the German, including quotes from German language publications and verbatim quotes from questionnaires, are my own.

Abitur University entrance qualification gained after 13 (in some East German *Länder*, 12) years of schooling upon completion of the Gymnasium; roughly comparable to A-levels (UK) or high school Diploma (USA) plus university or college admission processes (College Board Entrance Examinations, etc.).

The *Abitur* traditionally entitles students to enter the university of their choice. Due to large and ever-increasing numbers of prospective students, a national agency was established to channel applicants for admission to popular subjects into universities according to their grades. Applicants for Medical School are also required to take a national test to determine their suitability for this field.

Bundesland see *Land**.

Diplom Tertiary degree after seven semesters of study at a *Fachhochschule* or a *Gesamthochschule** (*Diplom I*), or after nine semesters of academic study at a German university, equivalent to the M.A.* degree (*Diplom II*).

Fachhochschule An institution of tertiary education below university level.

Gesamthochschule Comprehensive university, a university offering ways of entering degree programmes without the traditional formal university entrance qualifications.

Gymnasium Secondary school (high school, grammar school).

Land (plural: *Länder*)	State or province in the German Federal Republic. Educational policy is under the jurisdiction of the individual *Länder* which agree on a general framework of rules and regulations concerning the organisation and content of the different levels of schooling and training programmes and on the acceptance of the formal qualification obtained in any given *Land*.
Mittlere Reife	Qualification obtained after ten years of formal education, either in a *Realschule** (middle school), or in a *Gymnasium**; comparable to O-levels (UK).
Realschule	Middle school.
Ruhrgebiet	Area along the River Ruhr, flowing east to west into the River Rhine north of Cologne; heavily industrialised due to rich coal and iron deposits and mines and consequent steel production which used to be the main-stay of German industry; densely populated.
Studieren neben dem Beruf	Studying as a second job. This refers to mature students who continue to work in a full-time or part-time job and study in their free time.
Volksschule	Literally, People's School; originally grades 1–8, later *Grundschule* (grades 1–4) and *Hauptschule* (grades 5–10).

Note: * These terms are explained elsewhere in the list of abbreviations and glossary.

Chapter 1

Introduction

Since the earliest days of open and distance universities, women have been seen as forming one of their primary constituencies. Women have traditionally been under-represented in face-to-face higher education; their educational careers and aspirations are subject to interruption by the demands of childcare, and they often spend considerable amounts of time in the home, which is targeted as the natural place for distance study. Women should therefore feature prominently in distance education and their needs should be of primary concern to the designers of distance education courses. But is this really the case? What has been the actual experience of women undertaking distance education, and which factors are likely to influence their opportunities, choices and educational outcomes?

Has distance education been able to provide an avenue of social mobility for women? How do women's learning styles fit in with the way course materials are designed? What of assumptions about access to and control over the new information and communication technologies, which are increasingly becoming vital means of learning? And what of the provision of supplemental face-to-face tuition in learning support centres?

Based on empirical and comparative research, this book provides insights into the situation of women in distance education and on the opportunities as well as the risks involved in taking the chance of pursuing this educational path. It also addresses the issue of gender in distance education more generally and from a theoretical perspective, placing it into a feminist and sociological context. A wide variety of evidence from different countries supports the conclusion that distance education, while involving a degree of risk – to the stability of families and relationships and to personal esteem, etc. – nevertheless offers opportunities to women which, on balance, are worth taking. It is up to distance education policy-makers to provide a framework for women students which will limit the risks and maximise the opportunities.

Issues and focus: gender and distance education

On the face of it, distance education appears *per se* a 'woman-friendly' form of acquiring education and formal qualifications. There are two character-istics which are generally seen to render this mode of learning especially suitable for women, by making distance education compatible with other spheres of life: first, there is little or no attendance requirement; second, at the same time, there is a high degree of flexibility in learning schedules and time management. These characteristics have three distinct and undisputed advantages for the distance student:

1   Since the main part, if not the whole, of a distance teaching curriculum is designed for independent study and does not require classroom attend-ance, there is no need for students to live on a university campus. Study-ing at a distance can thus be reconciled with occupational and personal commitments and with living at home with a partner or family.
2   Since the learning material is sent to the student's home or workplace, and since tuition is provided mainly through the use of media (letters, telephone calls, electronic communication) distance students do not have to live in the same town – or even country – in which their school or university is located. While studying at conventional institutions often involves a move to the university town, studying at a distance enables students to maintain their place of residence, as well as family and work commitments.
3   Although distance teaching systems vary in the degree of flexibility, all allow students to set their own timetables for actual studying. For instance, there may be prescribed times for completing and handing in assignments, but students are free to choose when, in a given time-span, they work through the course, and whether they work continuously or with interruptions. Equally, although tutors and other teachers may set times at which they are available for consultation in person or on the phone, answering machines, fax services, and electronic mail (e-mail) provide round the clock access to the support services students may need.

It is easy to see why these factors are assumed to favour women in particu-lar. With respect to changing their geographic location in order to further their own educational or career goals, women have traditionally been less mobile than men. Images of the housebound mother of small children and of the dependent wife of a working husband are often called up in this context. Conversely, women might have to move away from a location near their school or university because their partner relocates to a different part of the country or is posted abroad. Women are also less able than men to leave a family home for any length of time in order to commute to school or univer-sity on a daily or weekly basis.

In being able to set their own timetables for their distance studies, women who are housewives and mothers of small children are seen as having no prescribed work schedule, and consequently they are assumed to be able to fit their course studies quite easily into a daily routine of housework and childcare. Distance education, therefore, is often considered to be especially suited to mature women who want to pursue an education while raising a family, or continuing to work in a lower level job, or both. The question then arises why women students are under-represented in a distance teaching institution, such as the German FernUniversität (FeU), and why they are less likely than men to complete their course of studies.

These questions formed a starting point for the institution to focus research into identifying factors making studying more difficult for women, contributing to their lower levels of female enrolment, and to drop-out rates which are often higher than those of their fellow male students. The goal of this research has also been to gain some insight into measures which could make the distance teaching university (DTU) a more attractive and conducive learning environment for women. Although the research presented in this book has been mainly concerned with the West German FeU, there are common patterns with the situation of women elsewhere. Sharing some of the findings and suggestions drawn from this research can therefore contribute to a better understanding of the situation of women in distance education.

In looking at distance students, we are confronted with two spheres of life which influence their learning environment: first, the teaching system which is determined by the institutional set-up and teaching modes preferred by the particular distance teaching institution; and second, the student's life situation which is affected by factors such as paid and unpaid work, family commitments, hobbies, age and health, and other factors of the student's private life.

Both of these spheres create opportunities as well as difficulties for the distance student, and these may be compounded or offset where they overlap. In this book I look at the opportunities and problems each of these spheres presents for women and for ways in which either the institution or the student herself can optimise the former and minimise the latter.

The FernUniversität as case study and illustration

As mentioned before, the German FeU was founded as a DTU in December 1974 and teaching started in October 1975. In 1978, when I started working there, the FeU was still a new institution bent on proving its academic standing and on providing tertiary education which was second-chance without the stigma of being second-best. All efforts were directed toward creating a distance teaching system which would provide the best possible conditions

for people who were part-time students while being in full-time employment. The vast majority – over 80% – of these students were men, many of
whom wanted to obtain a university degree in order to further their career
prospects or at least secure their jobs or occupational positions.

At the time, there was little concern with the under-representation of
women which was seen as a result of the limited range of subjects available for study. Apart from the Department of Education and Social Sciences, the FeU offered degrees in subject areas which were traditionally
male oriented: computer science, mathematics, electrical engineering, and
economics with a strong mathematical orientation. It was not until 1980
that gender issues were raised at the FeU, when FeU women staff got
together to describe and analyse the situation of women distance students
in an effort to find ways to improve enrolment and completion rates. The
beginning of this concern with the inadequate representation of women in
the FeU is marked by two publications. One was the December 1980 issue
of the FeU journal *mentor* which was completely devoted to the theme of
women in distance education. The second was a provocative – if rhetorical
– question asked in the FeU journal *con-tacte*: 'Is distance education
"hostile" to women?' (Bröhl 1981). Even though this shows concern with
the extremely low level of participation of women (over three-quarters of
FeU students were male at the time) the underlying premise was not questioned: namely, that distance education, by its very nature, is exceptionally
well suited to women who are, for example, housebound mothers of young
children. It was, however, an accepted fact that the attraction of the distance education mode for women was offset by the absence of suitable
degree programmes.

By then West Germany experienced the first wave of cut-backs in education and it began to seem highly unlikely that the FeU would expand its
range of departments and degree programmes as originally planned. Given
the assumptions about the reasons for their under-representation, the only
options open for increasing the participation of women were schemes to
attract more women into non-traditional subject areas, and measures to help
women students combine their studies with their duties as full-time mothers
and homemakers, for instance by providing child-minding facilities during
study group meetings.

My observations on distance teaching institutions are mainly derived from
the west German FeU where I have worked as a researcher and evaluator
for over twenty years, drawing on various papers and publications on the
FeU and on women-friendly perspectives in distance education (e.g. von
Prümmer 1993a, 1994, 1997a). It is usual in 'open universities' in industrialised western countries that women constitute upwards of 40% of the student
population, or even the majority of students as is the case at Athabasca
University in Canada. By contrast, the FeU has a predominantly male student
population, with the proportion of women ranging from as low as 17% in

the beginning to approximately 37% today. I feel that it is exactly in this under-representation of women that clues might be found more easily to what it is that constitutes a more women-friendly distance teaching system.

The institutional context

The name *'Fern'*Universität translates as *distance* university. The rationale in founding it was to provide access to higher education for people who wanted to gain a university degree late in life, which would be equal to the qualifications they would have obtained by studying at a conventional university. In Germany, this traditionally means a Master of Arts (M.A.) degree, since the division into undergraduate and postgraduate studies did not exist until very recently. Much emphasis was therefore placed on the academic standards which students had to meet, and admission to a degree programme was only granted to applicants who fulfilled the regular entrance requirements for university studies in West Germany. The FeU is thus not an 'open' university, in the sense of having degree programmes open to any-one wishing to enter them, or in the sense that entry to a course of studies may be negotiable, based on the student's previous work and experience. Nevertheless, the FernUniversität is open in other respects:

- although the FeU is a state university funded by the West German state (province) of North-Rhine Westphalia (NRW), it admits students from out of state and foreign students to the extent that only one-third of the student population (34% in the academic year 1997/98) are residents of NRW;
- students with or without formal qualifications are admitted to individual courses which they can study for their own personal development or for job-related reasons. Short of thesis supervision and admission to the final examination, these students are provided with the full tuition that degree students in this course would receive, including study centre pro-vision where available, and correction and assessment of assignments and examinations;
- students who possess the formal entrance requirements are free to enrol in any degree programme which is offered at the FeU and may be given credit for work done in other degree programmes or at other universities;
- in accordance with other such universities, the FeU charges no tuition fees, although students pay a nominal fee for receiving the course material;
- the course material, which consists mainly of written manuscripts sup-plemented in some instances by audio and videotapes and instructional computer disks, is self-instructional and designed not to require face-to-face tuition; and

- there are no compulsory tutorials or summer schools, and attendance requirements such as laboratory sessions, seminars, and examinations are kept to a minimum.

These factors are generally held to make studying at the FeU attractive to people in full-time employment, more often men than women, but also attractive to people, nearly always women, who are housebound with small children and whose geographical mobility is determined by their partners' career requirements or other family commitments. Nevertheless men, who constitute the majority of the first target group, but are almost completely absent from the second target group, have always constituted the large majority of FeU students.

In looking at the institution we have found three kinds of institutional factor which affect the enrolment and continuance of women distance students and are the subject matter of institutional evaluation at the FeU and of comparative international research: first, the range of subjects and degree programmes; second, the teaching system and organisation; and third, the character of the institution.

The range of subjects and degree programmes

In the academic year 1998/99 the FeU offered degree programmes at M.A. level (the *Diplom*) in four major subject areas: economics (political economy and business studies); computer science; electrical engineering, and mathematics. The FeU also offers M.A. programmes in the Departments of Education and Social Sciences and of Humanities/Arts. Until the early 1990s, M.A. students had the choice of only two major subjects, namely education (since 1975/76) and the social sciences (since 1985/86). In the academic year 1992/93 the range of subjects was extended and M.A. programmes are now available in seven major subjects: education, history, modern German literature, philosophy, political economy, political science, social behavioural sciences, and sociology (see FeU 1999a).

In keeping with developments in German higher education, the FeU is in the process of introducing degree programmes at B.A. level which are meant to provide quicker routes to formal qualifications, as well as internationally recognised first degrees. It remains to be seen how well these new degree programmes will be accepted by students and prospective employers and what, if any, gender patterns will develop in students' preferences for the new shorter degrees. So far, when comparing the high enrolment rates of women in Anglo-Saxon DE systems to the low participation of women in the German FeU, the argument was often put forward that women hesitate to commit themselves for the much longer timespan of an M.A. level degree programme. The new B.A. level courses should therefore be more attractive for women and show higher enrolment rates than the parallel M.A. or *Diplom* courses.

The relatively limited range of degree programmes at the FeU and, at least until recently, their strong emphasis on traditionally 'male' subjects has often been quoted as the major reason for the low level of women's enrolment at the FeU. But research has shown that this is not a sufficient explanation and that other factors are at work also (see von Prümmer and Rossié 1987).

As far as students' choice of subject is concerned, economics/business studies is the most popular degree programme both for women and for men, and each year approximately half of the newly registered FeU students enrol in this subject area. Women are under-represented in all *Diplom* programmes and over-represented in the M.A. programmes. This does reflect a traditional choice of subject, and although there has been a slight tendency towards a higher proportion of women in technical and mathematical subjects, the lowest percentage of women is still found in electrical engineering and the highest percentage in education (von Prümmer and Rossié 1990a).

What pointers does this provide for women-friendly perspectives? If the FeU wanted to provide courses and degree programmes which are more attractive for women, it could:

- make mathematical and technical subjects more accessible and interesting for women, for instance by actively recruiting women and by providing special bridging courses or more intensive tuition. A pilot scheme at the FeU has shown, for instance, that more women can be recruited into atypical subjects if special tutorials and other face-to-face events are offered locally (FeU 1993);
- broaden its palette of major subjects to include more courses of interest and of use to potential women students, including the introduction of a women's studies course. At the FeU a successful step was taken in this direction with a number of courses on the theme of *Frauen im Recht* ('Women in the right – women in law'). These courses were based on a series of lectures and were very popular with women students, although no real (or degree) credit could be granted for the successful completion of the course material (Schultz 1989, 1992). Meanwhile the programme has been discontinued due to a decision by the FeU's Department of Law;
- in accepting the still traditional preference of women for social sciences and humanities (i.e. Arts subjects), channel more resources into such subjects. Today, the opposite development takes place with most of the cut-backs occurring in these so-called 'soft' subjects while resources are concentrated in the 'hard' technological subjects which are apt to draw funding from industry.

The distance teaching system and organisation

The teaching system of the FeU is designed for so-called independent study and relies on self-instructional course material. The concepts of 'independent' and 'autonomous' distance learners have been widely discussed in the literature, e.g. in a recent report by Otto Peters, *Learning and Teaching in Distance Education*, in which he summarises autonomy and autonomous learning (Peters 1998: 63–71, 108–24).

Ideally, FeU students are supposed to take their bi-weekly packages of course units and work their way through the written material and any supplementary literature or tapes; they send in the required number of assignments, and in due course register for end-of-term and final examinations. They do this according to a self-imposed schedule and they do not waste their own – or the institution's – time. They have made a conscious choice to study at a distance, and they want to have as little contact as possible with the university or with other students. They make no additional demands on institutional resources; they get their degrees with a minimum of time and fuss (and can preferably be given credit for previous studies elsewhere); and as 'turbo-students' they contribute to positive graduate statistics and to the measurable success of the institution. This success, in turn, has become one of the criteria which the government uses to decide on the distribution of funds to state universities.

In German terminology this ideal–typical distance student, *der Fernstudent*, is male. Parallel research carried out by Gill Kirkup at the British Open University (OU UK) and myself at the FeU shows that this type of student is indeed male rather than female and that the learning style required for such a teaching system is alien to many women. Our research has shown that women tend to prefer a learning style which has been termed 'social learning', and in this our results bear out feminist theories on the learning styles of women, especially mature students (see Gilligan 1982; Belenky *et al.* 1986; Kirkup and von Prümmer 1990, 1992). The emphasis placed by the FeU on the self-sufficient and isolated learner has the effect of creating a hostile environment for women distance students who are more interested than men in elements of social interaction, in contacts with tutors and other students, and in cooperation with other learners.

Thus women students in both the OU UK and the FeU made more use of study centres and the provision of support services than did the male students, and they went to more trouble to achieve what is termed 'connectedness' with other students. In both studies, women had to overcome higher hurdles in order to attend tutorials or study groups. For instance, they had to organise babysitters and transport, being generally responsible for childcare and being less likely to own a car or have ready access to one. Yet they had a higher attendance level than the men who rarely had these difficulties, and they placed a higher value on local support services and on interactive elements. Our research suggests that women-friendly perspectives in a teaching system require the provision of interactive elements which would allow students to meet and to learn together and to share their experiences both of studying at a distance and of the ways their personal and professional lives interact with their studies. In contrast to conventional universities, with their inbuilt opportunities for meeting other students and staff, distance teaching universities (DTUs) need to institute an active policy of providing facilities for social learning and for promoting connectedness among its students, such as frequent tutorials, (compulsory) summer schools, or telephone conferences as well as space and encouragement for voluntary study groups, and easy access to study centres, to tutors, and to other students.

They also require changes in the character of tutorials, study groups, summer schools and other forms of face-to-face interaction, in order to accommodate the learning styles of women and to avoid alienation. Specifically, there should be a less competitive, more cooperative climate, and less concentration on strictly course and exam-related 'useful' work. Rather, students should be allowed to introduce 'outside' factors, such as problems at work or at home, which influence their ability to concentrate on their studies, and allowances should be made for disjointed attendance due to other commitments.

There is a tendency to see the above-mentioned ideal–typical· male student as the norm and the 'atypical' woman as somewhat lacking in independence, self-sufficiency, and competence. It is easier – and much less costly! – to be concerned with questions of how to help women adapt to the system rather than with questions of how to adapt the system to the needs of women. In times of increasing fiscal constraints it seems unlikely that the institutions would want to invest in aspects of the system which are costly and staff-intensive and which might be considered extraneous to the distance teaching mode. In fact, in the last few years we have observed an opposite tendency. For instance, some distance educators are propagating the so-called 'electronic campus' where computer-mediated communication replaces face-to-face interaction and personal contact with tutors and other students. Questions of feasibility apart, there is little indication that the needs of women distance students are sufficiently taken into account when electronic networks are introduced, either for teaching or for support service purposes, often with the express purpose of cutting down costs.

Institutional characteristics relevant for gender equality

In this section I want to mention just a few of the additional institutional factors which have been found to make it more difficult for women to enrol at the FeU in the first place, and once enrolled, to complete their course of studies successfully. These factors concern staff composition and course content and presentation, including language.

One of the least women-friendly aspects of the FeU is the invisibility of women on the teaching staff:

- it took ten years for the first female professor to be appointed in 1985, and as recently as February 1999 only five of the 86 FeU professors were women, an overall percentage of less than 6%;
- the overall gender ratio among the academic staff still is less than two women in ten, and women are more likely to be in temporary and part-time posts than their male colleagues;
- all management and decision-making posts in the faculties and most in administration are held by men;
- the overwhelming majority of course units is written by men, and most contracts for external authors are given to male colleagues in other universities;
- many more men than women are appointed tutors or counsellors, especially in mathematical and technical subjects, but also in the social sciences.

For a woman studying at the FeU this almost always means:

- she must deal with a man whenever there are questions of the acceptance of her formal qualification or credit for previous studies;
- she must negotiate her course load and schedule with a man;
- she will be assessed and supervised by a man during her studies and in writing her M.A. or diploma thesis;
- she will be in the minority in any study group or tutorial since the tutor as well as her fellow students are likely to be men.

In discussions women students often mention these factors as offputting since they feel that the male staff and fellow male students are unsympathetic to, and consequently unhelpful with, their specific problems. As far as term papers and thesis subjects are concerned, women report feeling pressured by male lecturers not to choose topics, methods and theories which are considered 'feminist', and if they do, they cannot expect competent and sympathetic supervision and assessment. With respect to the academic staff, feedback from women FeU students in questionnaires and group interviews indicates that women-friendly perspectives also require the presence of women lecturers and an active equal opportunities programme in order to achieve this presence.

With respect to course content and presentation, the FeU is as male-dominated as its staff composition. The German language makes gender exclusion more visible than does the English language, and it takes much more effort to write text in a non-sexist fashion (see Pravda 1994, 1997). In spite of some recent signs of increasing awareness of the problem, use of the feminine gender is almost totally absent from official communications, be they course material or information for students. Contrary to the findings of feminist linguistic theory – and to the statements of many women students –

the decision-makers still claim that the exclusion of women from written or oral and visual materials (video films, for instance) is not sexist and has no negative effects on the participation of women students. Both in fact – nearly two-thirds of the FeU students are men – and in the (almost) exclusively male language it uses, the FeU demonstrates that the typical distance student – '*der* typische Fernstudent' – is male. '*Die* Fernstudent*in*' – the female distance student – must consider herself subsumed under the generic, i.e. male terminology. But many women feel that being subsumed also means being subordinated. A more sensitive use of the language would definitely be more women-friendly.

This is especially true when the course material is sexist in its content as well as its language, and unfortunately this seems to be the case in a number of courses. An example from an economics course which concerns the question of what happens to firms when the founder is too old to carry on and has no children who could take over the running of the family enterprise illustrates this. According to the text, this situation could arise in cases where the son chooses a different career or the daughter marries a man who lives in another city so that both the son and the son-in-law cannot take over as head of the family firm. The course author does not conceive of a situation in which the daughter might be inclined and qualified to take over the firm, or in which the son might wish to move to another town with his new partner.

Our research as well as everyday experience shows that many women have no problems with such course presentation. They have either become used to reinterpreting the language in a way which allows them to feel included, or they do not question traditional male and female roles. Increasingly, though, women students report being disturbed and distracted by their exclusion and by the male bias in the materials they are expected to work with.

The FeU so far lacks an explicit equal opportunities policy which would serve to reduce sexism and increase the visibility of women both on its academic staff and in its materials. Such policies have been institutionalised in other DTUs, for instance in the OU UK, and we feel that they do contribute to a better learning environment for women distance students.

Development of the student population

The FeU started its first academic year with a total enrolment of 1,304 students. As Figure 1.1 shows, the following years saw a rapid expansion in student numbers, which reached 56,000 in the academic year 1994/95.

The student population developed in two distinct stages, the first era of growth encompassing the years until 1981/82, the second encompassing the years from 1982/83 to the present. The first drop in overall enrolments was due to measures taken by the FeU to reduce student numbers by restricting

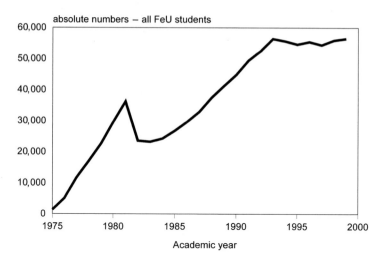

Figure 1.1 Development of FeU student numbers

access for one semester and by introducing fees for the study materials. These measures led to a total student population of 28,000 in 1982/83, a reduction of 9,000 compared to the previous year. After a short period of stagnating enrolment figures, from the mid-1980s student numbers started to increase again, at relatively stable yearly increase rates of 10%, followed by a slightly less dynamic period of growth after 1989/90. The absolute peak was reached in the years 1993/94 and 1994/95, when a total of 56,000 students were enrolled at the FeU. Since 1995/96 enrolments have been stagnating or been reduced in comparison to the high figures of 1994/95. While this parallels enrolment patterns in other universities, it remains to be seen whether this is a permanent trend or, as was the case in 1990/91, a short-lived phenomenon.

The renewed expansion after 1983/84 was accompanied by a shift within the student population. Before the introduction of fees for study material, a large proportion of FeU students were enrolled as visiting or guest students who registered only for selected courses rather than pursuing a full degree programme. New enrolments of distance students interested in continuing education declined by more than half from 1980 to 1983. This was a much more drastic reduction than the one in the degree programmes with a decline of one fifth of the previous enrolment figures. After 1983 enrolments in degree programmes expanded at a much higher rate, reaching twice the 1980 figures by 1989/90. At that time, enrolments by students not studying for a degree had only reached 80% of the figures at the beginning of the decade (von Prümmer and Rossié 1990a: 48–9).

As far as gender patterns are concerned, statistical analysis shows that the early increase in student numbers was directly associated with the rapidly rising number of male FeU students while the rate of growth was much slower for female students. At the same time, the shift from continuing education to degree studies was more pronounced among the women: by the end of the 1980s, the percentage of new students registering for a degree programme had doubled in the case of men and trebled in the case of women compared to the academic year 1980/81. This documents a deep and lasting change in matriculation patterns in the course of that decade.

Results gathered in surveys and in group discussions with FeU students, especially with women students, indicate that these changes are related to the introduction of fees for FeU study materials. Even though these fees may seem low in comparison to university fees charged in other countries, they place an additional burden on women who have to justify the expenditure of time and money if they wish to study at the expense of their families. In this situation, the very fact of registering as a degree student can be used to document a serious and legitimate purpose which is not usually associated with the status of non-degree students pursuing individual interests (von Prümmer and Rossié 1990b: 171–5).

Women students and staff

The under-representation of women students

One of the political goals associated with the foundation of the FernUniversität was the reform interest in providing access to tertiary education and to higher degrees for groups of people who were disadvantaged due to their social position or other factors. More or less explicitly, these 'other factors' referred to women, especially to housebound mothers of small children, whose family situation prevented their participation in all forms of education requiring attendance in fixed locations at given times (see Peters 1976: 21, 48, 152, 169). This assumption led to an expectation that women are more likely than men to avail themselves of the advantages of distance education and that their enrolment figures would be proportionately higher than those of men.

In fact, the first intake of FeU students counted 326 women and 978 men, i.e. exactly one quarter of the student population were women. This was much lower than had been expected considering the fact that at the time women constituted about one third of all students in West German universities. What is more, the proportion of women decreased even further during the first few years, reaching its lowest point of 17% in the second academic year 1976/77 (see Figure 1.2). The following years saw an increase in the number of women distance students, although not a linear one. In the current academic year 1999/2000 women constitute 37% of the student population of the FernUniversität, which is still nearly 10% less than at other universities (46.3%; BMBF 1998: 145).

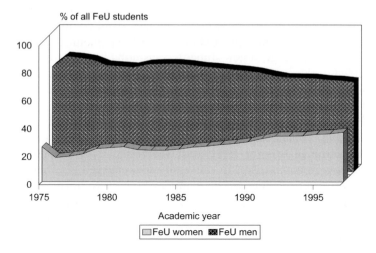

% of all FeU students

Figure 1.2 Development of FeU enrolments for men and women

In spite of the fact that the proportion of women registered as distance students has nearly doubled since the early years, it is still too low compared with the enrolments at conventional German universities and compared to other DTUs in western industrialised countries. Until the mid-1990s there has been a constant percentage of approximately four in ten women among newly registered university students in Germany. It is only since 1995 that enrolments of women started to rise, reaching 52% of all new students in Germany and 41% of new FeU students. Female enrolments in the OU UK, the oldest single-mode distance teaching university in western Europe, also developed along similar lines, reaching a ratio of just over half, after years of being just over 40%.

The observation of this persistent under-representation of women in a presumably women-friendly education system prompted the research focus on the situation of women distance students which we have pursued since 1983. Results of this evaluation research provide the empirical basis for the analysis of gender issues in distance education which are the substance of this book. One of the reasons quoted frequently as a possible explanation of the under-representation of women at the FeU is the limited course choice offered in the predominately 'male oriented' degree programmes.

While it is true that the subject areas covered by the six academic departments of the FeU traditionally attract more men than women, this is not a sufficient explanation for the over-representation of men. On the whole, the proportion of women enrolling in a given degree programme at the FeU corresponds to the enrolment patterns at other universities and shows the expected gender differences: it is highest in the courses offered by the Department of Education, Social Sciences and Humanities, lowest in courses offered by the Departments of Electrical Engineering, Mathematics, and Computer Science (see von Prümmer and Rossié 1990a). As early as 1985, a statistical analysis of the registration data of FeU students showed that in each and every one of the degree programmes the proportion of women was lower than in similar degree programmes at other west German universities.

Women staff

It often seems as if the issue of gender in distance education is only discussed in terms of students and the adequate representation of women in degree programmes and among graduates. But the environment that women distance students experience in their studies is also shaped by the visibility and importance of women working in the distance institution itself. The occasion of the twentieth anniversary of the founding of the FeU provided a welcome opportunity to bring the situation of women staff members as well as women students to the attention of decision-makers and the interested public (von Prümmer 1995b). As a starting point for this analysis we looked at the representation of women at different levels of the academic and non-academic hierarchies. Even the most basic statistical approach served to demonstrate that the FeU is not a specially women-friendly workplace and that both in the academic and non-academic sectors women are severely under-represented in the higher levels and in the secure positions, over-represented in the lower levels and in the relatively more insecure positions.

Considering the history of the FeU this may not come as a surprise: The founding committee, established by the NRW Government in 1974 for the purpose of working out the direction of the future DTU, did not count even a token woman among its 35 members (see Peters 1976: 46–7). The original governing body, including the *Gründungsrektor* (first Vice Chancellor or President), consisted exclusively of men.

Professors and academic staff

During the year preceding the opening of the FernUniversität, when the first course materials were developed and decisions were made about the character of the organisation and delivery of study materials and the support services, all members of the teaching staff in the academic departments were men. The only woman on the academic staff was a lecturer who as a single representative had no statistical significance. The first FeU catalogue of courses and personnel, published in the second academic year 1976/77, listed three academic departments with a total of 14 full professors, all men, and 52 academics in a variety of positions. The relation of women to men among the academic staff was 3:11 in the Department of Education, 2:17 in the Department of Economics, and 1:18 in the Department of Mathematics. In addition, one of three research assistants was female. Also, the FeU had four central units: the Library, the Computing Centre, the Centre for the Development of Distance Education (*ZFE*), and the Central Institute for Research in Distance Education (*ZIFF*). All four were then – and still are – headed by men while the non-academic staff such as clerks or secretaries were all women. The eleven academics working in the central units were all men.

In 1976/77 the FernUniversität had 24 study centres, 13 of which were functional, plus an office in Frankfurt/Main. Tutors/Counsellors ('mentors') were employed on a contract basis to support students in the four subject areas: economics (53), education (17), mathematics (11), and electrical engineering (4). Some of the mentors covered more than one study centre – in some cases academic staff from the Education and Social Sciences Department in Hagen doubled as mentors in a study centre. Less than 10% of the mentors were women.

In the twenty-five years since then the picture of an almost totally closed male academic community has undergone some changes. In 1985 the first woman professor, an ecological psychologist, was appointed, and in the academic year 1998/99 five of the 86 professors were female, one of them in the Department of Electrical Engineering, a rarity in Germany. This meant that the percentage of women among FeU professors overall was 5.8%, which is roughly comparable to other German universities. Currently the FeU boasts six women professors in three of the six academic departments: The Department of Education, Social Sciences and Humanities, the Department of Law, and the Department of Economics. The proportion of women in professorial posts is nil in the Departments of Computer Science, Mathematics and – again – in the Department of Electrical Engineering.

As far as the non-professorial academic staff are concerned, the situation has improved somewhat since the beginnings. Yet as recently as February 1999 women comprised just 18% of the 235 full-time academic staff members. The situation remains basically unchanged from the 1992 figures when only 32% of these women, but 42% of the men had permanent contracts, and 13% of the women compared to 21% of the men in this group had tenure as civil servants. Unfortunately, economic developments in Germany (and elsewhere) do not provide much hope for any improvements in the near future as there is a tendency to reduce permanent staff in favour of 'unprotected' contract work.

Non-academic staff

In contrast to the situation of academics, women constitute the majority of non-academic or support staff. As Figure 1.3 shows, the numerical dominance of 2:1 (407 women and 193 men) does not mean that women are equally represented in these positions or that they have equal opportunities for advancement.

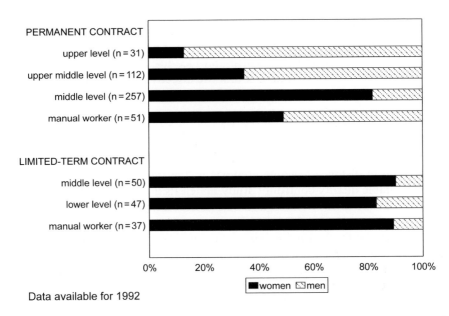

PERMANENT CONTRACT
upper level (n = 31)
upper middle level (n = 112)
middle level (n = 257)
manual worker (n = 51)

LIMITED-TERM CONTRACT
middle level (n = 50)
lower level (n = 47)
manual worker (n = 37)

0%   20%   40%   60%   80%   100%

women men

Data available for 1992

Figure 1.3 Proportion of women and men at different levels of the non-academic staff hierarchy at the FeU

In the first instance, nine out of ten men, but only seven out of ten women, have permanent contracts or tenure, which means that women are more likely than men to have short-term contracts and no job security. Figure 1.3 also shows two complimentary employment patterns which reinforce the disadvantages of women: more men obtain permanent or tenured positions and more men are hired or promoted into higher levels of the hierarchy and into better-paid posts.

Looking only at permanent or tenured positions we see that women hold the majority of positions on the middle or lower level of the hierarchy, while men hold the majority of the higher level and top positions. Only 1.4% of the women, but 16% of the men are on the highest levels of the non-academic staff hierarchy, followed by 14% women and 42% men on the next level below this. Three quarters of the women and one quarter of the men are at the middle and lowest levels. The percentage of men who are blue-collar workers or labourers is higher by six percentage points than that of women.

System evaluation: taking the measure of distance education

By definition, distance education systems have to use media to bridge the built-in distance between the institution and the students, especially if they are single-mode DTUs which do all their teaching in the distance mode.

These institutions have a need for an evaluation which provides insight into the quality of their teaching materials, staff and system and points out those areas requiring intervention and improvement. Dual-mode or mixed-mode institutions, which use both distance and face-to-face teaching modes, can get some of the necessary feedback in more direct ways from the on-campus students.

How to measure 'good' distance education: the role of evaluation

Evaluation in distance teaching contexts is 'the systematic and methodologically reliable quality control of study materials and study systems' (Peters 1981: 132). The institutionalisation of evaluation procedures is therefore an accepted part of the teaching and learning system of most DTUs. There is widespread agreement on the basic function of evaluation as expressed in the following statement by Mary Thorpe: 'Evaluation is the collection, analysis and interpretation of information about a programme of education and training, as part of a recognised process of judging its effectiveness, its efficiency and any other outcomes it may have' (1988, quoted in Schuemer 1991: 9).

Difficulties and dissension arise at each phase of the evaluation process with regard to the role of evaluation, the issues it should address, and the target groups which the results should serve. Policy issues are involved in decisons as to who collects, analyses and interprets what kinds of information, and who judges it by what standards or goals. These decisions are subject to historical changes due to internal developments within the institution as well as to social changes which put external pressures on the universities. This happened, for instance, when universities were asked to be more concerned with the quality of their teaching and to institutionalise procedures of quality assurance. DTUs reject the implicit accusation of a previous lack of concern with quality by pointing to their institutional research and evaluation. As Alan Tait (1995: 239) points out, there is a tendency for English-language publications to use the terms 'evaluation' and 'quality assurance' synonymously and to assert that DTUs have always carried out quality control of their study materials and systems: 'While quality assurance may be a recently applied term in the educational context, there is nothing new in open and distance learning (ODL) about systematic review and inspection of products and services to ensure their quality' (Tait 1993a: 241).

The experiences which distance teaching institutions world-wide have made with government-imposed quality assurance suggest that this is introduced more as an instrument of fiscal control than as a pedagogical tool and that politicians often see it as a way to camouflage or justify cut-backs in the educational sector:

We have a situation where Quality Assurance has been well established in Open and Distance learning at Higher Education level in both curriculum and presentation, but where the broader context of educational and social policy has created anxiety that the basic purposes of Higher Education, at least as they have been hitherto understood, are now at risk from government intrusion.

(Tait 1993a: 247)

In Germany, the politically instigated evaluation of universities, including the FeU is openly rooted in the wish to have more competition for resources and staff and to increase the effectiveness of university teaching:

Universities in Germany increasingly find themselves competing against each other for academics and for resources, external funding, and in some instances for students. Increasingly, there is even competition for the basic government funding . . . By assuring a quality standard in teaching the universities partially meet their responsibilities to society and to the students. They also discharge their duty for the efficient use of the financial resources with which they are provided in order to fulfil their tasks.

(HRK 1995: 1–2)

Evaluation is concerned with improving distance education, i.e. with helping institutions to provide 'good distance education'. This begs the question: what constitutes 'good' distance education?; followed by the question: how do we achieve good distance education?; and how do we measure the quality of our DE programmes? These issues, which cover a wide variety of subjects and theoretical and methodological approaches, have been addressed by distance educators and researchers as well as by policy-makers and administrators. As mentioned above, the term quality assurance, which originally covered industrial production, is often used as a synonym for evaluation in the educational context.

A number of conferences have revolved around these issues, for instance the 1993 Cambridge conference on the theme 'Quality Assurance in Open and Distance Learning: European and International Perspectives' (Tait 1993b); and the 1995 World Conference of the International Council for Distance Education 'ICDE' in Birmingham on the theme of One World Many Voices. Quality in Open and Distance Learning (Sewart 1995). The papers presented at such conferences display not only pedagogical concern but also question 'whether Quality Assurance can be accepted on its own terms, involving an essentially technical exercise for educators in its adoption and working-out, or whether far-reaching discussions about the nature of management, education and social change is necessarily involved' (Tait 1993b: 3).

As always, 'beauty is in the eye of the beholder', and what is seen as good or bad distance education depends on the standpoint of the teacher, learner, administrator, evaluator, or policy-maker and on the set of values, educational theories and personal preferences in which the individual or the institution grounds their work.

The evaluation of distance courses is a complex process. It involves decisions about:

- the criteria to be used in the evaluation;
- how to select them and define them;
- balancing the interests of the various parties – students, teachers, administration, funding agency, prospective employers;
- focusing the research questions in order to obtain a basis for suggesting decisions on course design, instructional material and the teaching system;
- the presentation of the data in ways which will ensure attention to it;
- the renewed evaluation of your own teaching.

It has long been accepted in the social sciences that there is no such thing as value-free, disinterested research, and this is true for evaluation which looks into the realisation of goals and intentions – be they manifest or latent, consistent or contradictory. But it is not necessarily involved in the definition of these goals and in the decisions on which goal to prioritise.

In my own work as an evaluator, I am guided by a concern to make distance education better for our students. As a woman working in a large-scale DTU where women are under-represented both among the academic staff and among the students, I am concerned with those aspects of our DE system and didactic approach which favour men and discriminate against women. As a feminist researcher, I am concerned with identifying such aspects in order to find ways in which to make the FeU a better place for mature women students. I therefore measure good distance education by its sensitivity to gender issues and by its ability to provide a productive and attractive learning environment for both women and men.

System evaluation at the FernUniversität

In the context of distance education a distinction is usually made between formative and summative evaluation. Formative evaluation accompanies the development of the course materials or of the study system and its components in order to judge the quality of the materials or programmes early on in the development and to influence the process if necessary. The goal of formative evaluation is to identify and correct mistakes and alter directions before the product or system is implemented. In practice, it is not possible to achieve an optimal product or perfect system (see Peters 1981: 132). For instance, as far as the FeU is concerned, formative evaluation would have meant that the written study materials were perfected before they could have been used for the first time, and this was not possible given the fact that there was less than one year from the time the decision was made to establish the university in December 1974 and the start of the first academic year in October 1975. The study material could therefore only be tested while already being used, i.e. through methods of summative evaluation. In the case of the FeU this meant:

> . . . that the quality control of the study material is carried out under the conditions of real teaching processes and results in the revision of both the material and the study system . . . With respect to the study system the advantage of an evaluation which parallels the actual teaching process lies in the fact that only in this way the distance education system as a whole can be examined. This is hardly possible through evaluation which accompanies the development of the material.
>
> (Peters 1981: 132–3)

While reducing the developmental stages for new materials, summative evaluation is not without its own problems. The major difficulty with this type of evaluation is the potential unwillingness of course authors and course teams to accept criticism of their finished product and to act on the evaluation results where they require revision. Defense mechanisms are activated which question the reliability and validity of the data or even the competence of the evaluators. Organisational factors may prevent the prompt response to evaluation results when, for instance, there is a supply of study materials in stock which need to be used up before a replacement can be considered or when there is a lack of resources and not enough staff to tackle the necessary revisions.

From the beginning the FeU instituted summative evaluation as 'accompanying research' which addressed three aspects of the distance teaching process:

1   Assessment of students, including assignments, grades, participation and success in examinations, final examinations and M.A. theses.
2   Course evaluation, including written study materials, audio-visual materials, computer-supported elements, face-to-face seminars and lab sessions.
3   System evaluation, including target groups, graduates, drop-out, elements of the study system such as the effect of fees, local support services, access to technology and computers and library services.

At first, evaluation at the FeU concentrated on the areas of assessment and course evaluation (see Bartels and Helms 1995); later it became increasingly focused on institutional research or 'Systemevaluation'. The methodological instruments used in evaluation research are those of the social sciences, mainly written questionnaires, telephone surveys, individual and group interviews, participant observation of seminars, video and computer conferences, interviews with experts, statistical analysis of student data banks, textual critique of the study materials sent in by students who judge the course units according to a catalogue of questions.

System evaluation, or institutional research at the FeU is directed at the whole system, i.e. at the institution as such, or at individual components of the system. On the level of the whole institution, the issues are concerned with the original goals associated with the FeU as an institution offering chances for educationally disadvantaged groups. This means that the evaluation looks into the social composition of the student population to see if all classes and both genders are adequately represented and to compare it with other universities. Since the FeU is the only DTU in Germany, institutional research also involves comparisons with DTUs in other countries such as the OU UK (Kirkup and von Prümmer 1990, 1997); or the Spanish Universidad Nacional de Educacion a Distancia (UNED) (Bartels and Nogales 1996). Both comparisons with other German universities and with other DTUs are necessarily limited, but nevertheless can provide important insights into characteristics of our own institution which need to be investigated further and contribute to a better understanding of the patterns found in the research data. This was the case, for instance, in the joint research done by Gill Kirkup of the OU UK and Ute Rossié and myself at the FeU in Germany which is presented in more detail later in this book (see especially Chapters 3 and 4).

At the level of components of the distance teaching system, the issues are concerned with specific elements, target groups, and functions of the DTU. This is by far the most extensive part of institutional research at the FeU and among other things comprises the investigation of communication in distance education, access and use of audiovisual and electronic media, opportunities and limitations of face-to-face seminars, access and use of study centres, conditions of success and failure, gender issues, the compatibility of distance education with other areas of students' lives, library services and many other aspects of the distance teaching system and learning environment of distance students.

Comments on the book and brief guide to chapters

Chapter 1, the 'Introduction' has set the scene for the discussion of issues in the following chapters by formulating the questions and focus of the book and by providing some background information on the German FeU which throughout will serve as a case study exemplifying the situation of women in distance education. Depending on the reader's own institutional and personal context, the women studying at the FeU will be seen as having more advantages or more difficulties than the women studying in other open and distance learning environments due to institutional and cultural or socioeconomic factors. Still, I believe that there are patterns of access and study behaviour which cut across national boundaries and that the findings and analyses presented in this book can be of use to those who want to understand their own distance education system.

In this I am encouraged by the fact that much of my work has been the direct or indirect result of joint research done by Gill Kirkup in England and by my colleague Ute Rossié and myself in Germany. Our comparative analysis has been very fruitful, not only for understanding the concrete data gathered in parallel surveys but also for informing other evaluation research we have each done for our universities. Also, our results have become part of an ongoing process of exchange between distance educators and researchers on gender in open and distance learning; in this process we develop our knowledge not only on the basis of our own research, but also on the basis of the theoretical and empirical work done by colleagues in other parts of the world. Here I want to mention specifically the valuable role of the Women's International Network (WIN) which brings together women from all over the world, mostly at distance education conferences, and which has been instrumental in creating the first book on (and by) women in distance education, edited by my Canadian colleague Karlene Faith in 1988. Its title *Toward new horizons for women in distance education*, was also its motto. The 'international perspectives' its subtitle promised were realised as women from all continents contributed their widely different, yet in many ways similar, experiences thus proving how much we can learn from each other (Faith 1988b).

The following is a brief guide to the chapters in this book: Chapter 2 'Distance education: studying outside the ivory tower' deals with different concepts of distance and with the question of how to overcome these distances. Its starting point is the issue of equal opportunities and the role of distance education in helping to achieve equity in the educational system.

Chapter 3 'Home study . . .', describes the learning environments of women distance students and the threats and potentials inherent in undertaking one's studying within the domestic sphere. Chapter 4 'Women studying at a distance . . .' focuses on women's learning styles and use of local support services. It presents evidence from comparative research which demonstrates the existence of gendered learning styles and the way in which these interact with the study system. Chapter 5 'Getting in touch' deals with communication and the new technologies which are increasingly seen as the future of distance education. Again, we find evidence that women and men have differing patterns, both with respect to their communication preferences and practice, and also with respect to their access and attitudes to information and communication technologies. This has consequences for their participation in the 'virtual university' envisioned by many to be the future of open and distance learning.

Chapter 6 'Minority women: class and gender in distance education' looks at women from working-class backgrounds who are held to be among the most disadvantaged social groups in Germany with respect to access to higher education. They serve as case studies for the goal of distance education in providing a second chance for educationally deprived segments of society. Chapter 7 'Distance education and the social mobility of women' is concerned with the goals of the women themselves, with the value they place on the university degree they are studying for, and with the role their distance education has for any ambitions they may have for upward social mobility.

Finally, Chapter 8 'Challenges, chances, changes: distance education for women', concludes the book and argues that distance education can indeed provide a chance for women to further their education, either for occupational reasons or for personal development, without forcing them to take the existential risk of giving up their job and income or abandon their family commitments. It is up to distance education institutions to ensure that women have the same chances as men to succeed. It is up to the women to take the chance.

Chapter 2

Distance education

Studying outside the ivory tower

In its simplest form, distance education is a form of teaching and learning which takes place at a distance from educational institutions. In the case of university level DE it could be said to take place outside the walls of the ivory tower, the proverbial bastion of academic dispute and pure intellectual knowledge. Can it therefore be assumed that DE is also more wordly than traditional academia, more concerned with social issues and equality of access?

Overcoming geographical distances

Distance education is commonly – and literally – associated with geographical distance and the isolation of people in remote areas. Students who live in areas without schools, colleges, and universities have access to these institutions through DE which does not require their presence in a classroom or on a campus on a regular basis if at all. One of the best-known examples of this understanding of DE is the Australian School of the Air which comes to children in isolated homesteads and allows them to stay with their families during their first school years.

Geography and isolation have been identified as limiting the educational opportunities of women, although the situation in Europe is usually not as extreme as that in Australia. The significance of distance for Australian women has been described by Pauline Heiler and Wendy Richards (1988) in the context of 'the implementation of an external course for isolated and rural women to draw them into the building and construction field' and thus provide new employment opportunities in the extremely gender-segregated labour market in New South Wales. Describing the conditions in Australia, the authors write:

> In part, because of the arid and inhospitable nature of much of its interior, Australia is one of the most highly urbanized countries in the world, and its relatively small rural population is scattered over vast distances . . . While some of these women [in New South Wales] live and work on

farms, the majority of them live in a few large regional centres and many small country towns and villages spread over seven thousand square kilometres within the state. Local conditions such as bad roads, inadequate public transport, and the generally higher costs of fuel in country areas restrict their mobility and access to the limited health, welfare and educational services available to them. Thus, for rural Australian women, distance and isolation usually go hand in hand, greatly affecting their chances to gain education, training and employment.

(Heiler and Richards 1988: 192)

Throughout the years, overcoming geographical distance has been the major concern of DE, but by no means the only one. Increasingly, other factors hampering access to traditional institutions of learning have become the focus of attention. Among these are personal barriers, such as a lack of mobility due to physical disability or private circumstances; and social barriers, such as exclusion from education on the grounds of class or ethnicity, gender or age. The gradual shift from the simple concept of distance education to the more encompassing one of open and distance learning also means a move away from distance teaching while placing more emphasis on 'open learning' and changes in the definition of DE. This shift is exemplified by a change of title of the journal *Teaching at a Distance* to *Open Learning* and marks the decade since the middle 1980s (see Tait 1993c: 2). This development has been furthered by the increase in dual-mode distance teaching institutions which offer courses both at a distance and in the classroom and which tend to blur the distinction between traditional and distance students.

Distance learning is moving beyond providing a 'second chance' system of education and training, towards becoming part of the normal fabric of teaching and learning. There is growing convergence between distance and conventional education and increasing popularity for 'mixed mode' delivery, which uses the methods and materials of distance learning for regular students.

(Jenkins 1995: 428)

The possibilities and processes of such a convergence have increasingly become a topic for distance education, as the growing use of information and communication technologies and multimedia applications blurs the distinctions of traditional classroom and distance modes.

Still, the main reason for establishing DE programmes, be it in single-mode or in dual-mode institutions, has always been the wish to extend access to education across geographical distances which could otherwise not be bridged. This was true for the OU UK, the first large-scale single-mode DTU in western Europe, and for the FeU established five years later in West

Germany. But although the FeU looked at the OU UK in order to learn from its experience, the two universities worked from different concepts of how to overcome the geographical distance to their respective students. The OU UK instituted a system of regional centres and study centres, with tutors and counsellors and local support services, in order to be in closer contact with its students. First-year students, by virtue of enrolling in foundation courses with weekly attendance requirements, were provided with decentralised tutorials within reasonable distance from their place of residence. Distance in this case was bridged by setting up classrooms away from the main campus. This is of course a very simplified sketch of the OU UK system of local provision. More adequate and detailed accounts of the organisation of support services at the OU can be found in the relevant literature (see Tunstall 1974, McIntosh *et al.* 1977).

The *Fern*Universität, taking its title '*distance* university' literally, designed its system to be independent of attendance requirements and study centres, operating from a central campus and making it possible to complete a degree programme with attendance only for certain examinations. The few study centres, most of which were established in the West German state of North-Rhine Westphalia, offered a limited range of optional support services, while the centre in Hagen maintained sole responsibility for the teaching and marking of assignments. The distance between the FeU and its students thus was bridged almost exclusively through the written study material and comments sent out and assignments, questions and forms sent in. The decision for this type of DE system was to have far-reaching consequences for women, as will be shown later.

Distance education and equal opportunities

The two concepts of distance education and equal opportunities are almost universally linked in the minds of educators, politicians, and students. The link has become even stronger with the bracketing of 'open and distance learning' in a single phrase and often referred to as ODL. Distance education has traditionally been seen as a way of providing educational opportunities for groups of people who would otherwise have no access to schools or universities. The distance which has to be overcome may be one of geographical location, physical handicap, social position, or gender, each of which alone or in combination with other factors prevents prospective students from attending classes and lectures in face-to-face institutions. This is exemplified in the following quote from a 1966 government White Paper on the possibilities of establishing an open university in Britain:

> At a time when scarce capital resources must, in the national interest, be allocated with greatest prudence, an open university could provide higher and further education for those unable to take advantage of courses in

existing colleges and universities. And it could do so without requiring vast capital sums to be spent on bricks and mortar . . . those who left school at an early age would have an added incentive to equip them-selves [through adult education] for higher study.

(quoted in MacArthur 1974: 9; and in McIntosh *et al.* 1977)

In Germany, the establishment of the FernUniversität was part of the educational reform movement meant to make higher education, both in the form of degree programmes and continuing education, more accessible for those sections of the society which were under-represented in universities and other tertiary institutions. This was expressed in the law with which the NRW state government founded the FeU:

These demands cannot be met by the conventional universities. In the long run only distance education can provide the necessary precondi-tions and offer the chance for adults to study while pursuing a career and paid work. In this respect the FernUniversität, which is a compre-hensive university ('*Gesamthochschule*'), will contribute to the opening of tertiary education and will overcome social and cultural barriers to higher education.

(quoted in Rau 1974: 118)

Providing a second chance through distance education

The term 'second chance education' soon became the catch phrase for this view of distance education. There is a danger that second chance may be perceived as only second best, a label which would in itself defeat the aim of providing equal educational opportunities. If people who complete a course of studies or a degree at a distance see themselves, or are seen by others, as having gained an inferior education, they will not derive equal benefits from their achievements. Distance educators, who are confronted with such opin-ions, tend to spend time and resources on proving that their teaching is at least equal to conventional, classroom-based teaching modes. In some cases, the curriculum and course loads, as well as the academic requirements, are even more rigorous than the ones at comparable institutions with face-to-face instruction.

In his account of the first five years, the founding rector of the FeU describes the guiding principle which was to:

. . . establish an academic reputation in the scientific community because genuine academic excellence in teaching and research is the sole guaran-tee for the acceptance of the university by the general public. This in turn provides the foundation for building a programme of continuing education and for experimenting with open access to university degree programmes for those applicants who do not meet the formal entrance requirements.

(Peters 1981: 15)

The quote illustrates a basic dilemma confronting the FeU from the first: the FeU had been set up in the context of the educational reform movement aimed at providing wider access to tertiary education. As a 'comprehensive university', it had to prove its academic standing and rigour to the traditional classical universities with their restricted access and philosophy of educating the intellectual elite. Furthermore, as the latest of the comprehensive universities, the FeU had been burdened with the additional and unprecedented task of providing university degree programmes in a distance teaching mode. Until the foundation of the FeU, DE in West Germany had been offered by private organisations only with courses providing secondary and vocational education, such as A-level preparation or technical diplomas, and continuing education. In East Germany the situation was different since distance education was part of the university system. Students were seconded by their employers – usually large state-owned factories – to enrol in distance programmes provided by dual-mode universities. This system came to an abrupt end with the dissolution of the German Democratic Republic and the unification of the two countries in 1990 (see von Prümmer and Stein 1991). Since then, the FeU has become the only university-level DE provider for the former East German states.

If the university-level DE offered by the FeU was unique in the West German tertiary sector, it was also considered unique in the world of distance education. A comparison with DTUs in English-speaking countries shows that the target groups of distance or open universities such as the OU UK are mainly undergraduates studying for a degree at Bachelor of Arts (B.A.) level. Until recently (1997) Germany did not have degrees of this kind, with university study leading directly to degrees at Master of Arts (M.A.) level as the basic academic qualification. The dilemma facing the new FeU arose from the need to establish its reputation as a real university in spite of – or because of – its character as part of the social reform movement.

The value which the institution placed on achieving a high academic reputation (see Peters 1981: 158) had consequences for the teaching system and for the students. One consequence was the fact that the degree programmes were structured mainly to conform to those offered at conventional universities, although they contained more interdisciplinary elements as required by the reform mandate. An example of this was the economics degree with its integration of the two subject areas political economy and business studies (Peters 1981: 29). In accordance with its character as a comprehensive university, to a greater or lesser extent the FeU programmes were set up to lead to the two degree levels of 'proper' academic degrees, after eight or more semesters of full-time study (M.A., *Diplom II*); and the lower level degree after at least 6 semesters (*Diplom I*; see FeU 1999a: 13). Another consequence was an effect created by the fact that the quality of the distance teaching was open to scrutiny by academics in all other universities. This occasionally led to the impression that the study materials had been written more with a concern about the reactions of the academic peers than with a concern about the pedagogy and the teaching of the subject matter to students, a phenomenon which has been evaluated both negatively and positively. For instance, students have commented negatively in the context of course evaluations, feeling that the material was sometimes unnecessarily difficult or lacking in pedagogical design elements (Bartels 1989: 4). By contrast, the founding rector pointed out advantages for the students due to the transparency of the teaching material which continually forces the academic staff to re-evaluate and improve their teaching (Peters 1976: 164 and 1981: 114–16).

The most important concept of the educational reform movement was the opening up of tertiary education for disadvantaged social groups, and the FeU was explicitly set up to provide such opportunities. Usually the means by which this opening up of universities is achieved is an admissions policy which does not require formal entrance qualifications. This has been done, for instance, in the OU UK which by its very name proclaims that it is open to students from all educational levels. The German FeU, by contrast, has no such open admissions policy. In the founding phase of this distance university as well as in the early stages of its development, the goal of establishing an academic reputation overrode the goal of providing university access for educationally disadvantaged groups. It was felt that the very reform mandate would be jeopardised by admitting students without the formal entrance requirements, since this would signal an inferiority of the degree programmes and the academic qualifications obtainable at the FeU (Ehmann 1978, Geiersbach 1981).

German distance education in the context of educational policy: a question of equity

In the mid-1960s West Germany experienced a widespread debate about the lack of equality in its educational system, especially with respect to access to higher education. Originally, this debate was prompted by a concern with the projected lack of skilled workers and qualified professionals which it was thought would inevitably lead to an economic emergency caused by a *Bildungskatastrophe* – a qualificational and educational catastrophe (Picht 1965). As the issue was taken up in the political arena, the focus shifted increasingly to the unequal opportunities of entering secondary and tertiary education and to the measures to be taken to improve the chances of all social groups for obtaining the education most suitable to each individual's capabilities.

The traditional German educational system, with its strictly separated types of school, has placed children into different educational strands from the age of ten, after only four years of primary school. Only the minority of a given age cohort took the entrance examination (roughly comparable to the British eleven-plus examination) and were admitted to the *Gymnasium* or secondary school. In 1972, for instance, only 19% of the schoolchildren aged 13–14 years attended the *Gymnasium*, then practically the only route to achieving university entrance qualifications in the form of the *Abitur* (roughly equivalent to British A-levels) (BMBW 1981: 11). Since there were no university entrance examinations, the *Abitur* was the only avenue leading to university degrees and therefore to professional qualifications in law, medicine and other academic fields.

Children who either never took this examination or failed to be admitted to the *Gymnasium*, later had the chance of entering a *Realschule* (middle school) and obtaining the *Mittlere Reife* qualification (roughly equivalent to O-levels) on which much of the training for white-collar jobs, such as administrators and bank tellers, was based. The successful completion of this educational level was also a way of eventually entering the *Gymnasium*, provided the student had exceptionally good grades and a good prognosis for success.

The vast majority of children remained in the *Volksschule*, as the basic educational institution was then called, and completed the requisite number of years until the school leaving age of fourteen (later fifteen). With this level of schooling, young people could continue their education by beginning an apprenticeship in a trade or blue-collar occupation, or as an office worker, or they could enter the labour market immediately as unskilled workers.

The system was very rigid and provided limited opportunities to change from a lower level school to one leading to more advanced qualifications. Decisions taken at a very early age could with difficulty be corrected and such missed opportunities affected people's life chances forever. In a political climate which had begun to propagate equal access to all educational levels and occupational positions, this was a matter for grave concern. It was especially disturbing that the selection process to secondary schools was based on class and social background rather than on individual potential. School recruitment in no way reflected the structure of society, and access to a *Gymnasium* depended on factors such as parental education and class, and students' gender, religious affiliation, and the region in which they lived.

This differential access to higher education was also reflected in university recruitment, where sons of middle-class academics were over-represented, while women, working-class students and students from rural backgrounds were severely under-represented. The most disadvantaged groups were those with a convergence of two or more exclusionary characteristics, and the 'Roman Catholic girl from a working-class family in a rural area' became the epitome of the educationally deprived child. In comparison with a boy of the same age living with his academically educated parents in a university town, this girl had to overcome odds of 1:45 in order to reach a secondary school and go on to a university (Peisert and Framhein 1980: 126).

The school system was seen as the continuation of the West German class system, and the issue of improving access to secondary and tertiary education became one of the major political goals of the Social Democrats (SPD) in the late 1960s and early 1970s. Equity in education, it was felt, could only be achieved by a fundamental restructuring of the educational system in order to make it more accessible and less rigid. In this, the SPD differed from the other major political party, the Christian Democrats (CDU, CSU) who wanted to maintain the structured system and improve access on the basis of individual merit.

For the fate of German distance education it is important to note that as a Federal Republic Germany has decentralised responsibilities for education and each *Bundesland* (state or province of the Federal Republic) is in charge of its own school system. The state of North-Rhine Westphalia (NRW), which has been governed by a Social Democratic majority since its beginning in 1947, is not only the most densely populated German province, it also used to be the industrial backbone of the country. The population in the *Ruhrgebiet* area, traditionally the coal mining and steel belt, was composed to a large extent of highly skilled blue-collar workers with a low attendance rate in institutions of secondary and tertiary education. The few existing North-Rhine Westphalian universities were situated outside this industrial region in cities such as Bonn and Münster.

In order to bring more children of working-class origin into secondary schools and then into universities, NRW introduced so-called comprehensives on both levels of higher education and founded a number of new universities, most of which were located along an east–west axis throughout the *Ruhrgebiet*. A history and analysis of these comprehensive universities was published by an insider, the rector of a comprehensive university, on the occasion of the 25th anniversary of the first *Gesamthochschule* which was established in 1967 (Rimbach 1992).

Comprehensive schools were intended to eliminate the very early decision for one type of school with its far-reaching consequences for subsequent educational avenues open to pupils in each sub-system. At the same time, comprehensive schools were meant to allow pupils to fluctuate between strands, thus making it possible to revise earlier decisions regarding the educational level they aimed for. The goal was to provide children from social strata which had traditionally only gone through the basic levels of schooling with an environment which would allow them to discover their intellectual potential; they would be encouraged to pursue their individual educational course, without regard to their class origin or any other inhibiting factor.

By analogy with comprehensive schools, the comprehensive universities were established in order to make the tertiary sector more flexible and to allow students with lower-level entrance qualifications to enter a degree course at university level. The new universities were deliberately built in traditional working-class areas in order to reduce the distance between these institutions of higher education and their intended target student groups. The university was no longer to be an ivory tower, far removed from ordinary folk, but rather a 'knowledge factory', close to home and easily accessible. In fact, students could continue to live at home and commute to the university, as their mothers and fathers commuted to the factory, the mine, or the mill.

The role of the FernUniversität

The establishment of the FeU was an extension of this philosophy, as is evidenced in the following quote from a government official involved in planning and setting up the FeU:

> The goal was to make it possible in principle to instigate processes of social change through the provision of tertiary distance education. It is not possible to tell yet whether the newly created FernUniversität will be able in the long run to overcome economic and social obstacles and resistance as well as ideologies and prejudices, thereby causing social reform.
>
> (Körnig 1979: 10)

Not only did it bring the university close to home, the FeU came *into* student's homes and eliminated even the need to commute to a campus. By offering degree courses at a distance the FeU helped to overcome distances in both location and attitude which were keeping whole social strata away from higher education. As a comprehensive university, the FeU was set up to provide a second chance for people who had embarked earlier on a different educational path. Studying at a distance meant access to university for people who had already established themselves in an occupation or profession, who had families and other commitments which they could not easily give up in order to pursue their education full-time and on-campus.

At that time, there were three major political arguments for setting up a single-mode state university, teaching exclusively off campus. They were:

1   The educational reform movement extended secondary and, consequently, tertiary education to ever-increasing numbers of young people, and the existing universities could not cope with the influx. The establishment of a DTU would greatly reduce the time and cost of providing thousands of badly needed study places since it eliminated the planning

and building stage necessary for a physical rather than a virtual campus. It was also anticipated that such a university could be run at a much lower cost-per-student ratio than conventional universities.

2   The FeU was a pioneering venture since distance education in Germany so far consisted exclusively of privately run correspondence schools which only offered courses below university level, such as O-level and A-level preparation, language and general interest courses, and vocational programmes. As a totally new type of university, the FeU was thought to lend itself to reform experiments, not only in the delivery, but also in admission policies and curriculum development.

3   One aspect of the educational reform movement was the concern with life-long learning, partly as an extension of the ideal of flexibility within the formal educational structure, partly as the provision of educational opportunities for personal development, and partly as an opportunity to keep up with the continually changing demands of the workplace. The FeU was seen to be a very good vehicle for this since it allowed its students to study without giving up their paid work or infringing on personal and professional commitments. 'Studying while working' (*Studieren neben dem Beruf*) was the term most often used to characterise this educational goal.

On the whole, during the twenty-five years of its existence the FeU has made progress toward meeting these goals. It has been especially successful in respect of the first goal, as is evidenced by the rapid expansion from the original 1,300 students in 1975/76 to an enrolment of over 55,000 in the 1990s. The pattern is not quite as clear-cut with respect to the second goal – namely that of extending opportunities for higher education to groups of people who had previously been excluded on the basis of their social background, or for personal reasons such as a disability or a life situation incompatible with on-campus studies. The latter group includes women in the family phase who study at the FeU in order to prepare for (re-)entry into the labour market. In those cases where students have no other chance to obtain a university degree, the FeU does indeed constitute a means to redress educational discrimination. The same is true for the third goal, which is definitely being pursued in those instances where students already have a degree and study at the FeU in order to improve their career prospects by increasing their qualifications (for instance by adding an M.A. or *Diplom II* degree to an existing lower-level *Diplom I*). While the B.A. and B.Sc. degree (Bachelor of Arts or Science) has only recently been introduced in Germany, there have always been lower-level degree programmes offered mainly by the *Fachhochschulen* which evolved from engineering colleges and technical colleges, and from teacher training colleges and seminaries. Traditionally, proper university degrees in Germany have always been at M.A. level, in some instances even at doctorate level.

Overcoming social distance: recruiting working-class students

The working class and the lower socio-economic strata are traditionally under-represented in secondary and tertiary education, and working-class girls are even more disadvantaged than boys from the same background. In fact, as Karlene Faith writes, the 'issues of gender and class are inseparable for women' and determine their opportunities – or lack of opportunities – both in education and in the labour market. It follows that 'women are caught in double (or triple) jeopardy: even when as individuals they overcome systematic economic (and/or racial) barriers, they still remain subject to those barriers that are engendered by sex discrimination' (Faith 1988a: 9–10).

In order to overcome the negative effects of this multiple discrimination, women turn to education as a means to achieve emancipation. This is often only possible if they find a way to reconcile their studying with their traditional duties as housewives and mothers. In Germany, too, it was expected that young people of working-class origin, especially women, would be over-represented among FeU students since this group has the most need to avail themselves of the 'second chances' offered by distance education.

A small study of in-depth interviews with three FeU women graduates, all of whom turned out to be from working-class backgrounds, strengthened the hypothesis that daughters of working-class parents who want to be upwardly mobile make up a disproportionately high percentage of all FeU students, enrolling at the FeU to a larger extent than at other universities (Raehlmann 1984). This was the basis for including questions on parents and socio-economic background into a large-scale research project on the situation of women and men studying at the FeU (see von Prümmer 1997a).

Definition of 'class' and empirical data on class background

For the purposes of this analysis of the socio-economic background of FeU students, the class position of individuals is defined primarily through their occupational position, supplemented occasionally by the inclusion of educational attainment (see von Prümmer 1997a: 116–78 for a discussion of gender and stratification and the problems of defining 'class' and the 'class position' of women).

In order to answer the question whether the FeU does help to reduce social inequalities the institution initially collected data on the parents of FeU students. The data are available for secondary analysis for the time period from 1985/86 to 1991/92 and provide information about the educational and occupational levels of the mothers and fathers of students registered at the FernUniversität during that time. If distance education were indeed a means for compensating educational discrimination, the proportion of students from a working-class background should be greater at the FeU than it is at other German universities. The FeU data can be compared to statistical data collected regularly in national surveys on the total student population in West Germany, published by the Federal Ministry of Education in its series *Das soziale Bild der Studentenschaft in der Bundesrepublik Deutschland*, referred to in short as the *Social Survey of Students*.

The social composition of the student population in West Germany in no way reflects the social composition of society as a whole, but shows an uneven participation of different social strata in higher education. Using the traditional class definition based on the father's occupational position, four classes are identified:

1   manual or blue-collar workers, the working-class, as the largest social group;
2   office or white-collar employees;
3   civil servants;
4   self-employed persons (including freelancers and entrepreneurs).

These four social groupings do not participate equally in tertiary education. In 1985, for instance, only 4% of the children of working-class fathers entered university while 18% of the children of self-employed fathers, 19% of the children of white-collar employees and a staggering 33% of the children of civil servants enrolled in a university degree programme.

As Figure 2.1 shows, the distribution of students in West German universities, including the FeU, in the academic year 1985/86 mirrors this uneven recruitment pattern. The year 1985 was chosen because detailed data is available from our survey on the situation of women and men in distance education. Also, the FeU survey modelled the occupational categories used to define class location on the *Social Survey of Students* (BMBW 1983, 1986). Figure 2.1 also shows the slight but noticeable demographic divergence between the FeU and the other universities which indicates a larger intake of working-class students as the group which is overall least likely to enter tertiary education.

For the purposes of this analysis I have defined the class background according to a student's own classification of her or his mother's and/or father's occupational position and, where appropriate, their educational attainment. (For a detailed discussion see von Prümmer 1997a: 116–78). Looking at the occupational status of parents of students at the FeU and at other universities from 1985/86 to 1991/92, we find that working-class students were highly under-represented in all universities, but less so among the distance students. In 1985, for instance, the overall proportion of manual or blue-collar workers among the male population in the West German labour market was 44%; the proportion of students with fathers who were manual

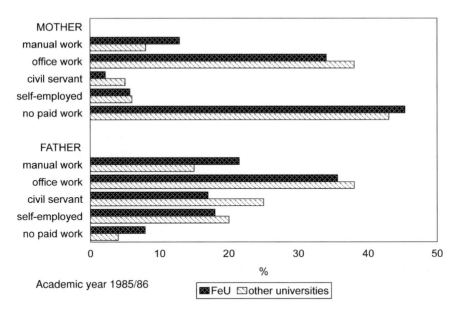

Figure 2.1 Occupational status of parents of students at the FeU and other universities

or blue-collar workers was 22% at the FeU and only 15% in West German universities. Not surprisingly, since women's participation in the labour market traditionally has been less than men's, the proportion of mothers in 'working-class' jobs was much lower in both types of institutions, although again the FeU attracted more children of such mothers (13%) than did other universities (8%). The comparison suggests that with respect to class background the DTU does offer more chances than conventional universities to working-class students who want to study for a degree.

Social class can also be determined by including additional factors such as highest level of schooling and vocational or professional education. The educational attainment of fathers and especially mothers is held to be an important element in a possible predisposition for or against further education. Compared to the general population, statistical evidence shows an over-representation of FeU students whose mothers (19%) and fathers (38%) have obtained the university entrance qualification and whose mothers (10%) and fathers (23%) have completed a university degree course (M.A. level or higher). Again, as Table 2.1 shows, the FeU exhibits a different recruiting pattern, with comparatively fewer students of better-educated parents registering in its distance education programmes.

The data can be interpreted as confirmation of the claim that distance education provides avenues to social equality. It is generally held that, among other factors, working-class families and families of lower social standing

Table 2.1 Highest educational level of parents of students at FeU and other universities

Highest level of schooling	FeU		Other German universities		Difference Δ	
	Mother 10,362 %	Father 10,362 %	Mother 14,394 %	Father 14,395 %	Δ Mother %	Δ Father %
Abitur (A-levels etc.)	9	21	19	38	−10	−17
Realschule (O-levels etc.)	26	23	32	22	−5	1
Compulsory schooling only	65	56	49	41	16	15
Sum	**100**	**100**	**100**	**100**		
Highest level of training/ occupational qualification	Mother 11,179 %	Father 11,179 %	Mother 13,794 %	Father 14,098 %	Δ Mother %	Δ Father %
University	3	11	10	25	−7	−14
Non-university tertiary (Polytechnic, College etc.)	2	9	4	14	−2	−5
Master craftsperson	5	20	7	17	−2	3
Apprenticeship, skilled	46	41	54	39	−8	2
No formal qualification/ don't know	44	17	25	5	19	12
Sum	**100**	**100**	**100**	**100**		

Sources: BMBW 1986: 99; FeU databanks 1985/86.

are characterised by a 'distance from education' (*Bildungsferne*); this contributes to their tendency to provide their children with the more basic levels of schooling and not encourage them to pursue higher education and careers which require academic degrees (Dickenhorst *et al.* 1992). The fact that FeU students are more likely to come from such an educationally distant background shows that progress is being made in bridging this specific type of distance.

Multiple discrimination: working-class women in distance education

It has long been an accepted fact that girls and women from a working-class background have even fewer opportunities than their male peers to enter secondary schools and later universities, and that they have therefore more need for compensation of missed opportunities. This leads to the expectation that the FeU should attract more daughters than sons of working-class parents. A comparison of women and men studying at the FeU does not produce any evidence to support such a hypothesis as up to 25% of the male students and only 18% of the female students had fathers in manual or blue-collar occupations. There are two contradictory explanations for this phenomenon: First, it is possible that working-class girls and women have better access to educational opportunities than has previously been assumed and their need for compensation is consequently less than expected. Altern- atively, the educational discrimination of working-class girls and women may carry over into distance education, reducing their chances to access even this route to pursuing university studies.

The following chapters will look at women distance students from a working-class background in order to pursue the question of multiple discrimination and the role of distance studying for overcoming educa- tional obstacles based on gender and class origin. To ensure readability it is necessary to identify this group by using a shortened label rather than the longer phrases which describe the 'women whose mothers and/or fathers had working-class occupations' or 'women from a working-class family'. In Germany, where the concern with gender issues in access to higher education was revived by feminist sociologists in the 1990s, we speak of *ArbeiterInnentöchter* – daughters of working-class mothers or fathers.

In this book I use the term 'working-class women' to identify this group, even though very few of these students would be considered 'working-class' on the basis of their own occupational position. Compared to their mothers and fathers, all of them have already experienced some social mobility, a fact which is documented by the very action of enrolling in a university degree programme at the FeU.

Overcoming the gender gap in educational opportunities

Persistent gender differences in educational opportunities

In spite of the educational reforms which have taken place during the last thirty years, women today still do not have equal access to all levels of education. In Germany, for instance, the participation of women declines steadily from secondary school through university enrollment, graduate and postgraduate study, and postdoctoral qualification to the hierarchy of uni- versity teachers (see Figure 2.2). This is evidenced by a secondary analysis of 1994 government statistics which I did for a memorandum on the situation of women in North-Rhine Westphalian universities (AK Wiss 1996: 15). At the start of this downward slope, girls now have achieved equal access and constitute just over half of all young people leaving the secondary school system with a university entrance qualification. The transition to university seems to have been more difficult and less automatic for young women. Until the 1990s they only made up 40% of the cohorts of newly registered

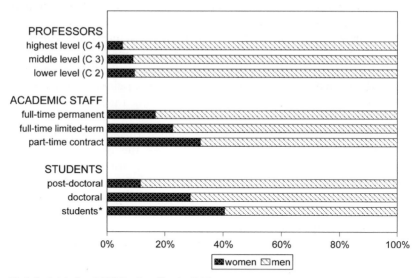

Statistical data for all NRW universities in 1994
* undergraduate and graduate students in 1995/96

Figure 2.2 Proportion of women at all levels of the university hierarchy

university students each year, a percentage which has since risen steadily and reached the 50% mark in 1995 (BMBF 1998: 144).

In the context of equal opportunities through DE there are two reasons for looking at women as a specific target group: as has been shown above, women are amongst those groups which are most discriminated against in the area of higher education and therefore should be most in need of the compensating opportunities which DE offers. In addition, women are not over-represented in all DE programmes as is to be expected. In Britain, where women now constitute more than half of the students registered at the OU, they still are a minority in subject areas not traditionally chosen by women such as technology (Kirkup and von Prümmer 1996, 1997).

In Germany women still constitute only 38% of the distance students registered at the FeU. They are not only under-represented in particular subject areas but compared to other universities the proportion of women is significantly lower in distance education than in the conventional system (46%) (BMBF 1998: 154). In order to explain these seemingly contradictory phenomena, it is necessary to look at women in distance education as a distinct group who might have different needs and require 'women-friendly' – rather than 'women-unfriendly' or exclusively male – perspectives in order to be attracted to and successful in DE. Quite obviously, distance education is not *per se* equally well suited for men and for women or – as has been argued – even better suited to women. As was pointed out in Chapter 1, and will be shown in more detail in Chapter 3, these claims are based on a superficial view of DE. This appears to be a particularly woman-friendly form of acquiring education and formal qualifications if one only looks at these two characteristics: DE combines a minimum of attendance requirements with a high degree of flexibility in learning schedules and time management.

From androcentrism to women-friendly distance education

In view of the contradictions between the image of DE as particularly women-friendly and the empirical evidence showing a gender-gap in enrolments and course completion rates, there is a concern with the latent or manifest androcentrism in DE which makes this form of education more attractive to men than to women. Consequently, as Gill Kirkup points out:

> When thinking about any distance education institution and its women students – potential as well as actual – it is useful to separate out issues of access from issues of content. A critical analysis of the institution should examine why women are unequally represented in sectors of the traditional curriculum and should also examine this curriculum to see how women and women's experience has been marginalized.
>
> (Kirkup 1988: 287)

In order to pursue this issue further we draw on data from a comparative research project on the situation of women and men studying at the West German FeU and at the OU UK. We had observed that the composition of the student population of the FeU differed significantly from that of other DTUs in western industrialised countries. The persistent and uncharacteristic under-representation of women in university DE in Germany made it obvious that there were differences between the two distance education systems which rendered the FeU less attractive to women – or more attractive to men – than was the case at the OU UK. Through the joint research we hoped to gain empirical evidence to determine which aspects of a distance education system render it more or less women-friendly.

Our research data has pointed to some areas in which institutional factors influence the recruitment and the successful study of women distance students. The following chapters will deal with these areas and show how they are relevant for women in distance education, and how an inherent androcentrism affects women's chances of entering and completing a degree programme. This analysis will point out ways in which distance teaching systems could be made more women-friendly.

Gender awareness: a test of 'good' distance education

The Importance of Gender as a Category in Open and Distance Learning (Kirkup 1995) cannot be disputed. In fact, I would argue, gender awareness is the criterion by which a 'good' distance education system needs to be judged. If gender is not seen as relevant, the system will not be equally accessible to women and men and will offer men more chances to succeed.

The reasons for the interest in gender in the DE context were summarised by Gill Kirkup of the OU UK in her keynote address to the 1995 Cambridge conference, entitled *Putting the Student First: Learner Centred Approaches in Open and Distance Learning*. I fully agree with Gill Kirkup when she says that these debates:

> ... on gender as one of the foundational categories of our intellectual world ... interest me for two main reasons. As an educator of women I need a model of the learner which helps me decide the significance of a student's gender in my day-to-day practice. As an educator working in open and distance learning (ODL) I need a model of the educational role of the new information and communication technologies (ICTs) which takes seriously the social and cultural significance of gender.
>
> (Kirkup 1995: 2)

In my own institution we are confronted with the effects of a DE system which does not take gender into account and in both content and delivery is aimed at a type of distance student who is more often male than female. The persistent tendency to ignore the relevance of gender and to continue almost unchecked with the androcentric DE system established twenty-five years ago must be held responsible for the low percentage and higher drop-out rates of women students.

It is true that 'equality of access' and 'equal opportunities' have become catch-phrases in educational policy and that the FeU, too, is in the process of formulating a policy of women-friendly perspectives for its students and staff. Unfortunately, it is equally true that women are still under-represented and that the learning environment at the FeU has not changed significantly to become more compatible with the circumstances of women's lives and with their preferred learning styles. On the contrary, due to the gendered character of technologies, the increased use of ICTs (information and communication technologies) brings with it the danger that women will be excluded even further from enrolling and from completing their degrees at a distance.

For the past fifteen years I have been doing research into the conditions under which women study at the FeU. I started out with the simple question of why women were under-represented, since in the early 1980s less than one quarter of our students were women. While the FeU aimed primarily at the

Table 2.2 Proportion of women and men in European DTUs

Distance Teaching University	Overall student numbers, abs.	Women, %	Men, %
OU UK (undergraduate programme)	87,000	50.0	50.0
FeU Germany (degree programmes)	36,000	31.0	69.0
UNED Spain	85,000	54.7	44.7
OU Netherlands	58,000	38.0	62.0

Source: Kirkup and von Prümmer 1997.

target group of people in full-time employment – mostly men – it was generally held that DE as a study mode is particularly suited for women because of their role as housewives and mothers, which was thought to provide flexible time management possibilities while preventing classroom attendance.

So far, our own research, as well as comparative research done in co-operation with Gill Kirkup of the OU UK, has confirmed that gender is an important category in the following ODL contexts: (1) the participation of women in distance education at various levels, including university; (2) gender-related enrolment patterns and course choices; (3) different learning styles of women and men; (4) gendered learning contexts; and (5) gender differences in access and use of technologies.

Unlike other western DE systems, the FeU has a disproportionately large share of male students, while women are under-represented (see Table 2.2). The proportion of women among FeU students has more than doubled from 17% in 1976/77 to currently 38%, but the participation of women in university level distance education is still lower than in other German universities where 46% of the overall student population and over half (52.4%) of the yearly intake are women.

In the face of claims that because of its flexible schedules and study environment DE is especially suited for women with family responsibilities, this under-representation needs to be explained and measures taken for a more equitable gender distribution. Much of the work I have done at the FeU and in collaboration with Gill Kirkup of the OU UK has been directed toward this issue.

At the time I began my research, the under-representation of women was usually explained in terms of the limited range of subjects available at the FeU at the time. It was frequently argued that, with the exception of education and the social sciences, the subject areas of our degree courses were traditional male domains and it therefore was 'natural' that men should be in the majority.

In fact, the enrolment statistics reflect traditional gender-related patterns of course choice at the FeU as well as at other universities in Germany and

Table 2.3 Proportion of women in subject areas/degree programmes at the OU UK and at the FeU

a) *OU UK women undergraduates in different faculties as a percentage of all students: comparison of most recent 1993 data with 1985 data*

Year	Arts	Social sciences	Maths	Science	Technology	School of education
1985						
%	66%	54%	26%	37%	16%	67%
abs.	11,371	7,654	3,395	4,246	2,702	3,283
1993						
%	68%	61%	24%	42%	17%	77%
abs.	14,686	13,239	3,695	5,499	2,778	2,828

b) *FeU women in different subject areas as a percentage of all students: comparison of most recent 1994 (summer semester) data with 1985/86 data*

Year	Economics/ business	Maths	Computer science	Electrical engineering	Educ, social sciences, arts
1985–6					
%	24%	16%	16%	5%	49%
abs.	2,101	164	658	81	1,268
1994					
%	33%	20%	19%	8%	55%
abs.	5,641	236	864	115	3,636

Source: Kirkup and von Prümmer 1997: 44.

in other countries. Even in the mid-1990s a comparison of the German FeU and the OU UK showed once again that men are more likely than women to choose mathematical and technical subject areas, while women tend to prefer areas such as education, social sciences and the arts (see Table 2.3).

Yet when I first looked at the enrolment patterns and compared these to choice of subject in campus-based degree programmes at other universities, I found that women had consistently been under-represented in each of the subject areas offered by the FeU (von Prümmer 1985; see also Chapter 1). Even though they constituted the majority in the degree programme leading to the M.A. in Education, a lower percentage of women enrolled at the FeU than at campus-based universities in West Germany. These findings clearly indicated that the limited range of courses was not a sufficient explanation for the under-representation of women. It gave rise to the question of what other factors were at work and what the university might be able to do to recruit more women.

One of the gender differences shown by our research, and a possible explanation for the under-representation of women, relates to the different learning styles of men and women students. The German DE system caters to the 'autonomous' and 'independent' learner who more or less happily studies on his own, working his way through the course materials provided by the university. Ideally, this student has *chosen* to study at a distance and does not want to be bothered with personal contacts and demands for attendance or interaction. There tends to be a feeling that any student requiring more attention – in the form of tutorial support, face-to-face interaction or other forms of personal contact – is somewhat lacking in those traits which characterise the successful distance student.

It is not a slip of the tongue that I speak of this ideal–type distance student as 'he', while I otherwise deplore the fact that the FeU still does not use gender-inclusive language. The joint research done by Gill Kirkup in Britain and myself in Germany has confirmed feminist theories of differential learning styles in men and women. At the FeU as well as the OU women distance students have shown more interest in support and connectedness with other students and in dealings between students and academic staff (see Chapter 4). On the basis of comparative data we have reached the conclusion that the German FeU provides fewer opportunities for interaction and collaboration than does the OU UK, and that this is one of the factors explaining why comparatively few women enrol in the German system. The ones who are enrolled tend to exhibit a study behaviour different from that of their male colleagues and oriented toward creating opportunities for meeting and working with other (women) students. For instance, women students have a higher rate of attendance in study centres, even though they have to overcome more obstacles in order to be able to participate, due to the fact that women are less likely to find the time and the transport to get to a study centre for tutorials and study groups. At the same time, women place a higher value on the local support services while men tend to instrumentalise them and see their value only in relation to immediate snags in their study progress or exam peparations. As we concluded in our first report entitled *Value of study centres and support services*, 'Women tend to make different demands on the institution than do male students, and they value and utilise the services in a different way' (von Prümmer and Rossié 1990c: 36).

It is important to note that in making these demands on the institution, women are not displaying a deficit in learner autonomy and independence as is often assumed. They approach their studies differently from male students, but their approach is no less valid and must be taken into account by a distance education system which actively wants to provide equal opportunities for men and women.

In looking for factors which might work against women enrolling and studying at the FeU, we also addressed the argument that distance education *per se* is women-friendly since it does not require attendance in class at set times. Due to their family commitments, mature women – especially if they are housebound mothers of small children – are thought to find it more difficult than men to organise face-to-face studying. This part of the argument is based in reality where women are the prime caregivers responsible for household and family commitments and is borne out by the situation of women distance students. The difficulties women face in organising their studies are compounded by the fact that many of our students are in full-time or part-time work in addition to fulfilling their commitments as housewives and mothers. These women find it very difficult indeed to make time to attend tutorials or study groups which take place outside their homes or even outside their hometowns.

The other art of the argument belongs in the realm of fiction as it assumes that housebound women in unpaid family work are supposed to have time on their hands and to be quite free in how they organise their schedules. For one thing, only a minority of women distance students do not work outside the home at all, even if it is only for a few hours and their main responsibility is to their families. Furthermore, in reality the everyday lives of family women are characterised by a degree of chaos and constant interruptions, where the mother is at the beck and call of her children (and sometimes her partner) and their immediate needs which tend to take precedence over the woman's desire for uninterrupted and concentrated study time. The fragmented character of housework and mothering has been shown impressively by Ann Oakley in her book, *The Sociology of Housework*, which first appeared in 1974 and was translated into German in 1978, and by Regina Becker-Schmidt, Uta Brandes-Erlhoff, Marla Karrer, Gudrun-Axeli Knapp, Mechthild Rumpf and Beate Schmidt, who studied family women working on assembly-lines. They published their findings under the graphic title *We do not own the minutes – the minutes own us*, a situation which the women faced in both of their workplaces, the family as well as the factory (Becker-Schmidt *et al*. 1982).

Our comparative research documents that the lives of women distance students with families today are no less fragmented and no more self-determined than the lives of the women in those early studies (see Chapter 3). FeU and OU UK women students comment extensively on the difficulties they have in trying to find or to make the time and the space for their studies. The men, on the other hand, are more likely to be granted the space and privacy needed to pursue their distance courses, as well as the support of their partners and family. While the DTU cannot interfere in the private lives of its students, our comparison of the OU UK and the FeU has shown that institutional provision does have the potential of helping or hindering the chances of women to combine a distance course with their family responsibilities and thereby contribute to more equal opportunities.

Removing the blinkers: overcoming androcentrism in distance education

In reading the literature on the pedagogy (or sometimes andragogy) of DE, in listening to conference presentations or – as was the case at both the 1997 and 1999 ICDE World Conferences – in looking at a podium of eminent distance educators and managers – one might get the impression that open and distance learning was primarily an enterprise run by men for men. True, in publications written in English we tend to find an observance of the rules concerning gender-inclusive and non-discriminatory language, at least if the authors come from Anglo-Saxon countries. But with the exception of some women's studies courses and equal opportunities programmes, as well as individual authors and conference participants (most of them women), even today there seems little concern with gender as an integral category in DE and with the adverse effects a seemingly neutral view of the distance education system and the student population has on women.

Gender differences do exist and they affect the ways in which women and men can participate in distance education (see Kirkup 1995; Burge 1997). The persisting androcentrism, which either ignores these differences or sets the male experience as the norm to which women have to adapt, limits the benefits which women can derive from the educational opportunities offered through open and distance learning. Androcentrism affords a blinkered view of the world by severely restricting the field of vision. The removal of these blinkers and the recognition 'of the female half of humanity and of sex as a central dimension in the study of society would lead to a more accurate picture of the social structure and to a better understanding of process' (Acker 1973: 936).

There is no reason to assume that the field of distance education differs from other academic disciplines such as sociology, of which Pamela Abbott and Claire Wallace write:

> Sociology is a male-dominated discipline, and this has fundamental implications for its theories, methods, research and teaching. Despite at least twenty years' criticism of the discipline for its malestream orientation and bias, little has changed . . . However, there has been some change. Sociologists can no longer afford to ignore women and gender divisions, and there is discussion about the changes needed for the malestream bias to be overcome.
>
> (Abbott and Wallace 1990: 1)

It is not to be expected that the necessary changes will occur automatically as had once been assumed, for instance in the case of class analysis and stratification research (see Acker 1973: 944). The change from an androcentric world-view to gender awareness would be so dramatic as to require a paradigm change on the lines of the scientific revolution described by Thomas Kuhn (1970). This is expressed, for instance, by Elizabeth Minnich who says: 'What we are doing, is comparable to Copernicus shattering our geocentricity, Darwin shattering our species-centricity. We are shattering andro-centricity and the change is fundamental' (quoted in Humm 1989: 9). The paradigm change is hampered by the staying power of established paradigms as well as the threats to existing power relations (Easlea 1973: 176ff). Giving up a paradigm means giving up the power to define 'reality'. This begs the question:

> If a paradigm shift can only occur within a shift in power, and if that means taking power in institutions that are already structured within the historical context of gendered relations of domination, what are the chances for the survival of critical feminist theories?
>
> (Acker 1989: 78)

What, indeed, are the chances of women of achieving such a fundamental switch in the theory and practice of distance education and to remove the restrictions imposed by androcentrism? By restricting the field of vision, blinkers protect the wearer from outside distractions, allowing a single-minded pursuit of a set course. As women teaching and doing research we have taken a chance and discarded the blinkers of traditional value-free sociology and pedagogy, thereby discovering the world beyond. We are in the process of challenging the old paradigm and providing evidence for the need to change. And we have the necessary faith, both in the new paradigm and in our ability to convert enough members of the DE community to make a paradigm shift happen eventually (see Easlea 1973: 176ff).

Chapter 3

Home study

The learning environments of women distance students

The enrolment and study success of women distance students is affected not only by institutional conditions but also by work-related and personal factors. One of the explicit goals of university-level DE is the provision of educational opportunities for mature students who are already in the labour market and want to study without giving up their job or career. This goal refers to the employment situation of men and women and calls for a DE system designed to fit in with the demands of paid work and even make use of resources students can access through their place of work. This target group is mostly male.

Another goal is the provision of educational opportunities for disadvantaged social groups without access to on-campus or classroom-based instruction. This target group, which also includes disabled and institutionalised persons, is often exemplified by the picture of the housebound parent of small children, and this latter group is nearly exclusively female. In fact, for a long time women distance students have been identified as housewives and mothers while women in paid work have been a neglected entity.

The foundation of the OU UK, for instance, was accompanied by the expectation that:

> the structure of the Open University, utilising as it does home-based study as the core of its learning system, is ideally suited to the needs of women who, housebound to a greater or lesser degree during the main years of child-rearing, nevertheless have some spare time which can be put to 'profitable' use.
>
> (McIntosh *et al.* 1977: 78)

As early as 1977, though, evaluation data showed that a DTU did not automatically represent a 'haven for housebound . . . housewives' and that this target group was under-represented at the OU UK from the beginning. Later evaluation studies provided some information about the reasons for these apparent contradictions, pointing to a glaring misconception in the initial assumptions about the learning contexts of women distance students and about the character of the work done by women in the areas of childrearing and domestic labour. The proportion of women studying at the OU UK was not only lower than expected, and too low in comparison to other British universities, but it also did not show the expected over-representation of family women not in paid work (for an account of the early years of the OU UK see McIntosh *et al.* 1977: 77–84).

The presumed equation woman distance student = housewife and mother proved to be a fallacy in Germany as well as in Britain. This was confirmed by surveys carried out at the FeU in 1985/86 and 1995/96 and comparative OU UK data collected parallel to the earlier FeU survey. Nevertheless, discussions about the participation of women in university-level DE tended to address this target group and to ignore the fact that the majority of the women enrolling in this form of education were in paid work and did not conform to the preconceived image of the full-time mother and housewife. While the issue of how to combine distance studying with employment was one of the most important considerations of distance educators, the emphasis was on the situation of the male distance students. The specific problems faced by working women were largely neglected, as was the even more difficult situation of women who had both workplace and family commitments.

The work situations of distance students

People who continue with their paid work while studying are in fact the major target group of distance education in the tertiary sector. In Germany, enrolment at the FeU is often referred to as *studieren neben dem Beruf* which signals the intended role of DE as a subsidiary activity to be pursued in addition to a job.

The work situations of women and men studying at a distance

The intention to provide study opportunities for people in the workforce is reflected in the high proportion of mature distance students who are gainfully employed. In the case of men, both the OU UK and the German FeU have been successful in reaching this target group: in 1986, the majority of male distance students – 80% of FeU men and 90% of OU UK men – were in paid work, most of them full-time. In the case of women the situation is different: only about half of the female distance students in the 1986 survey were in full-time employment and approximately a quarter of the women students at the OU UK (26%) and one-sixth at the FeU (17%) had part-time or occasional jobs (see Figure 3.1).

Compared to Britain, where a total of 78% of the women distance students at least held a part-time paid job, more women distance students in Germany

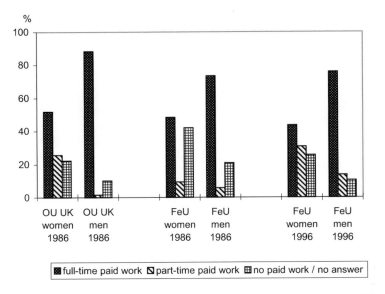

Figure 3.1 Work situation/extent of paid work: distance students in Britain and Germany

(32%) were not in any form of paid employment. This reflects in part the different age distribution in the two universities – OU UK students were generally older than FeU students – but also reflects national differences in the workforce participation of women (Kirkup and von Prümmer 1992: 4–5, 35, 47; BMFJ 1992).

It should be noted that later surveys at the FeU showed no significant changes in the employment patterns of men and women (see von Prümmer 1997b), although an FeU student survey carried out in 1996 shows a decline in full-time paid work of women as well as a lower proportion of women in unpaid housework and childcare, and a corresponding increase of part-time jobs. This finding may reflect social changes such as the high level of unemployment in Germany, coupled with an increased need to take on part-time employment, including hourly and occasional jobs.

To some extent the observed changes may also be a result of the 1996 sample definition which favoured so-called successful students who, as a group, exhibit lower work-force participation than distance students who were less degree-oriented (von Prümmer 1997b: 5). The structure of this latest sample allows us to correlate the extent to which students are gainfully employed to their study progress as demonstrated by their having passed the intermediate examination required to enter the advanced phase of a degree programme.

The differences between the so-called successful distance students and the ones who have not (yet) completed their intermediate examination are

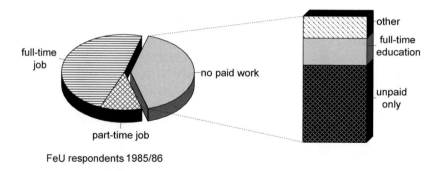

FeU respondents 1985/86

Figure 3.2 Work situation of women studying at the FeU

striking and demonstrate the difficulties of reconciling distance studies with the demands of a career. Three quarters of the successful group (73%), but only three-fifths of the other group (60%), had studied while being in full-time employment, a difference of 13 percentage points. Looking at men and women separately we find that the differences are much larger between the two groups of women ($\Delta = 18.2\%$) than they are between the two groups of men ($\Delta = 9.7\%$). This can be interpreted as further confirmation of the multiple pressures put on women because of their domestic and family commitments, which make it extremely difficult for them to concentrate on their studies while also working at a full-time job.

The 1986 survey showed that nearly half of the 579 women respondents (48%) had full-time jobs and 10% had part-time jobs outside the home (see Figure 3.2). Four out of ten women worked a few hours per week in low-paid jobs (7%), or were not in paid work at all (35%). Three-fifths of women distance students devoted themselves exclusively to unpaid family work. Men were much more likely to be in paid employment, three-quarters working full-time (74%) and 6% working part-time. Those men who did not earn money, were mostly (55%) engaged in full-time education other than their distance studies. Women who did not earn money worked mostly (61%) as unpaid mothers and homemakers.

Extent of paid work and household composition

Issues of unemployment aside, the extent to which distance students are able to work outside the home is related to their family situation and to the composition of the household in which they live. As Figure 3.3 shows this is where gender differences become glaringly apparent in both the OU UK and FeU data, especially when we are dealing with family men and women. Data from two surveys done in 1986 and in 1996 show that the social division

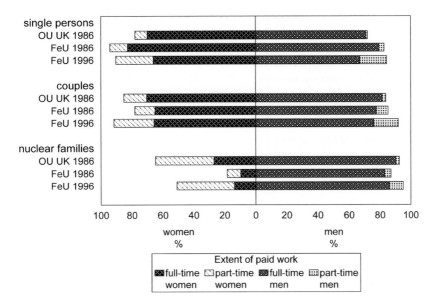

Figure 3.3 Extent of paid work by household composition: the OU UK and FeU

of labour has remained stable over this particular decade and that the role of the breadwinner is still assigned to the husband/father while the wife/mother takes care of the home and family and supplements the family income through part-time jobs.

'Homemakers': the responsibility of women for the private sphere

The differences in the extent to which women and men participate in the workforce reflect the fact that women are primarily responsible for childcare and for the household, as Figure 3.4 shows. Thus most of the men who did not hold a job were pursuing another educational programme (25% of 124 unemployed men). Only ten of the male respondents, that is 1.6% of the men, claim to be 'house-husbands', while one-fifth of the female respondents (20%) are housewives.

Regardless of the extent to which a woman is involved in paid work, she is nearly always responsible for the functioning of the domestic sphere and for bringing up her children, or caring for elderly or infirm relatives. It is often argued that modern western societies no longer have this rigid division of labour along gender lines. Men are said to participate in domestic and childrearing activities, and women are seen to participate in the labour

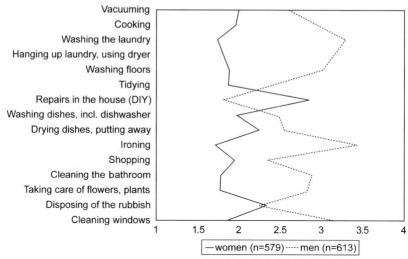

Vacuuming
Cooking
Washing the laundry
Hanging up laundry, using dryer
Washing floors
Tidying
Repairs in the house (DIY)
Washing dishes, incl. dishwasher
Drying dishes, putting away
Ironing
Shopping
Cleaning the bathroom
Taking care of flowers, plants
Disposing of the rubbish
Cleaning windows

— women (n=579) ···· men (n=613)

Comparison of means
1 = always or completely / 2 = Mostly or to a great extent /
3 = Occasionally or to a lesser extent / 4 = Never or not at all

Figure 3.4 Domestic division of labour: FeU students

market. In fact, even the most recent studies show that although men may help more with household tasks and childcare, they do not take equal responsibility or spend nearly as much time on the shopping, washing, and cleaning chores. Rather, as a representative survey on gender equality in 1992 confirmed, 'the traditional division of labour continues to exist in both the Western and Eastern German States' (quoted in BMFJ 1992: 77). In this respect, distance students are no different from their contemporaries.

In order to obtain a clearer picture of the extent to which women and men are involved in the day-to-day running of their households, we defined two groups of distance students and contrasted each of them according to the following criteria:

• childless couples, both partners in full-time employment (see Figure 3.5); and
• couples with children (nuclear family), woman in unpaid family work (see Figure 3.6).

This refers to women students' own work situations and to the work situations of the female partners/wives of male distance students. The comparative analysis of these groups demonstrates some expected and some unexpected patterns of domestic partnership.

Working from home: 'A woman's work is never done'

Distance education is sometimes described as an industrialised form of teaching and learning (see Peters 1997: 163ff and 1998: 139ff). This picture illustrates the production and delivery process of knowledge in large-scale DE systems. It fits the imagery of universities as thinking or knowledge factories which was part of the reform approach to higher education in the 1960s and 1970s and, in Germany, led to the foundation of new, comprehensive universities of which the FernUniversität was one.

By analogy with this picture of the teaching process, the learning process may be likened to a cottage industry or, in the jargon of the technological age, to teleworking. Students work from their homes rather than commuting to the factory or, in this case, the university campus. Instead of being provided by the employer/educational institution, the machine and tools/desk and computer are set up in the student's private environment. Responsibility for the workplace is privatised, as is responsibility for reaching the production/ teaching goals, and the home workers/students are thus in charge of their own success or failure. Any conflicts between working/studying and the private sphere with its family commitments have nothing to do with the employer/DTU and must be solved independently by the teleworker/distance students. The latter, most of whom also hold a job, have to reconcile their distance studies with their paid work as well as with their domestic responsibilities. This is more of a problem for women distance students since it is almost exclusively women who are faced with childcare and household chores.

Multiple commitments: juggling course loads, family work, and paid employment

As has been shown, to a large extent – though to a lesser degree than male distance students – women studying at the FeU are in full-time or part-time employment. Only one-fifth (20%) of the women respondents in our 1986 sample (and 1.6% of the men) said they were in 'full-time unpaid work', i.e. exclusively taking care of their homes and families or dependents. Regardless of their family status, nearly half (48%) of the women – as compared with three-quarters (73%) of the men – were in full-time paid employment (including self-employed). In the light of these figures, the image of the typical woman student being a housewife with no outside commitments had to be abandoned. Both men and women who enrol in a degree course while in paid employment must carry the double load of a job and their degree course. But men do not have to carry the multiple load of domestic labour and possibly childcare which women have to cope with in addition to their studies and employment.

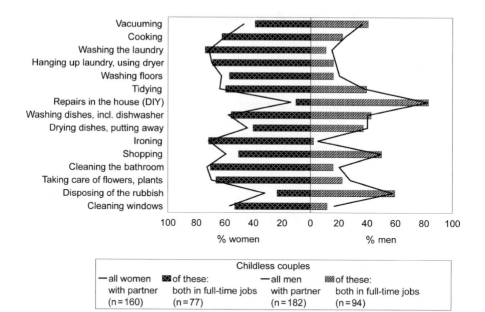

Figure 3.5 Responsibility for household chores: domestic division of labour with childless couples, both partners in full-time paid work

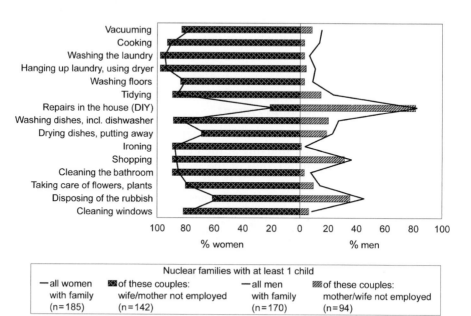

Figure 3.6 Responsibility for household chores: domestic division of labour in nuclear families, woman not in paid work

It is often assumed that working couples share the domestic and childcare responsibilities and therefore women who hold a job have fewer duties with respect to their roles as housewives and mothers. This assumption is patently false in the case of single parents where the full responsibility and workload falls on the one parent, usually the mother. In cases where there is a partner, the domestic and parenting work is not shared equally, and the double or triple burden of family and paid work nearly always is the woman's responsibility (see Figures 3.5 and 3.6).

Although we might expect two-income families, where both partners work outside the home, to organise the family work as a partnership, more women than men in this situation report that specific household chores are 'fully' or 'to a large extent' their sole responsibility. The only exception to this is the traditionally male area of home-improvement and repairs around the house. This is the exclusive responsibility of 80% of the men, in the case of male respondents their own responsibility, in the case of women respondents the responsibility of their male partner. With respect to housework, our findings bear out other research showing the continued existence of the traditional division of labour along gender lines (Metz-Göckel and Müller 1985). Periodically, there are newspaper reports about recent surveys which always conclude that this division of labour remains basically unchanged, although the rhetoric may be more concerned with partnership and women's right to work outside the home and to earn their own money.

While these findings may be disappointing they are not totally unexpected, unlike the connected finding that there are gender-related differences in what happens once a person has taken up a DE course. Considering the fact that women already bear most of the housekeeping and childcare load, it might have been expected that they are relieved from some of their duties upon registering as a student. In fact, the reverse is often true: many women distance students report an increase in the demands their partners and children make on them. Men, by contrast, often mention being relieved of household and childcare duties, being given uninterrupted time and space for studying, and having other active help from their partners such as the typing of term papers and assignments or the locating of literature.

The different circumstances of men and women distance students manifest themselves even in the case of childless couples: nine out of ten women living with a partner but without children (91%) report that the domestic division of labour has remained unchanged after they enrolled as distance students; only 4.4% of them experienced a noticeable relief from their responsibilities. The figures for men living with a partner and no children are 81% and 13% respectively. This confirms the fact that studying nearly always is an additional burden for women, who already bear the main load in the private sphere, while men students who might at best help with household chores, are relieved of the little they previously did perform.

It appears therefore that women do not have the same right as men to pursue their education, especially when this could be seen to interfere with their role as mothers and wives. This thought will be explored in more detail in a later section. The following quotes, cited verbatim from the 1996 questionnaires of women studying at the FeU (my translation), illustrate what it means to embark on a course of study in addition to employment and family commitments. They are taken from answers to the open-ended question 'Whom or what do you have to take into account/or what takes precedence when you wish to study?'.

> '*My working hours, not a normal 8 hour day. I only have time for my distance studies at night, after 8:00 in the evening until c. 1:00 at night and sometimes on a weekend.*
>
> *My family.*'

> '*Overtime.*
>
> *Children.*
>
> *Appointments in connection with the renovation of our house.*'

> '*Husband; family; job/career; childminder.*
>
> *In essence I work in the evenings, putting in 4–6 hours whenever I have the inclination and energy.*'

> '*At home I can only study after 9:00 p.m. when our daughter is in bed. Alternatively, I study during my night shift at the hospital, between 11:00 p.m. and 3:00 a.m.*'

Women in marriages or partnerships without children also experience more pressures through the cumulative demands of their career, their household and their partner. The following quote from a married woman student in full-time paid work shows these effects:

> '*Because of my job I am out of the house for more than 12 hours a day. Before I can start studying I need some time for myself to rest and wind down. I also want to spend quality time with my husband, talking things over. And of course there is the household which needs to be taken care of.*'

The quote is taken from the questionnaire of a 25-year old economics student who says that she does her course work in the evenings and at night, except during her holidays and weekends when she also studies in the afternoons. Usually she manages a weekly workload of ten hours during the week and an additional two hours on the weekend. This is much less than the twenty hours the FeU expects part-time students to spend on their course load. The following statements are typical examples of women students who have to fulfil commitments at work and at home and reconcile their distance studying with other spheres of life:

'*Everyday life (i.e. cooking the evening meals, doing the dishes) and weekend chores of cleaning our home and shopping have priority. Otherwise I cannot study with a clear conscience. I also make sure that I do not lose contact with the outside world (television, friends, social life) in order to avoid becoming a recluse and losing touch with the world during the 8 long years of studying.*'

'*Household.*
Partner, guilty conscience due to my neglecting him.'

'*Job responsibilities, overtime.*
Family situation, since my husband works mostly irregular hours.'

'*Household; partner; family; friends.*
My own disposition: after an 8-hour working day my stamina and my ability to concentrate is often much lower than I had expected. Often I am too tired in the evenings to get down to studying.'

'*My husband's working hours. He is a shiftworker, and on principle I don't study in his free time. We have too little free time together as it is.*'

The open-ended comments of these women distance students are systematically different from those of their male colleagues. When asked about circumstances which restrict their study activities, men refer mostly to employment-related factors and hardly ever mention family or domestic responsibilities. This is true for both single and family men and for men who live with a partner or wife without children. In this respect, distance students do not differ from other segments of society. It is not surprising that women in DE are confronted with many more problems in trying to combine their studies with other areas of their lives.

For instance, men not only can spend more time on their distance studies, they can also organise their time more freely than women who have to fit their studies around the demands of their multiple commitments. The effect is seen in gender differences in the answers to questions concerning the time management of distance study (see Figure 3.7). The answering patterns show that employment-related factors interfere more in men's study schedules and family-related factors interfere more with women's study schedules. This is true even for those women who have job responsibilities as well as family responsibilities.

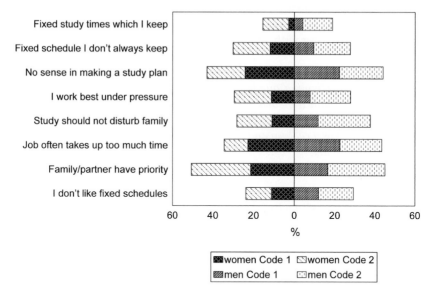

Code 1 = "corresponds to my situation exactly"; Code 2 = "corresponds to large extent"

Figure 3.7 Gender differences in time management with respect to distance studying

Women distance students with children

Distance students differ from other students in their age, their employment status and their life circumstances. They are generally older than students in conventional universities and quite often are family men and women with children and domestic responsibilities. The mean age of FeU students is 28.9 years for women and 30.6 years for men, i.e. the women tend to be slightly younger than the men. In comparison to OU UK students, both male and female FeU students are younger. In the 1986 surveys nearly one-third of the former (29%) but only 5% of the latter are under 25 years of age, and nearly one in ten FeU respondents (9%) but three in ten OU UK respondents (34%) were 39 years and older (see also Kirkup and von Prümmer 1992: 4, 47). Compared to other German students FeU women are considerably older, as Figure 3.8 shows.

Both marital status and household composition are age-related, the age groups in their mid-twenties to mid-thirties being most likely to have childrearing commitments. At the time of the first survey, one-fifth of the students at the FeU had children under three years of age (19%), 12% had children aged three to five, 11% had children aged six to thirteen, and 8% had children aged fourteen and over. In total, 426 out of 1,192 respondents had between one and six mostly younger children, and 390 of them lived in the same household as their children. Parents in the survey had an average

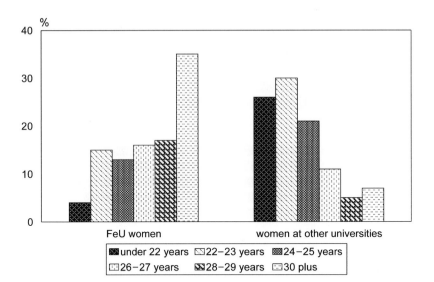

Sources: FeU survey 1986 and "11. Sozialerhebung" (BMBW 1986: 91)

Figure 3.8 Age distribution of women studying at (West) German universities

of 1.72 children altogether, an average of 1.65 children lived with their parent(s).

The age of the children is directly related to the age of the students themselves and to their gender. For instance, the overall proportion of students with children under three years is 11% in the age-group under 25 years, 22% in the age group 25 to 31 years, and 28% in the age group 32 to 38 years. Viewed separately, young women are more likely than young men to have very small children: only 1.7% of the men aged 24 and younger, but 19% of the women in this age-group have children under three years of age.

In an earlier section of this chapter we have seen that the extent of women's paid work is related to their domestic situation and that women distance students who live with a partner and with children are much less likely to work outside the home than men in similar situations (see Figure 3.3). These employment patterns are mirrored when we look at the age of children as a determinant. Here we find that only 6.1% of the mothers with children under 3 years and 8.7% with children aged 3–5 years work full-time outside the home. The same is true for 82% and 77% of the fathers who have children in these age-groups (data taken from the 1986 survey of FeU students). Figure 3.9 shows the extent of paid work in relation to the ages of the children in the household of women and men enrolled in a degree course at the FeU.

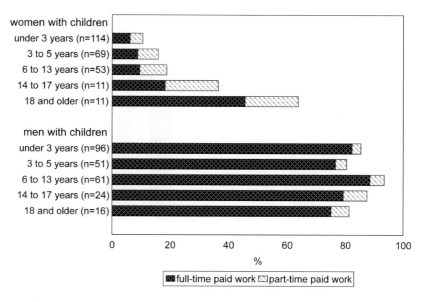

women with children

Figure 3.9 Extent of paid work of women and men by age of children

If the existence of children thus affects a woman's ability to pursue employment outside the home, it also has an impact on her everyday life and, consequently, on her ability to pursue a DE programme. The first issue arising in this context is the gender division regarding childcare, which is almost universally the sole responsibility of the mother. In our comparative survey we provided both male and female distance students with a list of people, including themselves and their partners, and childcare institutions, and asked them to tell us for each of them the role they play in their own childcaring arrangements.

The men and women in the sample were not couples, but the gender patterns in their answers were complimentary and strongly supported the contention that women and men, especially when they are mothers and fathers, do not have equal learning environments in their homes. The responsibility for childcare rests squarely on the women, be they distance students themselves or the partners of the male distance students filling in the questionnaire. Men are more inclined to perceive their own childcare arrangements as a partnership in which they take a fairly active role in bringing up the children, taking responsibility often, but not always, or investing much time in it. This does not always correspond with the answers they give for the mother's role in the childrearing, and it certainly does not correspond to the answers the women give for the division of labour in this area.

The women who share a home with a partner and with at least one child are the primary carers for children of all ages, with a slight lessening of the responsibility once the children are fourteen and older (see Figure 3.10).

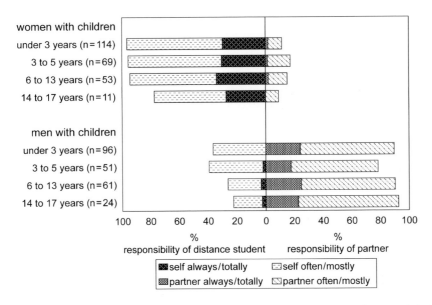

Figure 3.10 Responsibility for childcare by age of children: distance students and their partners

Even in cases where the woman holds a job in addition to her family and domestic work, there is no discernible reduction in the childcare responsibilities of mothers. This can be seen clearly in the patterns of childcare responsibilities presented in Figure 3.11 which compares distance students and their partners in different employment situations. Although some of the groups are quite small, the overall trend is clear: family women, whether they are full-time mothers and housewives or whether they also work outside the home, take on the care of their children while men have limited responsibilities in this area.

The findings do not reflect a German national characteristic, as can be seen when comparing the FeU data with answers given by OU UK women and men. These also show a persistent division of childcare responsibilities according to gender.

Flexibility versus fragmentation: the myth of women being in charge of their time

In an earlier section I discussed some of the ways in which the enrolment and study success of women distance students might be affected by institutional conditions. Problems may also arise out of a student's personal situation and learning environment. When mature students take up a distance education course they always take on an additional workload on top of work and family commitments. In the case of women who are housewives

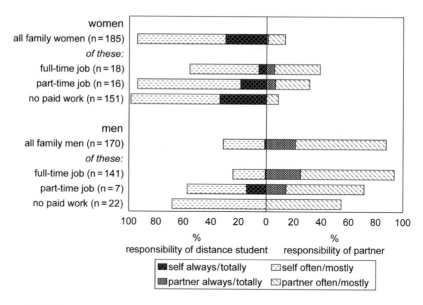

Figure 3.11 Responsibility for childcare by extent of paid work: distance students and their partners

and mothers, this is added to their domestic responsibilities as well as to job or career responsibilities.

As mentioned earlier, the often heard argument that distance education is especially suited for those women who are housebound mothers of small children, with restricted mobility but with plenty of spare time, is based on two characteristics of this teaching mode. Namely, the relatively high flexibility of the time and study schedule; and also the fact that the student can study in her home environment rather than in classrooms or lecture theatres in the institution. The following quote from an early text on the OU UK is characteristic of this view:

> . . . the structure of the Open University, utilising as it does home-based study as the core of its learning system, is ideally suited to the needs of women who, house-bound to a greater or lesser degree during the main years of child-rearing, nevertheless have some spare time which can be put to 'profitable' use.
>
> (McIntosh *et al.* 1977: 78)

The argument that distance education is a form of studying specially suited for housewives is based on the erroneous assumption that housework and childcare are undemanding tasks which do not require much planning or attention. The housewife and mother of small children, although housebound is assumed to be autonomous in the way she organises her learning environment and her schedule.

This view ignores the character of domestic labour and childcare, both of which are extremely fragmented and subject to external pressures. Specifically, it does not address the reality of those women who are mothers and have to be ready to react immediately to direct and indirect demands from their child or children. This has been demonstrated impressively in a study on women working on factory assembly lines published under the title *One is not enough – both are too much. Experiences of working-class women between factory and family* (Becker-Schmidt *et al.* 1984).

In her pioneering study on *The Sociology of Housework*, Ann Oakley identified the fragmentation of the work process as the core problem of domestic work and childrearing:

> This is a crucial finding. Housework is such fragmented work that almost never does the housewife report thinking about the task in hand. Whatever skills are needed, complete mental concentration is not one, and the effect of having many different tasks to do is a dispersal of the housewife's attention in many different directions. Children amplify this fragmentation effect. They make perfect concentration impossible and are often the cause of breaks in work activity. The extent to which children are thought about while housework is done is not only a reflection on housework's fragmented quality: it also signifies the basic difficulties which inhere in the combination of housewife and mother roles.
>
> (Oakley 1974: 84–5)

It is this fragmentation which characterises the situation of many women distance students and which differentiates it from that of the men who almost never carry the sole responsibility for children and household. Matriculation in a degree course does not change this situation as women distance students are frequently confronted with everyday emergencies which demand immediate intervention without any consideration for the need for uninterrupted study time. The resulting pressures are described vividly by Ingeborg Heinze, a student at the German FeU, mother of four children (aged, at the time of writing, $6\frac{1}{2}$, $4\frac{1}{2}$, $2\frac{1}{2}$ and $1\frac{1}{2}$ years), who had given up her full-time job after the fourth child. She explicitly contradicts the assumptions about the compatibility of childcare and distance studying:

> The second 'housewives' problem' is almost worse. It is the fact that, contrary to the opinions voiced by smart people, it is not possible to organise a household and family with small children in the best possible way to provide regular slots of free time for the housewife . . . My own experience tells me that there are a great many household chores which

are more sensibly tackled when the children aren't around, such as using the sewing machine, ironing, and doing repairs involving glue (!).

As a housewife one often gets the 'simple' piece of advice to set priorities. This is difficult to follow (unless it is absolutely imperative to hand in an assignment within two days) since it is an unwelcome characteristic of housework that those things that have not been done and are cluttering up the place are immediately obvious to everybody else, especially to one's husband.

Another disadvantage of distance studying is the fact that children obviously do not consider paperwork as real work (and I have heard that some husbands share this attitude!) . . . When I am sitting in my home office trying to study, I am constantly interrupted by my children calling out things like: 'I don't want to disturb you, but . . .', 'do you know where . . .', 'look, I can't find . . .', 'Mama, why . . . ?' In the background I can hear a lowered voice saying 'be quiet, Mama is working', answered by the understanding comment from my eldest son: 'Shit, Mama is always working when you need her!' . . . Yet I only get nervous when I'm trying to prepare for examinations. During those times things always turn out differently from how I had planned them.

In summary I'd like to say that the problems which face housewives become especially pressing and visible when they concern those aspects which cannot be organised. Here we deal with problems such as 'how do I escape from my children?' or 'how do I concentrate on the study material when the baby is crying?'. One solution I can think of is to put off studying until the children are old enough to attend kindergarten or school. But then, that is the time when women start thinking about a return to paid work, and then it is often too late to enrol as a student.

(Heinze 1980: 12)

I have quoted Ingeborg Heinze's story extensively since even today, nearly twenty years after it was written, this story reflects the learning environment of many women distance students who have brought it to our attention time and time again in interviews and surveys or in discussions we have with groups of students and with tutors and counsellors in study centres.

A different view is taken by Patricia W. Lunneborg in her study entitled *OU Women. Undoing Educational Obstacles*. She stresses the unsuitability of traditional universities and institutions of further education which are 'out of sync. with the realities of women's lives' and whose timetable 'does not take into account women's domestic and family responsibilities' (Lunneborg 1994: 101). By contrast, DE offers a way out of the dilemma because 'how else could a mother deliver her kids to school, drive them to violin lessons afterwards, go on to a class on constructing soft toys, and go to university – except by doing the OU?' (Lunneborg 1994: 103).

The book gives another example of a woman with a disability – partial deafness – for whom the OU provided:

> . . . a mode of study which allowed her to hold on to her job and be at home for her two boys. She also needed a way of learning that took deafness into account – as well as the fact that English was her second language.
>
> (Lunneborg 1994: 103)

This woman also held a job as a nurse. Considering the formidable odds against her studying at a regular university one must agree with Lunneborg's conclusion that the OU is an improvement over other alternatives: 'Traditional universities ask mature women to fit with them. The OU says, instead, I will fit with you' (Lunneborg 1994: 104).

While it is undeniably true that DE is more flexible and therefore more amenable to fitting around other commitments, our data show that the learning environment of women often makes it difficult to cope even with this form of studying. As long as the social division of labour places the childcare responsibilities and domestic work almost exclusively on women, a distance education system needs to be concerned with women-friendly perspectives in its organisation and delivery system in order to provide equal chances for men and women.

Studying at home: keeping women in their place?

Thus far I have described the learning environment in terms of outside factors such as the extent of paid employment and in terms of personal relationships and domestic responsibilities. In referring to the title of a paper given by Karlene Faith and Rebecca Coulter *Home study; keeping women in their place* (Faith and Coulter 1988: 195ff) in this section I want to address two aspects which affect women's chances to succeed in their studies. The first one concerns the literal side of the quote, i.e. the actual space and the physical surroundings women find or make for their learning activity. The second concerns the possible effect of distance education on the power relations by which society reserves the public sphere for men and relegates women to the domestic sphere.

The dual face of distance education: overcoming or reinforcing traditional role patterns

Up until the mid-1980s the relevance of distance education for women was discussed exclusively with reference to the opportunities it offered to participate in higher education. The focus was on those institutional characteristics which dispensed with attendance requirements and allowed flexible study periods. This undisputed advantage of DE was held to favour women whose life situations were characterised by restricted mobility in space and by unrestricted flexibility in time, i.e. women who were housebound mothers of small children.

Since 1982 the newly founded Women's International Network (WIN) provided a forum within the International Council for Distance Education (ICDE) for looking at other aspects of the role of distance education for women. One aspect referred to the above-mentioned cottage industry character of DE and the double-edged effect this has on the women who are working from home. On the one hand, it was an opportunity, as studying at a distance meant that women could pursue higher education and gain a degree even if they could not attend regular universities. On the other hand, it posed a threat as it was apt to cement the traditional social structures which prevent women from entering higher education in the first place, mainly through the gendered division of labour. This assigns the public sphere to men and consigns women to the private sphere. Seen from this angle, DE could reinforce the stereotyped role of women as responsible for domestic activities: the children, the household and, thanks to the distance study mode, the degree programme and study material. This does nothing for the emancipation of women and also does not help to overcome the isolation which characterises the situation of the housewife (Burge 1990: 12–13). In a contribution to the 1988 ICDE conference Karlene Faith and Rebecca Coulter asked the provocative question: 'Does distance education, then, reinforce women's confinement to the home and collude with gender role tradition, or does it provide the means for realizing women's aspirations for social and economic equality?' (Faith and Coulter 1988: 196).

A similar question had also been raised in 1988 by Nick Farnes about the liberating potential of paid work. In his discussion entitled *Open University community education: emancipation or domestication*, he warns:

> . . . the issue of whether domestic activities are necessarily domesticating and work automatically emancipating (or *vice-versa*) is of central importance in considering the changes students make in their domestic, communal, and paid work. We must be aware of the traps that these can present since certain features of wage labour contribute more to subordination and exploitation than to women's emancipation.
>
> (Farnes 1993: 190)

With regard to education, there seems to be nearly universal agreement that women must have better access to education on all levels, including primary, vocational and tertiary education as well as in improving adult literacy. The recognition that education is a basic human right of women as well as men is reflected in equal opportunities programmes such as the ones initiated by the European Union:

In many European countries, during the past ten years, there has been concern that women have not participated in post-school education, both vocational and academic, equally with men; and that they have been particularly under-represented in traditionally 'male' subject areas, for example engineering, law and management studies. This has been seen to contribute to gender inequality in the labour market, and also to a basic inequality of educational opportunity for women.

(Kirkup and von Prümmer 1996: 33)

The world conference on population in 1994 asserted the fact that education and vocational/professional qualifications are the basis of a self-determined life (see Sadik 1994). In this context, distance education plays an important role since it offers the two-fold opportunity: first, to extend education to large sectors of a society at relatively low cost; and second, to provide educational opportunities for girls and women without fundamental changes to the social structure and the traditional gender relations in the society. One case in point is the following discussion of the advantages of distance education:

If the student is a young girl who is needed to contribute to the welfare of the family by gardening, carting water or collecting firewood, these duties can be carried out and the study fitted around them. In towns, young girls, while not needed to carry water or even grow food, will still be required for shopping and childminding. The distance mode of study enables urban and rural females to fulfil their obligations to their families.

Married women who find themselves confined to the home through pregnancy, breast-feeding and child care can continue their education. No one says it is an easy way for women to continue educating themselves, but it is available and women need not venture out of their homes to do it.

(Martin 1988: 132)

The quote describes the situation in Papua New Guinea. Doing a book review on a conference report edited by Eileen Wormald and Anne Crossley in 1988, *Women and Education in Papua New Guinea and the South Pacific*, I first noticed the parallels in the situation of women in distance education in Papua New Guinea and in western industrialised countries (von Prümmer 1992). I was fascinated to see that there are only gradual, rather than fundamental, differences in the situation which we have found in our research of the circumstances of women in highly industrialised countries in western Europe. In Europe as well as in Papua New Guinea there is a social consensus which decrees that their family duties, especially childcare, take precedence over the educational rights of women. Distance education serves to ensure that women fulfil these duties even when pursuing their educational aspirations.

The other side of the coin is the potential of education to empower women to break through the confines of the prescribed domestic roles: on the formal level, education leads to qualifications which may be used toward gaining economic and social equality. On another level, education is *per se* the basis for a critical reflection of existing power relations and social hierarchies. If women are prevented from access to institutions of learning by the traditional gender role definition in their culture, DE may be their only alternative. In bringing the learning into the domestic sphere, DE keeps women at home, while at the same time providing them with a wider perspective and the means to enter the so-called male domain of the public sphere:

> For these women home study is, in many senses, an ideal solution for obtaining an education, and education, we would argue, provides women with some of the essential tools needed to challenge the traditional assumptions about their role and status and to transform their lives.
>
> (Faith and Coulter 1988: 196)

A woman's place in the home: kitchen, bedroom or study?

It has already been mentioned that distance education as home study privatises the learning process in a way similar to the way teleworking privatises jobs in production or in the service industry. Students have to furnish and equip their own workplace and take sole responsibility for creating a conducive environment in which to pursue their studies. This system favours those students who have sufficient resources and sufficient power to establish their own and undisputed space.

Traditionally, men are more likely than women to either own those resources or have access to and control over them. This is most obvious in the case of the modern technologies which are becoming increasingly prominent tools in distance education and will be dealt with in more detail later (see Chapter 5). It also affects the way in which men and women are able to claim their own space within the household:

> Creating adequate privacy for women means shifting long-existing power arrangements. An odd paradox emerges: women have inhabited the 'private realm' but lacked the benefits of privacy. Historically, women have worked to create private space and leisure for men.
>
> (Smith 1998: 23)

This is true in the case of distance students, and many women studying at the OU UK and at the FeU report study problems which they relate directly to the lack of a room of their own in which they can work through the study materials without being disturbed. Quite often, the students do not even

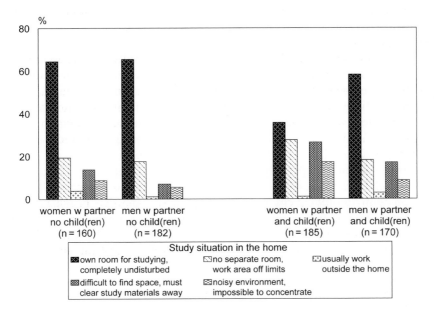

Figure 3.12 Study situation: couples with and without child(ren)

have a table or a corner set aside exclusively for study purposes and which is taboo for other family members. This inadequate situation happens frequently to the mothers and rarely to the fathers among the distance students. Compared to them, childless couples generally have better study conditions, irrespective of gender.

We have already seen how difficult it is for women to find the *time* for their studies. Figure 3.12 shows that it may also be extremely difficult for them to find the *space* which exacerbates the situation. Often this results in a lack of concentration and in conflicts with other members of the household which again add to the pressures inherent in studying for a degree at a distance. It is small wonder that women, more often than men, report having experienced problems with their studies during the first semester as distance students.

Changing the balance: empowerment through distance education

For many women, especially those outside the labour market or in low-paid, undemanding jobs, learning to organise their own studies and acquiring effective learning patterns is in itself a difficult learning process. This has been identified as one of the main problems facing mature students re-entering education after often long periods of abstinence, for instance by

Mary Thorpe and David Grugeon in their book *Open Learning for Adults*, who state that:

> ... there is the issue of learning to learn, especially where the familiar, often passive role of the traditional classroom and teacher-based student must be replaced by a more independent, self-motivating approach. Early difficulties are exacerbated in systems, like the OU, which use technologies still unfamiliar to most adults as a means of learning.
>
> (Thorpe and Grugeon 1987: 8)

For other women, especially if they are used to work in managerial or professional occupations, this may present little or no problem. What all women with families seem to have in common, though, is the apparent incompatibility of family and domestic responsibilites with serious distance education, and the need to learn to assert their right to be a student as well as a mother and housewife without feeling guilty. Unlike the men, women have to perform a constant balancing act and cope with 'the resulting feelings of guilt and anxiety' (Wellendorf 1980: 38). Yet this is deemed essential for the independent and autonomous learning habit required by any distance education mode to at least some extent because:

> ... communities have long relied upon women to perform domestic tasks, nurture men, raise children, care for the sick and the elderly, visit the poor, and maintain kin ties, when women think about devoting energy to other pursuits – including those which are personal and private – society becomes anxious and notices selfishness and excessive individualism with fresh interest ... Autonomy and liberty – as well as certain kinds of creativity and self-expression – are almost impossible without privacy, so establishing its place in a woman's life is a primary task of any bid for equality.
>
> (Smith 1998: 23)

Our research, and many discussions with women students, have shown that it is important for students to become aware of the potential pitfalls as early as possible and to develop strategies to counteract the combined effects of family and domestic duties, demands made by partners and other significant people, work-related pressures, and – last but not least – demands which originate within the student herself, as a consequence of the socialisation process of girls and women in our society. The conditions needed for successful studying do not simply 'happen' because a woman has registered as a distance student, and they are not usually 'given' to her. Rather, women distance students often find it necessary to negotiate the space, both literally and figuratively, and the support needed for studying in order to ensure:

- that uninterrupted work is possible at reasonable times and that study materials are not disturbed by others. Time for travel and attendance at tutorials or face-to-face seminars, as well as exams has to be available;
- that domestic and childcare responsibilities are lessened, both through other family members sharing in the work and through a re-evaluation of standards. This includes the woman student as well as her family: she cannot be a 'perfect' housewife and mother while she is carrying a double or triple load;
- that no questions are raised about the necessity of course-related expenditure. The woman must not feel that she has to justify the use of financial resources to pay for study fees, course-related travel expenses, or literature, and possibly childcare provision.

In discussions with women studying at the FeU the importance of recognising these patterns and taking steps to deal with their effects has been pointed out time and again. Contacts with other students, be they personal meetings, conversations on the phone, or the exchange of e-mails, can serve an important function in making a woman distance student aware of these processes, lessening feelings of guilt, reaching agreements with her partner and children, and helping to overcome inner conflicts.

While women face many difficulties in trying to combine studying with family and household responsibilities, enrolling in a distance education programme can also have a liberating effect: in creating objective circumstances outside the student's control, studying can provide a legitimate excuse to withdraw at least partially from the ever-present demands on a woman's time and emotional resources. A woman whose partner was supportive of – or at least not opposed to – her decision to register as a student is in a good position to call in his active support with respect to relieving her of domestic duties and possibly reorganising his own schedule to fit in with her timetable.

In recent years increasing attention has been paid to the question of the empowerment of individuals, especially women, through distance education. 'Adult change and development: learning and people's lives' (Morgan 1995: 319) gives an illustration of the way in which the student's home life has come to be seen as relevant for judging the success of distance education in a given social context. The research done by Alistair Morgan explores the:

> . . . outcomes of learning and the way students change and develop, when the experience of learning is viewed from the learner's perspective. The outcomes of learning can be conceptualised under three closely related levels of change: changes in conceptual understandings, changes in study patterns and skill in learning, and adult change and development – change in a social context.
>
> (Morgan 1995: 319)

Morgan's concern with placing distance studying in the social context is to identify 'some of the realities of the experiences of studying in the OU. The aim is to generate rich descriptions of people's lives and the way these interact with study, and to theorise the various forms of human change', in order to 'contribute to improving practice and improving learning' (Morgan 1995: 322).

Of course, looking at social contexts means looking at gender effects even if this is not the starting point for the research. It was therefore inevitable that the discovery of less than ideal settings led to a description of the difficulties of women students whose:

> ... relationships with their husbands can be seen as influenced by historical factors which shape the social structures of how they are subordinated ... It seems that some women students experience a 'double day', as they return to study with the OU combined with their domestic roles. Besides all the traditional expectations of gender roles, study has to be fitted in around these domestic labours ... It would appear that for some women students, to be engaged in OU study is perceived as a threat by their husbands. Studying is seen as changing the identity of the partner from being subservient and domesticated.
>
> (Morgan 1995: 321)

As feminist distance educators we cannot be satisfied with the finding that some 'women students have to contend with study under constraints of this nature' (Morgan 1995: 319). Rather, we look for ways in which we can support the process of change and contribute more directly to the empowerment of women. This goal has been pursued by women distance educators for a number of years now, and their concerted efforts can be summed up as a commitment to 'feminist pedagogy and women-friendly perspectives in distance education' (see the Women's Studies Center of Umeå 1993).

Undoubtedly issues of the domestic division of labour, including childcare responsibility, belong to the sphere of students' private lives and therefore might be considered beyond the legitimate reach of institutional interference. At the same time they profoundly affect women students' ability to enter programmes of further education, including DE programmes, and their chances of pursuing a course continuously and completing a degree successfully.

Although these factors cannot (and should not) be directly influenced by the university, the institution nevertheless can (and should) take measures to make it easier for women to come to terms with problems of incompatibility. Some of these measures could include:

- more flexible opening times and times for tutorials and counselling;
- help with the care of children or infirm relatives, either through the provision of facilities or through financial support; and

• providing students with the means to set up support networks, study groups and other forms of contact.

The last point is important because it allows new women distance students to learn from the experiences of others, both with respect to the problems they will be facing and to the coping strategies which have been developed and tested already. As an institutional researcher at the FeU I therefore consider it an important part of my job to share research results with the subjects of the research. By meeting groups of women students and their tutors/counsellors – the mentors who provide local support services in the German distance education system – in round-table discussions; and by giving presentations of our findings, we can disseminate the information and initiate discussions among women in which they can exchange not only their problems but also their coping strategies.

At the same time, the students and the mentors might bring up additional questions to ask of the data, point out possible interpretations which we have overlooked, and suggest areas for further research. The value of involving the students and study centre staff in the evaluation research has just recently been impressively demonstrated by Mavis Heron (1997) in her study of OU UK women entitled *In my own skin. Dialogues with women students, tutors and counsellors.*

Emancipation through distance education: observations from a pilot project

After unification, the decentralised East German DE system collapsed and the FeU became the only university-level provider of DE in the whole of Germany. There are other distance teaching institutions (which are privately owned) providing education at secondary school level, leading for instance to the *Abitur* (A-levels or high school diploma); or offering vocational courses, such as programmes for technicians and engineers, or language programmes for interpreters and translators. Compared to the FeU, these institutions tend to have a higher female enrolment rate, due to the type of courses and programmes they offer and due to the level of educational and vocational or professional qualifications obtainable. Among these there are a larger number of women who study in preparation for (re-)entering the labor market after a period of being full-time housewives and mothers.

In 1991, Isabell Herbst, a colleague working for the largest of these organisations, AKAD (Society for Continuing and Adult Education), was awarded a federal grant to run and evaluate a pilot scheme on further education for women with families through distance learning. The project was explicitly designed to put into practice and test some of the results and hypotheses for women-friendly perspectives in DE which had come out of our own and other research into the situation of women distance students.

I myself was asked to join the advisory board and to contribute both to the formulation of the research questions and to the design and methodology of the evaluation research.

The project was based on the premise that 'women in general have no difficulties with the distance learning method' and on the finding that 'women with families or single mothers are clearly overtaxed' (Herbst 1992) leading to a high drop-out rate. Concentrating on women who were mothers, study conditions were created aimed at being 'women-friendly', more specifically, friendly for women in the family phase of their lives. The project focused on two aspects:

1   With respect to didactic and methodological issues in distance educa-
    tion, the project aimed to develop and test measures for a reduction of
    women's high drop-out rates in West German DE systems.
2   With regard to opening up new perspectives for women's further educa-
    tion, and for designing women-centered programmes, the project aimed
    at providing adequate learning conditions for full-time housewives and
    mothers, so-called 'family women' (*Familienfrauen*), who are studying
    at a distance.

Briefly, the project involved a joint programme in which Mothers' Centres, a network of some 200 centres run by and for women with children, provided the infrastructure for study groups of women enrolled in a course or a programme at AKAD. The centres were local self-help organisations helping mothers of small children, especially single parents, to overcome some of their isolation by meeting other women in similar circumstances; to re-learn social skills and gain confidence, to re-enter public spheres outside their immediate family; and to free women from some of their domestic and parental responsibilities. Some of the features of these Mothers' Centres are the provision of childcare, including homework supervision for older children, and of hot lunches and take-away meals (for more details, see Herbst 1992).

The project setting included eight Mothers' Centres in West Germany, all located near AKAD seminar centres. On the part of AKAD, women enrolling in the pilot scheme were allowed special study conditions, such as reduced attendance requirements at seminar centres, the possibility of a temporary stop of study materials, and reduced fees. Small study groups were established which were fairly homogeneous with respect to courses and levels of previous knowledge. Each group was assigned a coordinator (or tutor/counsellor), who was available for questions and problem-solving but who was not in charge of the group. Groups were expected to meet on a regular basis for shared learning and for exchanges of problems and solutions concerning the subject matter as well as learning problems, but each group was autonomous in scheduling meetings/tutorials and in deciding on the pace and progress of their studies.

The project has shown ways in which distance education could be made more women-friendly (see Herbst 1993; Herbst *et al.* 1994):

- The provision of specific conditions, which allow the woman to concentrate on her studies without having to worry about caring for and feeding her children, does contribute to a more positive and relaxed learning atmosphere and helps to reduce drop-out rates.
- The Mothers' Centres also make it possible to meet other women and to socialise with students in similar circumstances, which meets the need for social learning of otherwise isolated women distance students. The majority of participants felt that this was a very positive feature of the pilot scheme.
- The small study group provides a stable and in most cases sympathetic learning environment, and the groups became increasingly independent and self-reliant. Problems could arise when individual women could not attend regularly for longer periods of time or lagged severely behind in their work.
- While the groups on the whole were seen to be a positive experience, in some cases there were personality conflicts which threatened to exclude a woman and force her to drop out of the programme, or which endangered the continuation of the whole group. In these cases the existence of the coordinator or tutor/counsellor, a woman who was experienced in group dynamics, was felt to be very important.
- There were problems in some of the groups which turned into 'chat clubs' where little or no work was done on the subject matter or course material, and consequently no study progress was achieved. This development made it necessary for the coordinators or tutor/counsellors to intervene and to steer the groups in the direction of working on the course material as well as being support groups for the emotional well-being of the students in order to avoid the group becoming dysfunctional with respect to the academic goals of the programme.

One of the most exciting results of the project was the fact that this type of distance education setting had a strong emancipatory effect for most of the participants. This showed in a variety of ways:

- The learning situation provided by the project helped to further the personal development of the student herself and of the small study group as a whole. Over time, the groups became very independent in their organisation of learning processes and also more assertive in their dealings with the DE provider AKAD, with the staff on the project (project leader and evaluator), and with the staff employed locally (course coordinator or tutor/counsellor).
- With respect to their private lives, most students developed the self-confidence and the strategies necessary to claim the space and time

needed for their studies. At the start of the project, students experienced the greatest difficulties in trying to combine their studies with their domestic and family duties, and were confronted with a lack of acceptance on the side of their partners and their children. With the help of the material conditions provided by the Mothers' Centres and the support provided by the study group they were able to accept the legitimacy of their wish to study and, consequently, to assert their needs at home. Attendance became less vital, and the existence of the centres and study groups was increasingly seen as a welcome and comforting supplementary feature to fall back on if necessary.

Although the project concentrated on a specific group of women, namely (single) mothers of small or school-age children, we feel that the findings can be generalised. The results support other research done on the needs of women distance students (see Kirkup and von Prümmer 1992; von Prümmer 1997a) and reinforce the claim that distance teaching institutions need to pursue an active policy of creating women-friendly perspectives, not only with respect to their teaching system as such but also with respect to the compatibility of distance education and women's life situation.

Home study: the pitfalls and potential of making education a private concern

This chapter has been concerned with the learning environments in which DE takes place. Open and distance learning involves a shift from the traditional places of learning in classrooms and on campus to locations outside institutions. The most frequently used learning space of distance students is their home. Making education a mostly private concern carries with it both risks and opportunities.

Modern society is still characterised by a gendered division of labour and the separation of the public sphere, which is seen as the male domain, and the private or domestic sphere, which is seen as the female domain. This fundamental gender division has wide-ranging effects, and impacts the ability of men and women to pursue their distance studies in a variety of ways. In fact, we can speak of gendered learning environments, with women distance students usually finding it more difficult than men to reconcile their education with their personal lives. On the whole, women have more domestic and family responsibilities, less privacy and fewer resources than men do, especially if they are mothers with (small) children. Often women work outside the home in addition to performing household and childrearing tasks while men in paid work tend to have few domestic and childcare responsibilities.

Looking at the domestic learning environment, we find that the woman distance student is less likely to have a room of her own, where she can study in peace and with concentration on her academic work. She is more likely to be constantly interrupted and to be exhausted by the double or triple load she carries because of her many roles as homemaker, mother, student, and possibly carer of elderly or sick relatives, employee, volunteer, all of which are demanding and time-consuming. Why, with all these drawbacks, should a woman be encouraged to embark on a DE course? Had we not better warn her that home study will only serve to domesticate her further and keep her, quite literally, in her place?

The answer, of course, is both 'no' and 'yes'. No, we should not warn her away from distance education; but yes, we should warn her about the possible pitfalls and at the same time provide information about coping strategies. Additionally, we should work toward a more women-friendly distance education system which will be more sensitive to the difficulties faced by women learners in trying to organise their studies around their family and work schedule. And we should point out the liberating potential of open and distance learning for women.

Throughout this chapter, we have seen examples of women who were prepared to take a risk, entering a DE programme even though their circumstances may not have been favourable for concentrated studying. Intellectual development apart, the very fact of studying challenges women to reassess priorities and reorganise at least some details of their lives. This may be a difficult and sometimes painful process, but it can lead to a more assertive renegotiation of the division of labour concerning domestic and family duties, and empower the woman to claim her own space and uninterrupted study time within the home. Some women report that their studying provides them with a legitimate excuse to break out of the old routines and roles. In many cases, contact with other distance students in similar situations has been helpful in putting domestic and mothering roles into perspective, and in being willing to take the risk of being less than perfect in these roles, even though they may previously have been the source of the woman's identity.

Chapter 4

Women studying at a distance

Learning styles and local
support services

The previous chapters have shown that both the distance teaching system and the different circumstances of women's and men's lives affect their chances to enrol in and complete a DE course of studies. This chapter deals with the learning styles of women and men and with the different ways in which they use the support services provided by the institution as part of the distance teaching environment.

Drawing on research data from Britain and Germany, this chapter is concerned with gender differences in students' approach to their distance studies and in the use of study centres and local support services. It is largely based on the joint analysis of data from parallel research done by Gill Kirkup at the OU UK and by Ute Rossié and myself at the FeU in the 1980s which offered the first empirical evidence of the relevance of gender in open and distance learning provision (see von Prümmer and Rossié 1990c; Kirkup and von Prümmer 1990, 1992; Kirkup 1995). Although the data on which this analysis was based is some twelve years old, it is by no means outdated. Surveys done in the intervening years have repeatedly confirmed the continued existence of gender differences in study behaviour and the importance of taking these divergent learning styles into account. A recent example is a study on interaction in DE which Mary Davoust (1996) carried out in Sweden and which showed 'a significant difference between men and women in the answers about the interaction. Women state a higher need in general.'

At the FeU the most recent evaluation of learning styles and support services was a 1996 survey on student use and appreciation of study centres and tutorial services. The results once again demonstrated the validity of our earlier conclusions that support and connectedness characterise the learning styles of women distance students in a way which differs from the learning styles of the male distance students (von Prümmer 1997b).

Learning styles of distance students: theoretical and empirical context

By its very character, the distance mode is open to scrutiny to a much greater extent than other types of university, where the teaching takes place behind the closed doors of lecture halls and seminar rooms, and where examinations are usually conducted within the walls of the ivory tower. As a new and different mode of learning and teaching, DE has always been open to experimentation and to didactical and pedagogical development. This is both because of the (mostly) indirect teaching methods required, and also the fact that distance students at tertiary level are mature adults. The recent flood of changes in education has happened in the wake of the technological revolution, which has already had profound effects on the dissemination of knowledge and on communication across time and space. I will touch on these in Chapter 5.

Much has been written about the didactics and pedagogy of DE, a recent publication being an overview by Otto Peters (1998) entitled *Learning and Teaching in Distance Education. Pedagogical Analyses and Interpretations in an International Perspective*. As a sociologist and an institutional researcher I am not an expert on teaching methods, pedagogy, or learning psychology. My concern is with the practice of DE following the application of these disciplines, and with their consequences for the adults studying at a distance.

This book, concentrates on women in ODL contexts and on the opportunities these modes of education offer them. In this context the question arises of whether we can identify factors which make learning at a distance either easier or more difficult for women and whether the pedagogy of teaching at a distance needs to become gender-sensitive to an extent that renders it women-friendly.

The focus on women as learners in a DE setting was a prerequisite for discovering the existence of both gendered learning styles and the consequent need for DE institutions to take the learning styles of adult women into account. It provided the framework for our analysis of the empirical data on women and men studying at a distance in Germany and Britain and has contributed to the increasing concern among distance educators, mainly women, with 'the importance of gender as a category in open and distance learning' (Kirkup 1995) and, more specifically, with 'women as learners' and with the consequent 'issues for visual and virtual classrooms' (Burge 1990).

In comparing data from the OU UK and the German FeU, Gill Kirkup and I were aware of the fact that the two DTUs are quite different in their teaching systems, although both are single-mode institutions with very large student populations. In spite of the different distance education systems and social contexts in the two countries, our preliminary data analysis showed similar patterns in the responses of FeU and OU UK students. There were parallels on two levels:

1   The comparison of men and women in each study yielded similar gender differences; and
2   The comparison of the responses of the two groups of women distance students yielded similar answering patterns. The similarities occurred with respect to the study behaviour, the use of study centres and the relevance which students assigned to local support services provided through tutors (mentors), counsellors, study groups, and other students.

Women distance students in both countries valued support and connectedness much more than their male colleagues did. This means that women are more interested in interpersonal contacts with other students and with staff members. They consequently visit study centres more frequently, have higher attendance rates at tutorials and study groups, and are more interested in face-to-face meetings with other students and teaching staff and in all forms of cooperative learning. In short, the comparative data analysis showed that, unlike the male students, women distance students in the FeU as well as the OU UK preferred to do their studying in a connected and social context.

By comparing the data from our two surveys Gill Kirkup and I realised that the gender patterns in the answers of the students in Britain and Germany were not simple coincidence, but reflected systematic differences in the learning styles of men and women. We found convincing arguments in the work of Gilligan (1982), J. Thompson (1983) and Belenky, Clinchy, Goldberger and Tarule (1986) which proved very useful for the understanding of the empirical phenomena in our joint surveys (Kirkup 1995). Jane Thompson's *Learning Liberation. Women's Response to Men's Education* provides a picture of the learning processes of women in face-to-face situations which are based on the principle of shared learning. In their preference for this learning style, the women distance students in Germany and Britain resemble the adult women in Jane Thompson's description of adult and continuing education.

Carol Gilligan's *In a Different Voice: Psychological Theory and Women's Development*, and Mary F. Belenky and her colleagues' *Women's Ways of Knowing: The Development of Self, Voice, and Mind* supplied the theoretical framework for the analysis of the observed gender differences. In referring to this framework we were not interested in joining the feminist debate on equality and difference or in using our data to prove one or the other position in this debate. We were interested in understanding the gender differences in the participation in distance education, including the under-representation of women students in Germany as well as the differences in study behaviour and learning styles in both countries.

Our situation as researchers on women in DE was characterised by the fact that before the mid-1980s gender issues had not been a topic for institutional research in open and distance learning contexts. The book *Toward New Horizons for Women in Distance Education*, edited by Karlene Faith in 1988, was the first international collection of contributions about gender relations in DE settings. Until that time, as Elizabeth J. Burge points out in her foreword to the book, a total of six papers with a gender focus had been published in the two major international journals, *Teaching at a Distance* and *Distance Education* (Burge 1988: xi). In her keynote address to the 1995 Cambridge Conference entitled *Putting the Student First. Learner-Centred Approaches in Open and Distance Learning*, Gill Kirkup described the history of gender research in ODL and its connection with our own work. The material collected by Karlene Faith supported our impression that our findings had a broader significance and were not limited to the OU UK and FeU contexts:

> Before the Faith book there had been a commonly accepted view that ODL is a type of education that is particularly suited to women . . . The historical material discussed above suggests that this view was reasonably founded in the knowledge that adult women have many more restrictions on their time and mobility than adult men, as well as their access to disposable income, which made ODL the most practical option for post-school education. However, there is often an implicit presumption that, apart from these material factors, women are the same as men with respect to their motivations to study and their intellectual styles, as well as their domestic circumstances.
>
> (Kirkup 1995: 10)

The assumption that equal opportunities exist for women and men to enter programmes of distance and open learning and that they have equal chances to complete a degree easily leads to a deficit model in the face of the under-representation of women among the students and especially among the graduates of DTUs. In an androcentric frame of reference, study behaviour and learning styles which are different from that of men are usually perceived as inferior or less mature, and consequently women have been seen as being on a lower level of intellectual and moral development. In this model, the action required of the institution to redress the gender imbalances is directed at bringing women up to the standard which is seen as universally valid.

It was the search for alternative explanations which led us to the above-mentioned work of Gilligan, J. Thompson and Belenky *et al.* They provide a frame of reference which does not measure women by a male standard of which, almost inevitably, they must fall short. The discovery that women develop in different ways from men allows us to accept the validity of their experience and to start looking into the previously neglected question of how DE systems can serve the needs of women students. In this model, the action required by the institution to redress gender imbalances is directed at changing the teaching system to suit the learning styles of women as well as those of men:

> This connected way of being for women comes, it is argued [by Gilligan], out of a life in which one's relationships with others are a crucial part of personal development. It is a positive way of being rather than an immature state on the road to 'separation' or 'independence' which is how it was previously described. Belenky *et al.* . . . describe women as 'connected knowers' who, when they reach the highest stages of intellectual development, *equivalent* to but not the *same* as those described by Perry, continue to exhibit a strong sense of relatedness to others. Something lacking in men at the same stage.
>
> (Kirkup 1995: 6–7; emphasis in original text)

The comparative findings on the study behaviour of men and women could all be explained using the concepts of support and connectedness: the fact that women visit study centres and use local support services more frequently in spite of having to overcome more obstacles, the higher value they place on social learning and connectedness with other students, the greater feelings of isolation in being a distance student – all of these fit into the picture of women having a 'connected way of being'.

The work of other colleagues on women in ODL has since confirmed the empirical and theoretical value of this model for gender analysis (in Germany – Bandlow *et al.* 1994; Herbst 1993; Herbst *et al.* 1994; in Canada – Burge 1988, 1990, 1997; Burge and Lenskyj 1990; in Britain – Kirkup 1988, 1995; Kirkup and Keller 1992). In a recent article, Elizabeth J. Burge sums up some of the newer findings:

> Distance education discussions about women's learning add to the already large body of research into women's learning in 'traditional' walled classrooms, . . . into the preferred relational styles of many women learners (compared to the autonomous styles preferred by many men learners), and the ways in which women come to know what they know . . .
>
> We can expect that when helping many women to make a successful comeback into higher education and develop learning to learn skills, we have to focus less on the three 'Rs' of receive, retain, and return, and more on respect, re-frame and re-apply, so that the relevant knowledge is generated and used.
>
> (Burge 1997: 6)

We will therefore continue to use this theoretical framework both in our individual research and in future comparative projects. One of the research issues which will become increasingly important for institutional and evaluation research is the rapidly developing field of information and communication technologies (ICTs). Already, studies have shown gender differences in access, control and use of the new media which in the traditional androcentric manner are explained in terms of the deficit model (see Chapter 5). We suggest that it is extremely important to apply the gendered learning style model to this field in order to develop the technologies in a way that ensures gender equity in the 'virtual university' of the future. For instance, we need:

> to look at different attitudes that men and women students have towards the new (and old) ODL technologies that we are experimenting with – if not fully committed to – in our various institutions . . . The model we have used is certainly not post-modernist and is open to criticism that it could be interpreted as essentialist. The question is whether it is supported by empirical data, and whether it can provide any help in deciding future strategies for both women and men using ICTs in ODL.
>
> (Kirkup 1995: 12)

The following sections of this chapter provide empirical data on the gender differences in students' use of study centres and local support services and the higher value women place on this support. The findings, some of which have already been presented in joint contributions (see Kirkup and von Prümmer 1996; 1997) and in FeU research reports (von Prümmer 1997b), are taken from our parallel surveys and from evaluation studies at the FeU.

Gender and study centre attendance

In order to evaluate the use distance students make of study centres it is necessary to look at the institutional provision of a local support infrastructure and at the services available to students in different regions of the country. These are based on the institutional policy regarding the role of decentralised services in a distance teaching system (see Groten 1992).

Provision of study centres in Germany

The geographical distribution of study centres in Germany as well as student numbers shows a regional disparity which is due to the fact that each of the states (or provinces) of the Federal Republic is responsible for its own education system.

In order to establish local support services outside NRW, the state government has to negotiate treaties with other Provincial (e.g. Bavaria) or

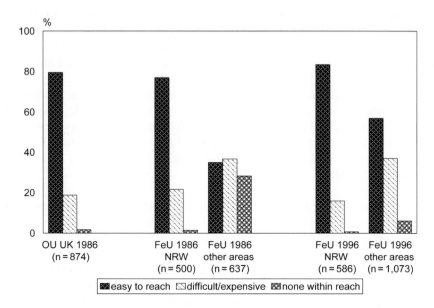

Figure 4.1 Ease of access to study centre: students in Britain, North-Rhine Westphalia and other German regions

foreign (e.g. Austria) governments. As a result, the situation in NRW roughly parallels that of the OU UK (see Figure 4.1), while other regions such as Bavaria offer only few opportunities for students to access local support (see Kirkup and von Prümmer 1990: 12–16; and 1992: 8–12).

The unequal geographical distribution is reflected in the results of a 1996 survey on study centre use, which showed that 83% of the students in NRW (the home state of the FeU), but only 57% of the students living in other regions reported living within easy reach of a study centre. Overall, two-thirds of the respondents (66%) lived within easy reach of a study centre; three out of ten (30%) lived not far from a study centre which would have been difficult to reach; and only 4% lived totally outside the catchment area of an FeU study centre (von Prümmer 1997b). This may be due to an increase in the number of study centres maintained by the FeU, but certainly is a reflection of the composition of the groups of respondents which must be considered biased in favour of study centre attendees.

Considering the uneven geographical distribution of study centres in Germany, these answers must be interpreted to mean that the survey, which explicitly concerned the use of local support services, addressed significantly fewer students who had no way of using these services in the first place and therefore do not feel competent to judge their value. In addition, there might be different interpretations of what it means to be 'near to' or 'within reach of' a study centre; and students who objectively live some distance from a centre might consider it 'within easy reach' because they are used to travelling long distances, or because they have fast and comfortable means of transport.

Patterns of study centre attendance

The decision to attend a study centre is influenced by a number of factors rooted both in institutional provision and in the personal circumstances of individual students. It should be noted that the data reported here do not permit statistical conclusions about the situation in East Germany due to the small number of respondents from the former German Democratic Republic – only 66 respondents from the five new states participated in the survey. Apart from the constraints put on distance students through their employment and family responsibilities, study centre attendance is dependent on factors such as availability and access to study centres, and on students' knowledge of local support services and on their view of the possible benefits and costs associated with attending.

The following quotes illustrate the way in which students feels that insufficient information prevents their making full or better use of the local support services offered by the university. All the comments in this chapter, which are a very small sample of the comments given in answer to open questions, are from women students who participated in the 1996 survey on the use and value of study centres and tutorial support at the FeU (von Prümmer 1997b).

'Students should be informed about all seminars and tutorials relevant for preparing for examinations, regardless of where in Germany they happen to be held. As a student one is quite willing to sacrifice a weekend and travel long distances in order to get the best possible exam preparation!'

'I wish to have more information about seminars and tutorials in other places, not just my own study centre. In this way I could plan my schedule to fit them in. Since I am currently commuting between Dortmund and Düsseldorf every day, I could easily attend different study centres and profit from their services.'

'Since a large number of courses are offered in my subject area by the Department of Education, Social Sciences and Humanities, there are many courses without tutorial support. If I had more detailed information about the tutoring/counselling offered in neighbouring study centres (and if the FeU employed more tutors/mentors), this would alleviate the situation somewhat.'

Other students refer to the expected benefits in relation to the expenditure of time and money involved in attending study centres and face-to-face sessions. The following quotes from students who do not frequent a study centre show that they are likely to discontinue their attendance or to attend only specific events if they consider the costs to outweigh the gains for their study progress. There were also those students who no longer attended tutorials in the study centre during the semester but who felt that they would benefit from more concentrated sessions such as weekend seminars:

'I find weekend seminars or week-long summer schools, which are specifically directed at preparing for the examination in a given subject, much more useful than non-specific evening tutorials which cover a whole range of topics. These seminars offer the chance to get away from one's daily domestic stress and to study specific issues intensively. Also, in these cases one gets the most benefit out of the journey, which is usually quite time-consuming. On top of this I find it difficult to find a childminder on weekday evenings.'

'I am very unhappy with the fact that [the state/province of] Hessen does not offer tutorial support to the same extent as does NRW. In order to attend specific seminars for the exam preparation in my subjects I have to travel to Aurich or other towns in northern Germany. This is a very great outlay both financially and timewise.'

'Tutorial support in my study centre is mostly limited to first- and second-year courses. But it is in those study centres which are quite a distance from the centre in Hagen, that support in more advanced courses is essential. I am certain that many students would attend weekend seminars with teaching staff from Hagen and that they would consider them worthwhile even if they had to travel long distances. As it is now, many students, especially those living in Baden-Württemberg and Bavaria [southern Germany], have high costs and time-consuming journeys, even having to take leave days, in order to attend one-day seminars which are scheduled for workdays.'

'There should be more week-end seminars outside of NRW to avoid discrimination of students living in other states/provinces and who have to invest much more money and time and need a lot more motivation to attend. Such seminars are very important since they often are the only human contact with the FeU.'

'If you come from a rural area and have children it is nearly impossible to attend tutorials or seminars on a regular basis as the costs (childcare) and time (long distances) are too great.

Absolutely desirable: weekend seminars (Friday–Sunday) in all FeU study centres (including Frankfurt).

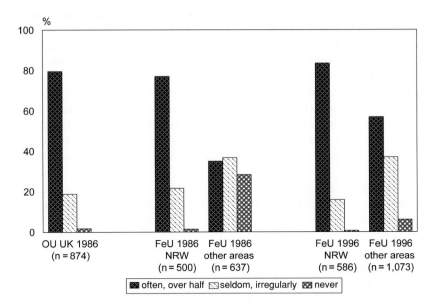

Figure 4.2 Frequency of attendance: students with easy access to a study centre

There are study centres in northern Germany which do wonderful work but are too far, which leads to high costs and the question of childcare.'

The 1986 data on geographical distribution showed no differences in study centre attendance between women and men enrolled at the OU UK or at the FeU in Germany. Yet in both countries we found that significantly more women than men report longer journeys to their study centre with 36% of the men, but only 29% of the women taking less than half an hour to travel. At the same time women were more frequent users of the local services. This was as true in 1996 as it was ten years earlier and can be demonstrated by looking at those distance students who report easy access to a study centre (see Figure 4.2) and thus may be assumed to have equal chances of attending.

The most recent figures show that half of the FeU students with easy access to a study centre visit it on a regular basis, with 9% more women (56%) than men (47%) being regular users. Fewer than four out of ten FeU students attend a study centre on a casual basis, and women (36%) and men (39%) are nearly equally likely to report occasional visits. In accordance with the earlier findings, men were more apt to refrain altogether from attending (11%) than women (6.5%) even when a study centre was within easy reach. Other factors related to frequency of attendance are major subject area and students' motivation to obtain a university degree through their distance studies.

Attendance in study centres also depends on the means of transport students use for travelling. This is most often the car owned by the student or by a family member, and here we found that women are less likely than men to have full control over this important resource. A comparison of 1996 survey data to earlier findings shows more use of public transport. This may be due to better transport provision or changed locations of study centres. It may also reflect social changes such as an increased concern with environmental issues which leads to a shift away from the use of private cars. The quantitative data and the quotes in this and the following sections of this chapter are taken from the 1996 FeU survey on study centres and tutorial support.

As was the case in previous research, students often experience transport problems in conjunction with other factors. Some difficulties faced by women in this respect are expressed in the following quotes:

'It is relatively time-consuming (a total of 2 hours travelling time for 80 km, parking problems).'

'This is due exclusively to the travelling situation as public transport is poor or non-existent. The study centre is only accessible for local people or for people with a car. Therefore I rarely can attend tutorials. Getting a lift is an exceptional happening.'

'I am very satisfied with the services and equipment provided in the study centre, as well as with the staff who are very helpful. The reason why I attend so rarely is in no way the fault of any deficits on the part of the study centre. Rather, it is due to my personal/domestic situation: two children aged 7 and $8\frac{1}{2}$ years, a husband working shifts, only one car in the family, and a circle of friends and acquaintances who have little tolerance for my studying.'

'Regrettably there is no tutorial support I can use!!! I can reach a study centre easily (only 20 minutes by car) but it only offers tutorial support and face-to-face seminars in first- and second-year courses. To reach the nearest study centre which provides tutorial support in advanced courses I have to drive for over an hour. But some seminars or tutorials start so early (5:00–6:00 p.m.) that I cannot get there in time after work, due to the long drive. This is the reason why I attend this study centre rarely, although I would like to go more often.'

'During the advanced phase of my degree programme I have used a study centre quite often, but so far this has been limited to exam preparations in one subject. The problem is that the study centre which offers relevant tutoring/counselling can be reached only by car without too great a loss of *time. Since I cannot drive myself, attendance is difficult for me. So far, the tutorial support which I have been able to use has been good and helpful for my exam preparations.'*

The role of local support services for beginning students varies between the different academic departments of the FeU, and this is reflected in subject-related attendance patterns. Students enrolled in the Economics Department, for instance, find a wide range of course-related and exam-oriented tutorials available at most study centres. Regular attendance is therefore possible in regions with study centres. Students enrolled in degree programmes in the Department of Education, Social Sciences and Humanities on the other hand, are offered a range of individual seminars and tutorials on a one-off basis. It is therefore not surprising to find that 53% of the economics students but only 38% of the humanities students (education, social sciences and humanities) attended the study centre in their vicinity. Within each of these two degree areas, women with easy access to a study centre were more frequent attendees than men, the difference being 14.9 percentage points in economics, and 10.9 percentage points in the humanities.

Because of the small numbers of respondents, especially women, in the other degree programmes we looked at all students living near an FeU study centre, even if they themselves felt that getting there is time-consuming or expensive. In this case, all academic departments showed the same gendered attendance patterns with more women visiting study centres on a regular basis than men. This is true for:

- the Department of Economics (women 51.8%; men 39.5%; difference $\Delta = 12.3\%$; n = 1.053);
- the Department of Education, Social Sciences and Humanities (women 34.0%; men 24.2%; $\Delta = 9.8\%$; n = 255);
- the Department of Computer Science (women 41.5%; men 38.6%; $\Delta = 2.9\%$; n = 168).

Since only ten women enrolled in the Department of Mathematics and nine women enrolled in the Department of Electrical Engineering participated in the survey, no gender analysis is possible for these degree programmes. Again, this data confirms the fact that women distance students tend to overcome larger odds in their willingness to participate in face-to-face learning processes and meet with other students and teaching staff, as the following student quotes illustrate:

'If only there were tutorial support for law courses! And if only my study centre had a meeting room (lounge, cafeteria) where I could bring my child and work without too much hassle.'

'Since entering the advanced phase of my degree programme I have not been to a study centre, as the three study centres in my area don't offer tutorial support for courses in mathematics and computer science (unfortunately!!). I really wish these services could be improved. PS: A suggestion – all study centres should be equipped with computers which allow access to the library catalogue, just like the terminals in the FeU library in Hagen.'

'The study centre would have played a larger role in my studies if there had been more tutorials/seminars in my field.'

One of the most important factors influencing a student's decision to spend the time and effort visiting a study centre is their determination to complete a degree (degree orientation). Four out of ten women (40%), and three out of ten men (33%) studying at the FeU say that it is 'absolutely necessary' for them to obtain their degree as a result of studying. A look at distance students who live near a study centre and have used local support services on a regular basis confirms the importance of degree orientation, especially for the male respondents as 47% of these women and 44% of these men are degree oriented, which is an increase of 7% (women) and 11% (men) compared to the general student population. Put differently, 62% of the degree-oriented women and 58% of the degree-oriented men visited a study centre regularly, while only 52% of the other female students and 40% of the other male students did so.

Students who were seriously working toward a degree used the study centre for reasons such as the following:

'When I prepare for my final examination I would like to have intensive contact [with the study centre] to accompany my work on the thesis (but so far I have not taken any initiatives in this direction).'

'Since I have a full-time job I depend on the competent counselling and tutoring my "mentors" provide in order to achieve my degree.'

Others judge the study centre as very important for their study progress but did not always find the local support they needed:

'In my opinion tutorial support is as important for advanced study and for completing the degree at the FeU as it is in the first- and second-year courses. But unfortunately Munich hardly offers anything at this level! I have a full-time job and therefore cannot "tour Germany" as so many of my fellow students do in order to attend as many tutorials and seminars as possible at other study centres. In addition, subjects which are not compulsory for all students, are often not supported by tutorials at all. It would

be better if the FeU could spread its local support services more evenly throughout the country so students outside NRW could profit equally from tutorials and seminars!'

The following quote exemplifies why students who study 'just for fun' still may find the study centre useful:

'I have always profited most from tutorial support when it managed, through the use of examples, to connect the knowledge I learned from the course work to its practical application. I suspect that I am not the "typical" distance student. I like my job and am highly motivated to do it well. Studying for a degree at the FeU is a "hobby" I pursue in my free time, purely for my own enjoyment. Nevertheless, I want to use the knowledge gained through my studies later in my work context.'

The findings also support another observation from previous studies (see Kirkup and von Prümmer 1990: 26–7), namely that men tend to instrumentalise their study centre visits to a greater extent, weighing the costs of attendance against the expected gains of getting help with their assignments and exam preparation. Women, by contrast tend to make use of local services in order to connect with other students, even if the benefits for their study progress are not immediately apparent. This is not to say that women, who have many demands on their time and energy, are not interested in the benefits to be gained regarding their study progress. But more often than men, these academic factors are interwoven with motivational factors and the support derived from common experiences, as the following quotations show:

'It offers the opportunity to meet other students and to exchange experiences on "distance education".'

'There were at least a few other students studying the same subjects on a similar level so discussions about the subject matter were possible.'

'During the early stages of distance study it is especially important to have contact with other students: it helps in gaining confidence and motivation. Tutors and counsellors need to be aware of the fact that beginners tend to be insecure. During my first year at the FeU I studied micro economics and made an effort to attend the study centre in Munich (at the time there was no underground and the journey was lengthy and complicated as well as unsafe in the dark). But the behaviour of the other students and the mentor in the tutorials so shocked and terrified me that I quit attending after the second time and didn't come back for two years. It was as if they came from another galaxy. Fortunately, the tutor I had when I made a

second attempt was super, which is the only reason I attended tutorials more often.'

'Tutorial support was very important for me. In the beginning, the tutorials were the only opportunity for meeting other distance students. Not only did the tutorials help me to understand the subject matter, they also showed me that other students had as much difficulty with the course as I did. Also, I was lucky in that a stable group of students formed after the first three semesters and that this group existed until we completed the degree programme. (I am now in the process of writing my thesis.) Some courses, such as theoretical computer science, I would not have been able to complete successfully without the tutorials. Sometimes, though, I had to attend study centres 75 km or more from my home. But this has almost always been worthwhile.'

'It is important to have someone with whom you can talk over general issues of distance studying or the subject matter of specific courses. Especially for distance students it is very important to have the opportunity to talk subject matter through and not only read it on your own at home.'

'Very important:

Better comprehension of the subject matter.

Studying becomes less of a burden.

Higher motivation through other students.

It is simply easier than sitting at home, alone with your course materials, trying to learn when many questions remain open. In the beginning of my distance studies I lived near a study centre and experienced successes such as passing end-of-term examinations. Now I live a long distance from any study centre. Since I have two children, my time is extremely limited. Studying on my own I lack the motivation.'

'In the study centre it is possible to meet other students. I had the opportunity to ask specific questions concerning the study materials (even if it was not always possible to get answers) and I could measure my own study progress against other students.

For me studying with others meant that I studied much more effectively and I enjoyed participating in the seminars and tutorials.

On balance, attending the study centre was very important for me!'

'During the first years of study, the study centre was (almost) the only opportunity for meeting other students and thus for forming study groups and finding "comrades-in-arms". In a study centre one can ask questions

and learn to discuss the subject matter (!). There is a big difference between writing down the answers to assignments and reporting them orally. Also, fellow students build you up and motivate you and help you measure your study progress.'

'When I first started studying at the FeU I used the study centre frequently because I found great difficulty in knowing how to deal with the study material. The demands are so great that I would never have completed my intermediate examination on my own. I profited most, though, from contact with my fellow students as I was fortunate to become part of a good and effective study group.'

'My friends and acquaintances have only a very hazy idea of distance education and I needed the tutoring/counselling in the study centre to stop me from getting too discouraged. In rural areas distance students are on their own and rely on their study centres to provide basic services, such as help in obtaining secondary materials and literature.'

'The study centre offered the only opportunity to meet the tutors and other students in seminars and tutorials. The study group which my tutor organised and conducted made it possible to study effectively and goal-oriented in preparation for the intermediate examination which I passed successfully. These regular meetings were important for my motivation to continue.'

'Going to the study centre is useful because:

it makes the structure of the degree programme clearer; it makes it much easier to plan study-related activities; and it is a great help in working through the course materials and assignments or with study problems in general;

it helps with preparation for written and oral examinations;

it gives you confidence (because you can join in the discussion) and it makes you feel appreciated (very important as you are otherwise very lonely);

it provides contact with fellow students and opportunities for exchange.'

'The study centre is a place where you can go in order to clarify questions arising from studying the course material. Also, the contact with other students helps you not to feel quite so "small" and ignorant since you see that others are in danger of being defeated by the same problems. The help of a good tutor (although there are others) is very important and motivating. On the whole I have enjoyed my visits to the study centre, mainly because I was no longer anonymous but had concrete people with whom I could get in touch. My study group also was very important because of its disciplined and goal-oriented work.'

Obstacles to attending

In the comparative study, open-ended answers from both German and British distance students were found to identify:

> ... the following major factors: work pressures, family commitments, and combined pressures from both areas. Both men and women are subjected to pressures through their paid work which often requires long hours, shift work, frequent travelling, or professional changes and new or expanded areas of responsibility. A large proportion of women respondents in both institutions were working full or part time: at the OU 77% of the women compared with 90% of the men, at the FeU 58% of the women compared with 79% of the men.
>
> (Kirkup and von Prümmer 1990: 18; 1992: 15–16)

As with earlier research, the 1996 FeU survey also demonstrates that factors other than geographical access and transport influence students' use of local support services and that these factors have a different impact on women and men studying at a distance. Controlling separately for the extent of paid work (see Figure 4.3) and for household composition (see Figure 4.4) we find confirmation of the fact that the pressure of family and personal commitments combine to make it extremely difficult for women to fit visits to a study centre into their schedules (see Kirkup and von Prümmer 1990: 18–20).

With respect to students' paid work this manifests itself in a response pattern whereby women who hold full-time or part-time jobs with more than half the usual weekly hours (at least 19 hours per week), more often than men in the same employment situations, report frequent visits to a study centre. And while men's attendance rates increase as the extent of their paid work decreases, the opposite is true for women, as Figure 4.3 demonstrates quite clearly.

The housewife and full-time homemaker obviously have the most problems fitting a visit to the study centre into their days. Thus, there is a tendency for single women to visit study centres more often than women with commitments to a partner and family, while similar patterns do not show in the responses of male, distance students reported in Figure 4.4. It is fair to conclude that these divergent patterns are based in the gendered division of labour which traditionally leads to an inverse correlation between women's occupational and family commitments (see Chapter 3 for more details).

This can be seen in the reasons given by women distance students for their difficulties in organising study centre attendance, difficulties which frequently arise as a result of their family and domestic responsibilities, sometimes coupled with paid work. Not surprisingly the consequent multiple commitments interfere with the requirements of distance studying, especially when the element of travel to a certain place by a certain time to attend tutorials or participate in group work is involved. For example:

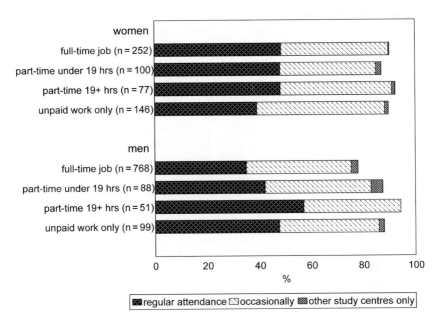

Figure 4.3 Study centre attendance of men and women by extent of paid work

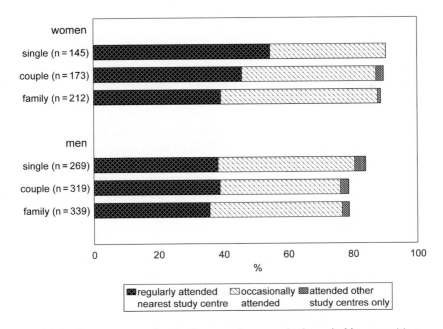

Figure 4.4 Study centre attendance of men and women by household composition

'*In my opinion tutoring/counselling is extremely important since without it it's nearly impossible to study effectively and successfully. I have had to relocate frequently and therefore have been to many different study centres which showed great variations with regard to the qualification of the tutors in the subject matter. Another important function of the study centre is the exchange of information between the students (e.g. regarding sending material and information or old exam questions). The weekend seminars are especially effective as are the "qualification weeks" organised by the study centres in northern Germany. Regrettably, none of the study centres I attended offered childcare. This poses a serious problem for women students with children, especially when they have to travel a long distance and the tutorials or seminars start early (usually before 6:00 p.m.).*'

'*For me the study centre was very important. I would like to attend more often if this were at all possible (time, two small children). Face-to-face seminars or meetings make it easier to learn (less time needed than in studying at home in order to achieve the same learning results). Motivation is greatly increased. It is possible to get insider information (e.g. old exam questions, most frequently covered exam topics).*'

'*In my view, tutorial support and study centre services (especially computer and Internet access . . .) are the most important help for distance students throughout all stages of the degree programme.*

Because I did not have childcare for my two small children I could only attend infrequently!!'

'*I have stopped using the study centre since I cannot organise childcare for my daughter for just a few hours and my child is too young to be left with a childminder for longer periods of time.*'

'*Even after completing the intermediate examination I am in desperate need of tutorial support. I find it difficult to learn solely from studying the written text, and this presents no less of a problem in the more advanced courses than it did in the introductory materials. Regrettably, there is not much tutorial support for advanced students. Now that I have a child I can no longer afford trips (a 60-minute journey) to NRW (too time-consuming and expensive).*'

'*As far as tutorial support is concerned Bavaria is a "developing country". Up till now I have had a full-time job. Now that I have a baby I find it nearly impossible to attend tutorials or seminars for exam preparation since hardly anything is offered in Munich and I cannot travel to Nürnberg with my child. (The father cannot breastfeed the baby.)*

Seriously, too many of the face-to-face seminars the FeU offers take place in northern Germany, and thus are much too expensive. Also, in my opinion, the large number of study centres in North-Rhine Westphalia does not fit the character of a "Fern" (distance) university.'

'I have two small children and therefore often cannot attend because of lack of time. It would be ideal to have tutorials or seminars on a Sunday morning which would have the additional advantage that one is rested. Evening hours are always very inconvenient. Often it is difficult to concentrate.

Regrettably, the FeU does not yet offer tutorial support in all subjects. Successful participation also is dependent on the individual tutor.'

'I always had the problem of finding childcare since I was not allowed to bring my children to the study centre. This required a great deal of organisation, even for very short visits.'

'The study centre is too far away (75 km) and as a single mother I have great difficulty getting there (childcare!!).'

'In my view the study centre is very important and I regret that I have no opportunity to visit it. We have three children (4 and 2 years and 14 weeks old). Thus travelling on the train is too difficult, and the study centre does not provide childcare. My studying happens mainly at my desk at home.'

'I did not use the study centre because of the long journey, the lack of atmosphere, the lack of facilities for bringing children, and the scheduling of activities in the evenings which meant that I would have needed a car.'

Some women mentioned the lack of facilities for disabled people, such as provisions for deaf students, or for wheelchair access:

'The nearest study centre is located on the top floor of a building in the city, and there are 150 steps. No elevator which makes it inaccessible for disabled students!'

As has been shown in Chapter 3 and confirmed in the above quotes from the women in the 1996 survey, the study situation of distance students is shaped to a large extent by their personal and family commitments. Since the household, childrearing, and caring responsibilities are regarded mostly as women's work, it comes as no surprise that single women, who can organise their time more freely, visit a study centre more frequently (regular attendance: 55%) than women living with a partner (46%), and that women living in a nuclear family, i.e. mothers with small children have the lowest attendance rate (39%) of all women respondents.

Yet in all three types of similar personal situations, men are less frequent study centre visitors than women, and their attendance rates vary little between the categories. This indicates once again that men are less affected by their commitments to a partner and children and that they are less interested in using the local support services. The gender difference is evidenced especially clearly in the case of single students: only 38% of the single men, but 55% of the single women living near a study centre report regular visits, a difference of 16.2 percentage points.

The use and relevance of study centre services

While the previous sections were concerned with study centre attendance in general, we now look at specific student services available to varying degrees at the FeU study centres. In the 1996 survey we asked students to indicate which of twelve support service items they had used 'often', 'seldom', or 'never' in the course of their first four semesters of distance study. Students were also asked about the relevance of each of these items in relation to their study success by rating it 'very important', 'not very important', or 'totally irrelevant'. Finally, students were asked about the conditions which would have induced them to attend a study centre at all or more frequently.

Functions of study centre services

The basic statistical analysis of the data shows that the most important function of study centres is to help students prepare for examinations and to provide specific advice and tutoring in the concrete subject matter. These services have been used by two-thirds of the respondents and judged as very important by 60% of them. Students who have completed the first phase of their degree programme are more likely to have used these two support offers and to value them more highly than do the less successful students. This may be an indication that study centres can play an important role for study progress. It may also be an indication of the higher commitment of degree-oriented distance students to succeed in their studies and to invest the extra time and money which study centre attendance usually requires.

Students were not only asked about the frequency of their use of study centre services but also about the importance they attached to any given service. The answering patterns show even more clearly that FeU students place the highest value on those local support services which are expected to help them prepare for examinations and on course-related tutorials in their major subject. These were also the most frequented of the events taking place in study centres (see Figure 4.5).

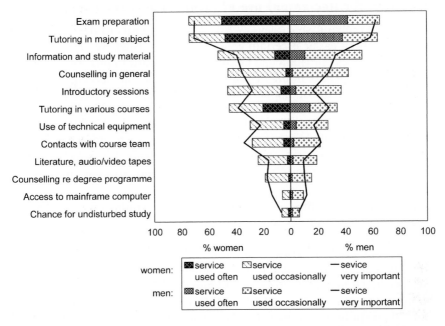

Figure 4.5 Use and importance of study centre services: women and men with access to a study centre

Nearly two-thirds of the respondents considered these items to be very important for their study success (64% and 61%), very few students considered them irrelevant (3.7% and 4.0%). Two other items were also judged important although they were not used as often: tutorials on courses which were not part of the major subject and contact with departmental course team members/teaching staff. These items ranked fourth and sixth in importance but only sixth and eighth in frequency of use. The answering patterns to these questions suggest the existence of intervening factors, although there is a close connection between the frequency of use and the importance a given item has for students' chances of succeeding in their studies.

The gender analysis shows that women use all but one of the study centre services more than their male colleagues, the differences being greatest in regard to tutorials in the major subject and in other subject areas, introductory face-to-face events, exam preparation, and in contacts with teaching staff at the centre. The one item which was frequented more by men is on-line access to the mainframe computer or to the Internet, although both genders used this service only infrequently. As Figure 4.5 documents, women also place a higher value on each of the study centre services. Of those students who consider a given item very important for their study success, women are more likely than men to avail themselves of the support offered by the institution.

Conditions for (increased) use of local support services

In the 1986 comparative survey, we asked whether visits to the study centre would have been easier if certain conditions had existed. We found similar gender differences in Britain and Germany with regard to provision of child-care, different opening hours or hours for tutorials, and accessibility of the study centre by road or public transport. In all cases, women were more likely to feel that given these conditions attendance would have been easier. This was especially noticeable with respect to childcare provision in the case of mothers of children under fourteen years of age (see Kirkup and von Prümmer 1992: 17–19). The fathers of young children, however, tended to feel that this facility would have made no difference to their study centre attendance.

Following up on this, the 1996 FeU survey contained a battery of conditions which students were asked to rate on a five-point scale from, '1 = completely right' to '5 = completely wrong' with regard to their own situation and ability to visit a study centre.

The answers demonstrate a rather pragmatic attitude toward the support services offered in study centres (see Figure 4.6). Students are most inclined to consider attendance if they had more time and if they thought they could ensure their study success by using the service. They also weigh the expected cost and effectiveness and want to be sure that study groups and tutorials or counselling will be immediately useful for their study progress, for doing assignments and for exam preparation. With the exception of the item 'I would have visited a study centre (more often) if it had been necessary for study success', more women affirmed that the conditions listed would have facilitated their use of local support services. The items with the most noticeable gender differences were provision of childcare, again a totally irrelevant consideration for the male respondents, different opening or tutorial times, and better accessibility.

Similar patterns occur when students are asked to state which conditions would have induced them to participate (more frequently) in tutorials or face-to-face seminars, either in the study centre or in a location chosen by the academic department. Students, who were provided with a list of twelve statements with the same five answer categories, were asked to state how well each of the conditions described their own situation. In all cases, more women feel that they could have attended tutorials or seminars if these conditions had existed. The gender differences are greatest with regard to childcare, times of meeting, ease of access, and the wish to have more access to competent advisors on the subject matter.

Importance of tutorials and seminars

Students may be motivated to participate in tutorials and seminars by a number of reasons. The 1996 survey therefore included a list of reasons

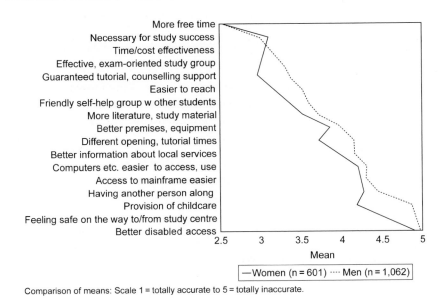

More free time
Necessary for study success
Time/cost effectiveness
Effective, exam-oriented study group
Guaranteed tutorial, counselling support
Easier to reach
Friendly self-help group w other students
More literature, study material
Better premises, equipment
Different opening, tutorial times
Better information about local services
Computers etc. easier to access, use
Access to mainframe easier
Having another person along
Provision of childcare
Feeling safe on the way to/from study centre
Better disabled access

Mean

—Women (n = 601) ···· Men (n = 1,062)

Comparison of means: Scale 1 = totally accurate to 5 = totally inaccurate.

Figure 4.6 Conditions for (increased) study centre attendance by gender

which respondents were asked to rate as 'very important', 'not so important' and 'totally irrelevant' for their decision to attend face-to-face sessions. Once again, the most important function of tutorials and seminars is the direct help students require in order to understand the subject matter and to prepare effectively for their end-of-term examinations. In keeping with the character of such sessions, students are less likely to attend them in order to receive general advice and information.

The answering patterns fit in with results from earlier studies and show that women value all items listed more highly than their male colleagues. With the single exception of the 'contact with teaching staff/course team' (in or from Hagen), there is a higher percentage of women labelling the items listed as very important for their decision to participate. The gender differences range from 8.6 to 19.7 percentage points and are highest with regard to 'more contact with other students' ($\Delta = 19.7\%$); renewed motivation to continue studying ($\Delta = 19.5\%$); competent instruction and help in the subject matter ($\Delta = 17.5\%$); subject-related cooperation with other students ($\Delta = 17.4\%$); and receiving up-to-date information on the course ($\Delta = 17.1\%$). Figure 4.7 presents the gender differences in the answers of those students who have some experience with tutorials and seminars, having attended at least one session during the first phase of their degree course at the FeU.

The open-ended answers relating to both the reasons for attending tutorials, seminars and weekend sessions and to deficits in this area, indicate the importance which the women distance students attach to these elements.

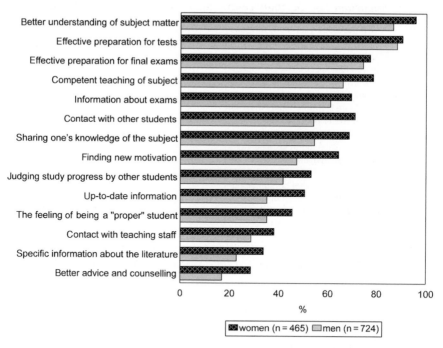

Figure 4.7 Importance of study centre services by gender: students who have used the services

They also sum up the general feelings about local support services. The most frequently mentioned aspects have to do with motivation and self-confidence, with isolation and loneliness, with information deficits and difficulties with the subject matter, and lastly with preparing for assignments and examinations. Again, the quotes presented here are only a very small selection of the comments made by women students:

> '*For me tutoring/counselling and the study centre are both very important. I would not have done as well in my intermediate exam if it had not been for the tutorial support I had. It is extremely important for me to have a specific person to contact when I cannot grasp the course material. Otherwise I would most likely give up too quickly and drop out of the degree programme.*'

> '*I am certain that I would not have completed the first phase of my degree programme without tutorial support. This was extremely important with respect to understanding the subject matter and practising the tests and examinations. The records of previous exams were very helpful in preparing for the intermediate oral examination.*'

'*The importance of the study centre and tutoring/counselling for me lay in:*

my need as a beginner to learn how to work through written course materials and the specific counselling concerning the structure of my degree programme;

the opportunity it gave me to control my study progress by comparing myself with other students to see where I stood;

exchange with other students;

preparation for written and oral examinations;

and in the continuing renewal of my study motivation.'

'*Contacts with tutors and fellow students are absolutely necessary in order to avoid being overwhelmed by feelings of loneliness when sitting alone at one's desk.*

In the study centre, up-to-date information is always available and help is provided so the students can find their way through the complexities of the degree programme.

Study centres and tutorials connect the students and the university.'

'*For me, the exchange with fellow students and the tutorial support from a highly qualified tutor have been very important. Working completely alone, it is impossible to learn how to participate in discussions and how to do presentations!*'

'*In my view, the exchange with fellow students and tutors about course content is absolutely essential for understanding the subject matter, especially in respect of its relevance and applicability in practice.*'

'*In my opinion, the study centre is of the greatest importance both as an institution and as an information centre and, especially, as the place providing tutorial support. Regular attendance at tutorials helps me to understand the subject matter of my courses. As a student I can turn to the tutor/counsellor when I have questions concerning course content. Usually these questions are not only answered but placed in the larger context of the subject matter. I am thus enabled to connect the topic in question to a wider range of ideas and subject areas and develop new perspectives leading to a deeper understanding.*'

'*Both the study centre and the tutoring/counselling are extremely important for distance students:*

Study centres provide help with solving a variety of problems and meeting like-minded others.

Tutoring and counselling serve as psychological supports necessary to complete the course, and provide help with the subject matter. This has a positive effect on the grades one gets in assignments and examinations and motivates the students to participate actively.'

'The study centre and tutoring/counselling have been very important for me during the first study phase, both with respect to mastering the subject matter and for meeting other students, professors and course advisors/ lecturers. In this way distance education was not quite so anonymous, I was not left to cope on my own and had a better chance to master the subject matter.'

'The existence of a study centre in my immediate neighbourhood was the precondition for my decision to register as a distance student. For me it is essential to have opportunities for communication in working through the subject matter and the written course materials, and in the matter of motivation!'

'The most important function of tutoring/counselling for me was the regularity of studying and the content-oriented discussion of different views on the same subject matter. This helped me to form my own opinion on the course topics and to clarify issues which I had not understood. Equally important was the contact with other students in similar circumstances.'

'The tutorial support in a study group was more important than using the facilities of the study centre on my own. During the early stages of my distance studies the tutor/counsellor played an important role in giving me advice when I had difficulties with the subject matter (understanding the course materials) and in suggesting literature. Working in a study group was highly motivating.'

'The study centre is a substitute for a face-to-face university and acts as a bridge between the "single-combat" situation of the individual distance student and the requirements of learning how to work in a team which is essential in today's world.'

'Immensely important. I would have given up long ago if it had not been for the study centre and tutorial support. I probably would not have gone beyond the first two semesters.'

'In my view the study centre and tutoring/counselling are very, very important. Home alone I often lack the motivation to continue studying and would have given up long ago without these support services. In the study centre I meet other students who have similar problems. Together we find

the strength to carry on, to keep on "fighting". Otherwise one often feels left alone, without anywhere to turn in the case of problems. But the study centre and the tutors/counsellors are a great help, something of a "substitute" for a face-to-face university.'

'I use the study centre mainly to photocopy study materials which help me to do the assignments. I attended tutorials in order to meet other students. They also helped me to clarify and structure course contents which were illogical or confusing. It often happened that I only became aware of the importance of a guiding principle or of connections between topics because we covered them in tutorials. Without these services I would not have succeeded in my studies, even though I am very ambitious and highly motivated.'

'During the first phase of my degree programme I participated in a small study group in my major subject of education which was led by a wonderful woman tutor. We met regularly once a month, wrote a term paper together, and finally studied for the intermediate examination together. The group was very important because we motivated each other and because of the support from the tutor. The fact that we were all in similar circumstances (women with children) also had a positive effect.'

'The social aspect of study centre services is very important for me. In order to be able to study I have given up social contact which would arise from other areas of life, such as children in school or involvement in village life. It is therefore very good to meet other people in similar situations through my studies.'

Implications

This is not the first time research on gender issues in distance education has brought to light the differences in the learning styles of women and men. In this chapter of the book I have presented some additional quantitative data and a selection of the many written comments from women in a recent (1996) large-scale survey on the uses and relevance of local support services for students of the German FeU.

It would not be correct to suggest that all women want to use study centres and can only be successful if they have the chance to learn in face-to-face situations and self-help study groups. Clearly, this is not the case since the majority of students in Germany, if only for regional reasons, do not have the option of using local support services or connecting with other students. Others, regardless of gender, may prefer to study on their own, some because this is their individual learning style and some because this is the way they can best organise their lives.

Yet the empirical evidence strongly suggests implications which the existence of gendered learning styles has for DE institutions. This has become
clear especially in the comparison of two major DTUs with different provision of local support services. At the OU UK, for instance, first-year students
enrolled in foundation courses have traditionally been advised and encouraged to attend weekly tutorials in a nearby study centre and also were
required to participate in a compulsory summer school. At the German
FeU, where two-thirds of the students are from outside the catchment area
of the state in which the university is located and where it can set up study
centres on its own initiative, students were expected to study independently,
i.e. on their own and with a minimum of institutional support at the local
level.

In our comparative data analysis, Gill Kirkup and I identified these differences as one of the major reasons for the different participation of women
in the two universities: the percentage of women studying at the OU UK
was around 40% in the beginning of the 1980s and has since risen to more
than 50%, making it higher than that of other universities in Britain. By
contrast, the percentage of women studying at the FeU, was just over 20%
in the early 1980s and has since risen to 38%. Although this is quite an
increase in the representation of women distance students, it is still lower by
10% than the figures for other German universities. A more women-friendly
distance education environment, it seems, would provide at least some options
accommodating the needs of women students for support ad connectedness
and facilitate personal contact and social learning.

Chapter 5

Getting in touch

Communication and the new technologies

By definition, DE is characterised by the fact that teachers and learners are separated from each other by time and geography, neither of them having to attend classroom activities at a given time or place. In the absence of face-to-face encounters and personal communication, the subject matter has to be transmitted via written materials or other media, and technically mediated communication must be substituted for direct verbal exchange.

The rapid developments in information and communication technologies (ICTs) have profoundly affected the use of media in distance education where new technologies have become a prominent focus and visions of the virtual campus are coming to appear quite realistic. In the beginning most DTUs, including the OU UK and the German FeU, relied on written course material as the primary teaching medium, a historical fact which is documented in the term 'correspondence education' as synonymous with DE. The written materials were supplemented, to a greater or lesser extent, by audio and video components in the shape of cassettes or radio and television broadcasts. Students and staff communicated mainly through written communication, and interaction between them was face-to-face or by telephone as the only technically mediated form of communication.

The introduction of ICTs first happened gradually, paralleling the developments in the industry, starting from slow and tentative beginnings with very expensive and cumbersome equipment and moving with ever-increasing speed. At the FeU, for instance, we have come a long way from the early experiments with btx (videotex) and with the first applications which allowed students to tap into the university's mainframe computer. Today, the FeU is present in the world-wide web (www) and aiming to reconstruct itself as a virtual university, utilising all the ICT features inherent in the www and other technologies.

The increased replacement of traditional media through ICTs raises issues of access to distance education since these technologies are more expensive to own and use and may not be a viable option for everyone interested in pursuing a degree at a distance. ICTs also change the way in which communication and interaction takes place, and consideration must be given to the preferences and learning styles of students to avoid a systematic exclusion of specific target groups. In the context of gender issues, this chapter is especially concerned with the access of women distance students to the new media and the opportunities they have to use them in accordance with their communication preferences.

Communication in distance education

A study on Communication in Distance Education was carried out at the FeU in the academic year of 1992/93 in order to obtain empirical data on the existing patterns of communication between the university and its students as well as the preferences and wishes of students and staff for future developments. Some of the data have been newly analysed with a focus on gender issues for the present purpose (for details on sample definition and methodology, see von Prümmer and Rossié 1994). The research question was prompted by two factors: on the one hand, institutional research at the FeU had shown some deficits in the availability and organisation of communication channels; on the other hand, expected developments in the use of information and communication technologies were assumed to have a profound effect on this aspect of distance education. The following sections on communication draw on the data gathered in this survey.

The role of communication in distance education

While it is generally agreed that DE as a mode of teaching and learning requires some form of mediated communication in order to bridge the distance between the institution and its students, there is less agreement on the kind of communication best suited to DE and providing the best possible study conditions for distance students. The discussion is influenced by the philosophy of distance education which formulates the principles of its role and character and by practical considerations of finance, organisation, and didactical applications.

For example, the approach to communication prevalent at the German FeU, is based on the principle that the mature students who choose this form of studying prefer to do so as independent and autonomous individuals. It follows that teaching materials are designed for self-study and compulsory or necessary contacts between students and staff are kept to a minimum. In this, the FeU differs from the OU UK, where students in foundation courses have been strongly encouraged to attend weekly tutorials in addition to a compulsory summer school.

Chapter 4 discussed findings which show that women and men differ in their learning styles and that women are more likely to prefer 'support and connectedness' even when studying at a distance. This learning style relies on communication as the basis of making contact and forming study groups and support networks. It follows that the role of communication and the direction a distance teaching system takes in providing channels for communication and interaction between students and staff and between groups of students has gender implications. As we have shown, the under-representation of women at the FeU must be attributed at least partially to the fact that there is much less institutional provision for support and connectedness here than, for instance, at the OU UK where about half the student population are women. The question for the future is whether the new technologies hold more of a threat or more of a promise for women distance students: will women be further alienated because they have fewer resources and find the technologies less accessible? Or will they be able to utilise the interactive elements as their own 'weaving looms' (Burge 1995) to create networks and strengthen their connection to other students?

Communication preferences of distance students

In the 1993 survey we asked students' personal communication preferences as well as their preferred mode of getting in touch with the FeU. Both are connected, but the data also reveal a certain pragmatism as students adapt their personal preferences to the existing limitations of actually available and feasible means of communication.

The data from the FeU survey do not support two of the main underlying assumptions about the communication needs of distance students: first, students who choose this mode of studying are often assumed to be more interested in indirect forms of communication than in direct or face-to-face interaction. Their preferred mode of studying supposedly is that of the isolated autonomous learner who is provided by the institution with the necessary course material and with sufficient information for the successful completion of the course and examinations. Second, at an institution like the FeU, which teaches mainly through written material, there is a tendency to view students as people with an exceptional interest in all forms of written communication, including the new media of electronic mail and computer conferencing.

Personal communication preferences

The survey results show clearly that distance students who are studying for a degree at the FeU have a marked preference for personal interaction with the academic staff and with other students (see Figure 5.1). They are less interested in forms of written communication, including electronic mail (e-mail) and a number of students even reject these outright (see von Prümmer 1995a).

Contrary to popular assumptions about distance students, nearly all respondents had a clear preference (answer categories were: 'decided preference';

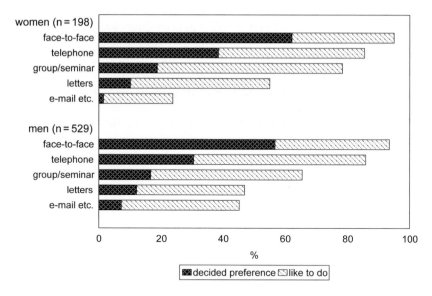

Figure 5.1 Personal communication preferences of distance students

and 'like to do') for interpersonal contacts, with face-to-face meetings being most popular (94%), followed by talking on the telephone (86%) and group meetings/seminars (69%). Written exchanges, traditionally the primary mode of communication in correspondence studies, were much less popular, with only half the respondents liking to write or receive letters (49%) and even fewer liking to correspond via the new medium of electronic mail (39%). In fact, a substantial minority of the students stated that 'under no circumstances' would they use the medium of the post (7%) or e-mail (17%).

Interestingly, the data reveal only slight gender differences in students' preference for types of personal interaction which involve just themselves and one other person, namely face-to-face talks or telephone conversations. Differences emerge with regard to group situations and letters, as women are more inclined to express a liking for these forms of communication. Larger differences occur with regard to forms of electronic communication which women are more inclined to reject and men are more inclined to like.

Communication preferences in dealing with the university

Students were also given a catalogue of 'personal' and of 'technically mediated' modes of communication and were asked to name which they would choose ('definitely', 'probably' or 'never') in their dealings with the university. The items were separated into communications on the 'personal level' and on the 'technical level', the responses showing a marked imbalance between

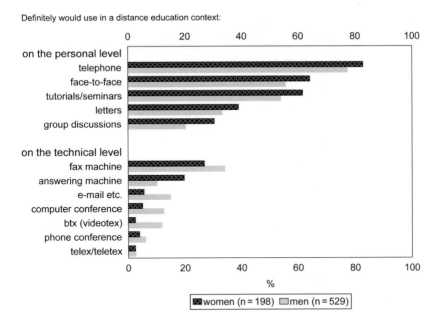

Definitely would use in a distance education context:

Figure 5.2 Communication preferences in distance education contexts

the two sections. In dealing with the FeU, respondents would 'definitely' use items of personal communication, mainly the telephone (79%), face-to-face conversations (58%) and seminars (56%). The answering patterns for both men and women corresponded to their personal preferences and, with the exception of the telephone and fax machine, were heavily biased against using ICTs (see von Prümmer and Rossié 1994).

Clearly, students adjust their communication preferences to the realities of distance learning: in practice, their strong liking for face-to-face interaction becomes much less pronounced and takes second place to the telephone as a realistic means of communication in the context of studying at a distance. The telephone, though a technological innovation without face-to-face facilities, provides an element of personal interaction in that it allows simultaneous exchange and direct conversation with a 'live' person. Communication through technical means is not only less popular, it is quite often not considered viable, or is rejected outright. The only exception here is the increasingly popular fax machine which students obviously see more as an extension of the telephone than as a separate and strictly technical means of communication.

Compared to their female colleagues men showed less preference for personal interaction and a stronger inclination to use technologically mediated communication modes (see Figure 5.2). The data is in keeping with earlier observations on gendered learning styles and has in turn been supported repeatedly in subsequent research at the FeU in Germany as well as in ODL institutions in other countries (see Chapter 4; see also Kirkup and von Prümmer 1990). Mavis Heron's (1997) research report of women students and staff at the OU UK is a recent example.

It is to be expected that the rapid technological developments will have had an impact on the availability and practicability of ICTs in distance education contexts. Further research will show how this affected the communication preferences and practice of distance students.

Communication patterns in distance education

The research results show a disparity between people's communication preferences and practice which may be due to constraints operating on different levels. For instance, students might find it difficult to impossible to meet staff in person because they lack the funds or the time to travel, or staff might be tied up with other commitments and unable to meet with (many) students in person. The disparity in answering patterns prompted questions about the actual communication practice of distance students with a view to identifying possible deficits and areas requiring intervention from the institution. The research on these topics carried out at the FeU in 1993 therefore contained batteries of questions on the communication behaviour of FeU students, including information on the frequency and cause of contacts and on the person or department contacted. Students were asked to state, for each of four activities listed, whether they had undertaken them 'once', 'two to four times', 'five times or more', or 'never' in a given semester. The answers to these questions show some congruence and some disparity with the stated communication preferences (see von Prümmer 1995a).

In this study, the reported frequency of correspondence and face-to-face interaction is nearly identical, a result that was not totally expected given the distances and difficulties involved in meeting one's teachers and fellow students 'in person'. Six out of ten respondents had met with members of the academic staff in person or had attended at least one tutorial or seminar (63%) and an equal number of respondents had corresponded with the university at least once (62%).

The overall answers presented in Table 5.1 show that the telephone was by far the most important instrument of communication and e-mail by far the least used of the four. Nine out of ten students say that they had telephoned the university at least once during the semester (91%), and only 8% of the FeU students had contacted the university electronically.

Our findings on modes of contact correspond to the findings reported for Australian distance students in a recent survey on student contacts and satisfaction with the modes of contact used. According to this study, a proportion of 'students do not make contact by e-mail', a fact which the authors explain in a variety of ways:

Table 5.1 Modes of communication used for contact with the FeU

Type of communication	Used once, %	Used 2–4 times, %	Used 5 times or more, %	Used at least once, %
The telephone	12.5	37.0	41.3	90.8
Face-to-face meeting	19.8	31.6	11.6	63.0
Written correspondence	16.5	33.1	12.8	62.4
E-mail	2.3	4.4	1.2	7.9

The telephone is still the most popular contact instrument. It may be that the telephone is still the most efficient means of two-way communication. Although e-mail is also two-way communication, it depends on factors such as whether staff read their e-mail regularly and how quickly they respond to it. Most staff apparently find it harder to ignore the ringing of the telephone. The telephone may also be seen by students as a substitute to a lecture whereas e-mail is just more study book style writing. There may also be a belief that the telephone is a private instrument whereas there is the likelihood that a number of people may have or be able to gain unauthorised access to e-mail systems and therefore there are some suspicions about privacy. It is also possible that messages can be reproduced under other people's names and it may be difficult to check who sent them.

(Park and Nooriafshar 1997: 11–12)

These hypotheses about the reasons why students are more inclined to use the telephone in their dealings with the university differ somewhat from our interpretation of the communication patterns of FeU students and would have to be explored in further research. In our experience, students use telephone contacts because they can actually talk to a real person, thus simulating direct and personal interaction. In addition, our data to a large extent reflected the FeU situation in 1994, when electronic communications such as e-mail and computer conferencing were new technologies not yet widely available. A similar study done today would, in our opinion, yield higher percentages of students using e-mail, paralleling its increased importance for course delivery and teaching and the increasing familiarity of many students with ICTs.

Using preferred means of communication

If we look only at those students who claim to have a preference for a given form of communication, we get a better idea of the extent to which they are able to realise this preference in their distance studies. The data show that

in order of preference

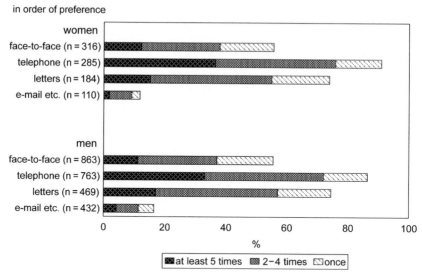

Respondents with a decided preference or a liking for the given mode of communication

Figure 5.3 Use of communication modes by students with a preference for the given mode

FeU students use the telephone whether they have a preference for this form of communication or not. In spite of many open-ended comments about the cost (e.g. peak period rates) and inconvenience (e.g. lines busy) associated with the telephone, it seems to be the basic method of bridging the gap and getting in touch with FeU staff and students. Its efficiency is enhanced when a fax machine is hooked up.

Personal interaction is very important for distance students, both in terms of their preferences and in terms of actually attending face-to-face meetings. By contrast, only half of the students state a preference for written forms of communication, and if they do, they are more likely to correspond with the university than those students who are not so inclined.

It has already been shown that distance students do take into account the fact that their chosen form of studying restricts their opportunities for dealing face-to-face with other students and the FeU staff. The need to compromise is further evident in the reported patterns of interaction in study-related contacts with the FeU.

Figure 5.3 demonstrates the striking divergence of the preference and actual use of e-mail on the part of students contacting the FeU. Looking only at students with a preference for e-mail as a mode of communication we find that 80% of them have never actually used this mode. Keeping in mind the gender differences in students' preference for a given form of

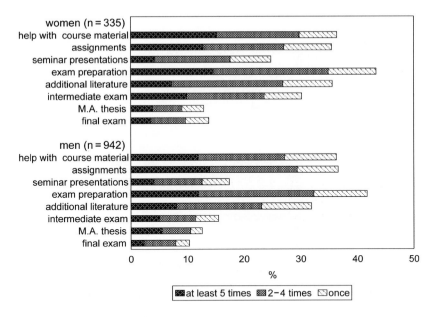

Figure 5.4 Reasons for contacting the university

communication, the answering patterns of men and women show marginal differences with respect to the extent to which they can realise their wish to use this preferred form of contact.

Reasons for contacting the FernUniversität

Distance students, with their work and family commitments, have many demands on their time and on their personal and material resources which are bound to put restrictions on their ability and willingness to do more than is strictly necessary in order to achieve their study goals. They are therefore likely to need a valid reason for initiating contact with FeU staff or with other students and they must expect this contact to contribute to their successful studying.

Evaluation studies have repeatedly shown that one of the most important functions of study centres and support services is the help they provide for assignments and exam preparation (see Chapter 4). This is reflected in the answers to a question in the 1993 FeU survey on the reasons why students contacted the university (see Figure 5.4).

Since the 1993 FeU survey sample concentrated on 'active' distance students, i.e. students who had already documented their intent to complete the degree by sending in assignments and sitting for examinations, Figure 5.4 includes information about contacts relating to final examinations

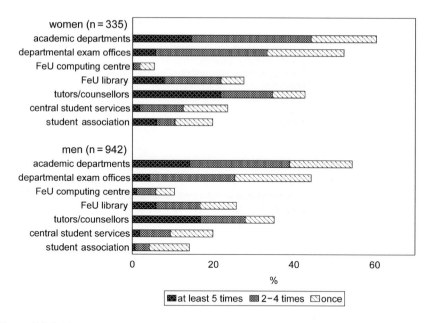

Figure 5.5 FeU personnel contacted in the event of study problems

and thesis supervision. The relatively low percentages with respect to these items are due to the fact that they are only relevant to students who have already completed a substantial portion of their degree course. Interestingly, the only significant gender differences show women contacting the university more frequently on matters such as seminars and intermediate examinations. Students are required to pass an examination at the end of the introductory or foundation phase of their degree programme, usually after the first four semesters of full-time study, later if they are part-time distance students. The intermediate examination is the prerequisite for the advanced phase of the degree programme, for admission to upper-level seminars and the final exam, and for being assigned a supervisor for the M.A. thesis.

In accordance with the findings on gendered learning styles men were less likely than women to contact the study centre and use local support services (see Figure 5.5). Thus 42% of the women but only 34% of the men reported communicating with a tutor or counsellor at least once during the semester. Women were also more likely to have direct contact with faculty on the main campus in Hagen and with staff in the departmental examinations office, men were more likely to contact the university computing centre.

With regard to personal meetings or face-to-face contact, nine out of ten FeU students in the 1993 survey had participated in activities in study centres or had attended at least one face-to-face event in connection with

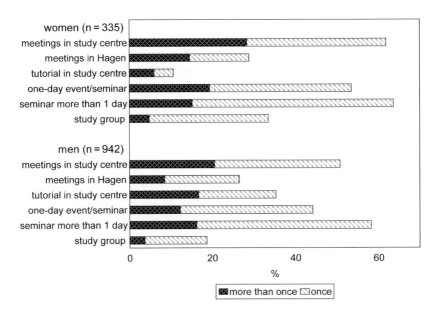

Figure 5.6 Participation in face-to-face activities

their FeU studies. This very high percentage is related to the sample which, as mentioned above, contained a large group of active distance students working seriously toward a degree. While there were few gender differences in the more general question, women were much more likely than men to participate in specific activities offered in study centres and in self-help study groups (see Figure 5.6). The differences were especially great with regard to the frequency of visits to a study centre for general information and tutorial support and to participation in study groups.

The results of the survey on communication preferences and practice fit in with other findings collected in the course of twenty years of evaluation research at the FeU and can legitimately be viewed as a valid basis for policy decisions regarding the communication needs of distance students. They support the argument that adults do not primarily enrol in DE programmes in order to pursue their degree studies in isolation. The women, especially, place a very high value on interpersonal relationships and on face-to-face communication. The results also show a certain pragmatism in the activities students actually engage in. As described above, students are influenced by various constraints on their time and resources which may curtail their making use of communication opportunities. In addition, students are motivated by the perceived costs and benefits of communication, and by their previous experiences regarding the effectiveness of their contacts with the university or with other students.

Experience with technically-mediated communication

It is stating the obvious to say that students must have access to a given communication technology in order to utilise it for their dealings with the university and to become experienced or expert users. It is equally trivial to say that what happens when students do use the technology will colour their perceptions of the technology's suitability for communication purposes and their willingness to intensify its use in their distance studying. Nevertheless, within distance education institutions we often find a certain lack of concern with the attitudes, both of students and staff, toward the increased use of ICTs as regular means of communication. It is often assumed that techno-logical progress is inevitable and the benefits of information and commun-ication technologies will eventually lead all distance students to obtain the equipment and the experience necessary for successful studying in this new learning environment.

Our research shows that students tend to be more sceptical than this and that often their previous encounters with the technologies have not been wholly convincing. In order to make informed decisions about the increased use of ICTs in distance education – possibly even the transformation into virtual universities – it is necessary to be aware of the problems associated with the new technologies as well as with the opportunities they offer. A knowledge of the difficulties encountered by participants of an e-mail dialogue or computer conference, for instance, should be helpful in reassessing the design, the structure, or the tutorial support provided and to identify tech-nical snags and pedagogical shortcomings. In this sense, we can underwrite the motto of the conference *Media Prosperity '98*, which stated: 'Resistance is futile: Potentials in the Technological Future', concentrating on develop-ing the potentials rather than blindly being pulled along by the irresistible attraction of technology (AMTEC 1998).

Experience of distance students with ICTs

When we did the communication survey (1993) few FeU students had much, if any, experience with ICTs which played no significant role in their every-day lives. The only technologies of which students claimed to be expert users were the telephone with answering machine (24%) and the fax machine (30%), as Figure 5.7 shows.

Those students who were at least to some extent familiar with the technologies did not judge them universally effective as media for their communication with the university as Figure 5.8 demonstrates. In addition to the experience they had with given ICTs, respondents had been asked to judge each of a list of technologies as 'highly effective', 'useful', or 'not effective enough'. It is the fax machine which was considered the most useful tool, with nine out of ten users (n = 433) judging it highly effective

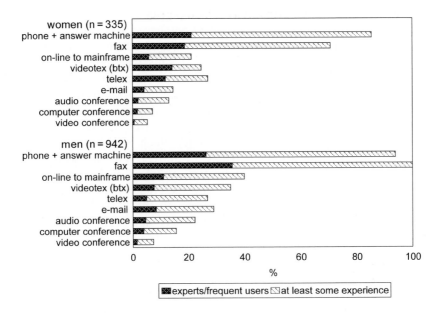

Figure 5.7 Extent of experience with ICTs

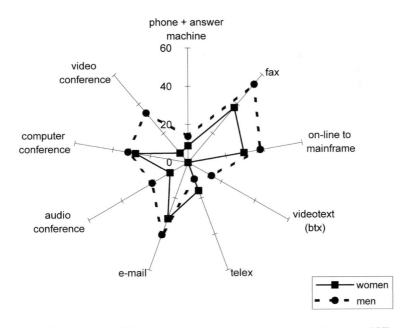

Figure 5.8 Effectiveness of ICTs: student with experience of using the given ICT

(48%) or useful (43%). Considering the high percentage of students who had at least some experience with this telephone-based technology, it seems plausible to assume a correlation between use and effectiveness of ICTs in the sense that people who have positive results when they use a given medium are more likely to use it again for future communication needs.

Conversely, people who have been frustrated are likely to try a different technology in their next attempt to reach the university. That this is not a simple correlation becomes clear when we look at two other results in Figure 5.8. The telephone with answering machine, which is the most often used instrument of communication (see Table 5.1 above), is by no means considered a very effective mode of communication: only 11% of the users (n = 479) judge it highly effective, and a further 58% experienced it as no more than useful. Computer-mediated communication, on the other hand, although not yet used by many distance students, was seen in a positive light. E-mail, for instance, was judged to be highly effective (39%) or useful (50%) by nine out of ten users (n = 124) of this technology.

Women commenting on communication and technologies in distance education

Perceived deficits in communication opportunities

Many students made use of the opportunity offered by an open-ended question to let us know which means of communication they had missed in their contacts with the university. It seems that problems were caused mainly by the fact that the telephone hours scheduled for advice and counselling from the teaching staff were totally inadequate both in the length of time staff were available, and in the time slots scheduled for student contacts. Also, the students could not always reach someone even if they did try to call during the scheduled periods.

Many students said that they missed the personal contact with professors and other teaching staff, as well as the opportunity to meet with other students. These complaints were sometimes accompanied by (more or less realistic) suggestions to help overcome these perceived deficits. Other suggestions were directed at ways in which the technical problems could be minimised. A number of students addressed issues of content and presentation and expressed the wish to have more information on the courses and organisation of their degree programme. The following quotes illustrate the types of comments as well as the suggestions for improvement made by women distance students with regard to problems in communication with the FeU:

'The students services department does not have enough telephone lines. Since they have started putting students on hold, calling the FeU has become too expensive. The academic departments don't offer enough time slots for calling in, one or two hours per week is not sufficient. Often it is not

possible to get hold of the teaching staff responsible for the courses. Week-end seminars, which are offered for exam preparation, happen too far away and too infrequently.'

'I don't miss opportunities for personal contact but for extended calling hours. I would appreciate the publication of a comprehensive telephone book for the whole institution since I often have to look up phone numbers in a number of different brochures. By the way, these information materials would benefit from being more concise.'

'I would like to get through to an answering machine which provides information on calling hours and to receive return calls.'

'On the organisational level it would be useful if departments and staff whom I need to contact were actually available (for instance, I cannot get through to the departmental examinations office even during the posted calling hours!) → It might be sufficient if services which are offered in theory were available in practice!'

'There should be opportunities for students, who are preparing for the same examinations (intermediate or final exams) or who are working on similar topics for their term papers or theses, to get together → i.e. the FeU should institutionalise intensive and focused seminars for specific groups of degree students.'

'I would appreciate more face-to-face seminars in which it is possible to meet other students and to exchange our experiences as distance students. For me, one of the greatest deficits of this form of studying is the lack of someone to turn to when I have organisational problems. The "muddling through on your own" study system is extremely time-consuming.'

'I would like to have more opportunities for self-help study groups with fellow students who are at roughly the same point in their study progress and exam preparations. This is unlikely to happen because of the varied demands of employment and studying, plus possible family commitments and differences in students' life circumstances rooted in the social structure.'

'It should be possible to meet other students who are enrolled in the same course or are engaged in similar activities (for instance, preparing for the same exam). The contact lists provided by the FeU upon request usually arrive too late and are inadequate. This system of bringing students together must be improved if it is to serve its purpose.'

'There should be an opportunity for a brief talk with the examiner either before or after the oral examination.'

'*There should be more face-to-face seminars, spread out regionally throughout the whole country, and there should be more opportunities for discussions about the course content.*'

'*What is needed is an answering machine and more accessible information
on the regulations governing exams:*

Who is the person I should contact in the academic department?

What are the prerequisites for being admitted to take the exam?

*Can I suggest an exam topic, or will the topic be set by the examiners
without consultation?*

*I often felt as if I had overlooked the one all-important piece of informa-
tion which would have provided the answers to all my questions.*'

Student comments on using the technology

A number of questionnaires contained open-ended comments on the uses of
technologies and the experience students had with more or less technologically mediated forms of communication. Even in 1993, there was a basic
acceptance of the new media and a willingness to buy the necessary equipment if the university made sure that the returns would be worth the invest-
ment. But the comments also show students who are sceptical or even totally
opposed to the idea of making computers and technologies indispensable.
The following quotes by women distance students exemplify these divergent
attitudes:

'*As the mother of two small children I personally feel very isolated from
other students. I would like to have more personal contact and interaction.
Because of this I am against technically mediated communication. This
does not free one from the isolation of the distance student but pushes one
even further into it!*'

'*Considering the special circumstances of the distance student (being engaged in "single combat", having little or no contact with other students),
meetings in the study centre or face-to-face seminars and tutorials brought
me help with the subject matter, a good friend, and motivation, as well as
raising my spirits. All of this would be lost if distance communication were
to be extended at the cost of face-to-face provision. I realise that my
situation may be exceptional – there are three study centres within a
30 km radius and five study centres within a 60 km radius. I therefore
think that the FeU should maybe look for a compromise, developing technically mediated communication routes for those students who are going it
alone (really fighting "single combat") and at the same time opening new
study centres and expanding the existing ones.*'

'A word of caution: do not exclude students who do not have the advanced technical equipment. Studying at a distance is hard enough – and expensive enough – already!!'

'In my view, technical communication means will increase the isolation of the distance student. Rather, more face-to-face contact is essential.'

'Computer-mediated communication is nothing desirable. For me the telephone is almost too impersonal since the structure of distance education offers so few opportunities for interpersonal communication anyway. Of course, those students interested in it should have the chance to use computer-mediated communication. But this should not become the main institutional goal.'

'In principle I don't have any problems, financial or otherwise, to upgrade my computer to the standards necessary for on-line communication. But so far I have found that the financial outlay has not paid off: for instance, I connected a modem to my computer to use during the practical programming course. But soon after that course was finished I disconnected it again since I had no use for it in my studies.'

Issues of access and control over technologies

The congruence or disparity between communication preferences and practice is at least partly associated with opportunities for realising one's preferences. Distance students, who like to meet teaching staff in person, often cannot afford the time or money required to visit study centres or attend seminars. The less favoured telephones and letters, on the other hand, are widely accessible, and students are competent users since these media are part of their everyday lives. In 1993 two thirds of the respondents had access to a fax machine (29% unrestricted and 39% by arrangement), a technology which today is likely to be a standard piece of equipment for FeU students. At the time of the survey, only a quarter of the FeU respondents had at least some access to those technologies which require linkage to computer networks (27%), while the majority could not make use of these media at all (68%). Since then there has been an increase in the availability of computers and internet access, but in Germany high rates for providers and telephone transmission still restrict the use of these technologies.

Distance teaching universities such as the OU UK and the FeU monitor the state of equipment available to their students in order to make informed decisions about the extent to which they can employ modern technologies as integral and required components of their teaching system. Continuing research at the OU UK shows how rapidly computers and ICTs are spreading and how quickly the state of equipment available for distance studying changes. This has been documented in the PLUM (Programme on Learner Use of Media) reports on computer access which the Institute of Educational Technology (IET) has been doing for some years now (Laurillard 1995; Taylor and Jelfs 1995; Kirkwood 1995). Many of the findings have a bearing on the chances of women distance students since they show the existence of gender factors in relation to access and usage of technologies.

Gendered access to personal computers and ICTs

Research on access to personal computers and to information and communication technologies has been carried out in Britain and in Germany. First it must be noted that in both countries many more students today have access to these technologies than was the case a few years ago. This is due to the rapid expansion of multimedia PCs, computer-mediated communication systems, ISDN and the world-wide web which has taken place in these two industrialised countries within the last few years. Being part of the electronic community, distance educators and administrators may be tempted to assume that their reality is the same as that of their students and that they only need to tap the seemingly unlimited possibilities of technology in order to provide the optimal learning environment for all distance students.

In fact, as even the most recent research shows, there still are segments of society which are excluded from this technological advance, and for whom the necessary equipment and connection costs remain prohibitive. There are national differences in the availability of technology but also class differences within individual European countries. In Britain, for instance, where:

> ... the data have been analysed by social class there is a significant social inequality with respect to household electronics with 50% of 'professionals' having access to some form of computer in the household and less than 10% of the economically inactive (many of whom are likely to be single parent mothers). Gender is compounded by socio-economic inequality.
>
> (Kirkup 1997: 6)

Gendered access to computers

The gender inequalities mentioned carry over to the availability of technology for distance studying since women traditionally have fewer resources than men and tend to have a greater distance to technology as well as more demands on their time and energy. It is therefore not surprising that distance students in both Britain and Germany show similar gender patterns, with men having more access to such technologies and more control over their use in the context of their distance studies.

In Britain, as Gill Kirkup and others reported in their contribution to the 1995 ICDE Conference, women distance students had less access to computers, mainly because men were more likely to be able to use a PC (personal computer) at their place of work. In addition, men also were more likely to have the unrestricted use of the household PC for their studying and in general be more familiar with ICTs and media (Kirkup *et al.* 1995).

A more recent gender analysis of the OU UK computing access survey of 1996 shows that the gender gap still exists and is likely to remain in evidence for years to come. Referring to other national and international surveys, Gill Kirkup and Jason Abbott state facts which cannot be overlooked in policy decisions on the future uses of technology in distance education. They see their report as part of:

> a history of analysing gendered inequality in computer access and use among OU UK students and students elsewhere in distance and higher education. It demonstrates that, despite an increase in the quality of computer access amongst OU UK students in general, women students continue to have a significantly poorer quality of access, on a variety of measures. They are also less enthusiastic about an expansion of the technology into more areas of their studies.
>
> (Kirkup and Abbott 1997: 1)

Comparative research in Germany showed that FeU women also had less access to computers and the new media than men studying at the distance. In 1996, for instance, twice as many FeU women (22%) as men (11%) did not have access to a PC at all. As Figure 5.9 shows, men were much more likely to be able to use a PC at their place of work, partly because of their greater participation in the workforce and partly because of the nature of their paid workplace which tends to have more sophisticated software and equipment, including on-line facilities, and fewer restrictions on using the technology for applications which are not job-related.

Where students did have access, PC standards were fairly high for both women and men, but the latter tended to have more advanced communication technologies. In 1996 most PCs at work and at home (72% each) were equipped with processors of the 486 and 586 or Pentium variety, 84% had a colour monitor, 83% featured Microsoft Windows, and almost all were connected to a printer (99% at work and 91% at home). While these basic features show little gender differences, the computers available to women both at home and especially at work were less well equipped than those of men in terms of using multimedia products or links to on-line services or the FeU computing centre.

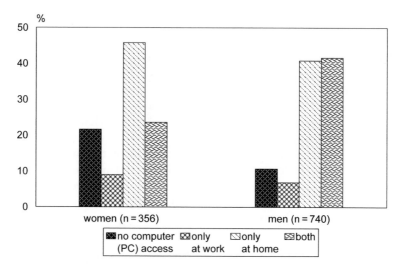

1995 FeU survey

Figure 5.9 Computer access by gender

Decisions about computer purchase

The most revealing question in terms of access to new technologies refers to who in the household is responsible for the decision to buy a computer (see Figure 5.10). Eight in ten men say that this decision was their own, one in ten men says it was a joint decision with his partner/wife. Women, by contrast are more inclined to leave this decision to their partner/husband: only half the women with privately owned PCs say that they made the decision to buy a computer by themselves (51%); one-fifth bought the equipment as a result of a joint decision (21%); and one quarter of the women distance students left the decision completely up to their partner/husband (24%). This last is a situation which happened rarely in the case of the men, as only five men left the purchasing decision completely in the hands of their wives or partners (0.9%).

A joint analysis of the research data from the OU UK and the German FeU led Gill Kirkup and myself to conclude that the new educational forms and media pose both threats and opportunities for European women (Kirkup and von Prümmer 1997). The threats arise mainly out of the unquestioning introduction of ICTs into distance and open learning which often neglects to take into account the differential needs and resources of specific social groups. Based on our research we express our view that now:

> . . . is a good time to stop and consider the implications a full-scale shift to technological course delivery and learning designs might have for

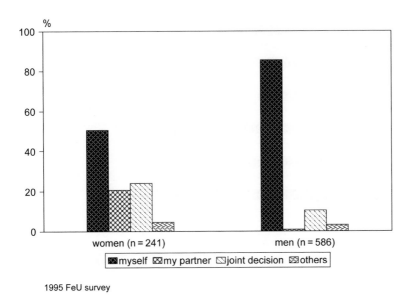

1995 FeU survey

Figure 5.10 Decisions about computer purchase by gender

different target groups. Empirical data could help determine which technologies, pursued in which way, would either serve specific target groups or further handicap them due to their restricted access or other factors.
(Kirkup and von Prümmer 1997: 54)

The research results reflect three factors which influence access to technology. The first factor is economic since women generally have less control over the family income and tend to be in lower-paying jobs. The second factor is based on gender effects in the education and socialisation of girls and boys, resulting in women being less knowledgeable and/or less confident with respect to their own technical competence, and therefore more willing to leave such expensive decisions to their male partner. The third factor is that men are more likely to use the computer more extensively and that it therefore seems justified that they should choose the kind of equipment purchased for use by themselves and their other family members.

Tools and toys: gendered uses of the technology

Another difference between men and women distance students is the way in which they approach the technology, for instance with regard to learning how to use the equipment and software (see Figure 5.11). Men are more likely than women to follow the 'learning by doing' road, i.e. they like to

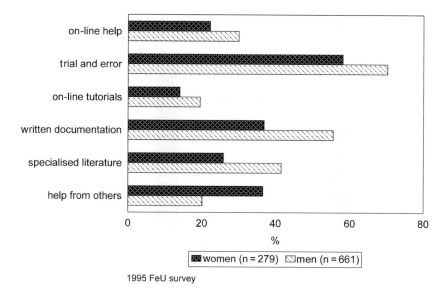

1995 FeU survey

Figure 5.11 Preferred mode for learning to use the technology

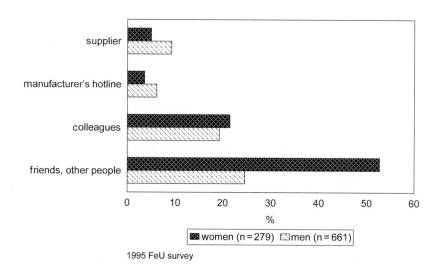

1995 FeU survey

Figure 5.12 Preferred sources of help with difficulties in using the technology

play with their new toy, something which women quite often simply have not got the time for even if they did have the inclination.

Men are also more likely to study the written documentation, on-line help or other handbooks, again a time-consuming undertaking. Women are more inclined to look for help from other people (see Figure 5.12).

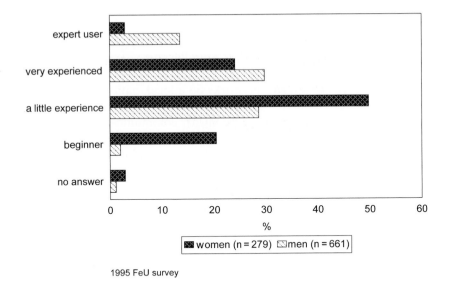

1995 FeU survey

Figure 5.13 Own estimate of competence in working with computers

It is in keeping with these findings that women are much less inclined than men to say that they enjoy working with the technology. We have already seen that women approach the technology differently and have different learning styles. If the systems are set up and run according to these preferences, women might find it easier to take the plunge and incur the cost, both financially and in terms of overcoming the emotional and social barriers, of 'getting into' computers. As it is, women distance students are less likely to consider themselves competent users of the technologies, while men are quite likely to consider themselves expert computer users (see Figure 5.13).

This is another fact which distance educators might keep in mind when planning the increased use of ICTs and educational media for their course delivery and communication channels. It may legitimately be assumed that the fun people have using the equipment is one of the determinants of their willingness to work with the educational media, being much less inclined to have reservations when they get enjoyment out of doing so. This, in turn, depends at least in part on factors which the institution can influence, such as an interface and software ergonomics.

Another gender difference in the approach to information and communication technologies has been noted with respect to what is commonly referred to as the electronic super-highway. It seems that women are less attracted to the concept of a high-speed motorway with the concurrent restrictions of travelling in an isolated vehicle on a road with limited access, prescribed lanes and unpredictable speeds, making detours and getting into traffic jams (see Menzies 1994). Rather, and this ties in with our findings on women's learning styles in general, and in relation to getting used to a computer, women tend to take a different view of the world-wide means of communication and dissemination/collection of information. Taking the names Inter'*net*' and world-wide '*web*' literally, some women see the potential of these services as an 'electronic weaving loom' (Burge 1995: 151) on which they can create women's networks on a local, national or world-wide level. WIN (the international network of women in distance education) is a case in point, although at this stage we mostly communicate and collaborate through the basic means of e-mail, a technology accessible to many women who do not necessarily have the most advanced, sophisticated information and communication technologies.

Implications: gender aspects and electronic communication

Due to the gap between the communication preferences of FeU students on the one hand and the institutionally supported types of communication on the other, students are frequently not able to interact with teaching and administrative staff or with other students according to their personal inclinations. Distance students need to be pragmatic in adapting their communication patterns to institutional requirements and provisions. Their actual communication patterns are the outcome of various interacting factors such as:

- personal likes and dislikes, abilities and disabilities;
- access to different types of communication, cost of using it and time needed;
- perceived benefits; and
- institutional requirements and provisions.

On the part of the institution there are two assumptions underlying the debate about communication in distance education:

1   Students who seriously study for a degree via distance education are prepared to compromise with respect to their personal communication preferences. DE students utilise those channels of communication which are both available and effective in terms of time and cost.
2   As communication technology advances and becomes less costly and more easily accessible, DE students will readily use communication channels such as e-mail and the new interactive (multi)media to further their studies.

Still, it could be argued that students are more likely to be motivated and successful in pursuing their degree when there is a high level of congruence

Table 5.2 Communication preferences and practice by gender (FeU 1994)

Type of communication		*a* Personal liking, %	*b* Preferred use, %	*c* Actual use, %	Difference *c minus a,* %
Written	women	55.0	38.9	63.7	8.7
correspondence	men	46.9	33.1	61.9	15.0
Telephone	women	85.4	82.8	93.9	8.5
	men	85.8	77.3	89.7	3.9
Face-to-face meeting	women	94.9	64.1	60.6	−34.3
	men	93.4	55.6	63.8	−29.6
Group discussion,	women	78.3	30.3	60.1	−18.2
seminars	men	65.4	20.2	51.8	−13.6
E-mail	women	23.7	5.6	3.0	−20.7
	men	45.2	14.9	9.8	−35.4

a personal liking = decided preference + like to do
b preferred use = definitely would use in DE context
c actual use = used at least once in dealing with the university

between the type of contact available and their personal preferences. Assuming that distance education does require some form of interaction between the student and the university, in the interest of quality assurance, the institution should be concerned with providing communication channels which are suited to the communication needs and preferences of its students. Considering the available information on distance students, this concern must necessarily extend to gender issues.

As far as student preferences go, it is noticeable that both men and women distance students lean toward personal interaction rather than technologically transmitted communication, although some differences can be observed. These fit in with other data on gender-differentiated communication preferences as Table 5.2 shows (von Prümmer 1995a).

The results are consistent with earlier findings that women are more interested in social learning but that they face more problems in order to be able to meet face-to-face with staff and other students. (See Chapter 4; see also Kirkup and von Prümmer, 1990; von Prümmer and Rossié, 1990c.) The data on electronic communication shows twice as many men interested in e-mail without necessarily putting it into practice. This could suggest that women distance students approach technology more practically than men and are less inclined to find it fascinating *per se.*

One result which needs to be explored further occurred with respect to electronic communication. The overall use of e-mail was almost negligible (8% in 1993) and increased only marginally when we looked only at those students who reported a preference for this form of technology (18%). This contrasted with the fact that four in ten respondents (39%) stated a personal liking for electronic communication – but not in relation to their distance studies, where only one in ten (12%) would 'definitely' use e-mail. The data from the FeU survey suggested that the way students could communicate with the FeU through electronic media was not sufficient or satisfactory and most likely not attractive enough to offer a real alternative.

This could partly be explained through a lack of access to computer networks, as only 27% of the respondents had unrestricted (14%) or limited (13%) access to the FeU computer. Furthermore, only half the students with electronic access to the FeU had at least some experience using the technology, and only one-fifth (21%) of those students who did have a way of getting into the net claimed to have extensive experience with the system.

In order to log into a computer network, students need to have the right kind of hardware and software. The FeU caters to IBM-compatible personal computers (PCs). At the time of the survey on communication in distance education three quarters of the active students (77%) either owned or had access to a PC, most of which were of the 486 or 386 variety (45% and 23% respectively). While the percentage of FeU students with a PC was high compared to the population in general, only 15% of the students with a PC, i.e. 11% of all respondents, also had a modem, which is the prerequisite for data transmission and electronic communication. A current survey on computer access and use is expected to show much higher figures due especially to the increase of high-speed telephone networks and the decrease in telephone charges.

One of the factors impeding women's embracing the new technologies is their comparative lack of access to the more sophisticated ICT equipment. Figure 5.14 shows that there is still a need for redressing this imbalance as equality of access is necessary for equality of making use of the chances offered by the new media.

It seems that a few years ago students expected more results from investing in a fax machine than in a PC with data transmission facilities. Two-thirds of the respondents had unrestricted (29%) or limited (39%) access to fax facilities, and 43% were experienced users of this form of communication. Both methods of technically mediated communication allow round-the-clock access to staff at the centre, and the initial financial outlay as well as the costs of transmission are much lower for fax than for computerbased telecommunication.

Considering the speed with which both computers and on-line providers have spread in the last five years, it is to be expected that distance students today have better equipment and easier access to ICTs, and that this development has been accompanied by a corresponding shift in communication modes and, possibly, preferences in student–staff or student–student interaction. These issues, including their gender implications, are currently explored in a FeU survey on students' access to and usage of computers and ICTs for their distance studies.

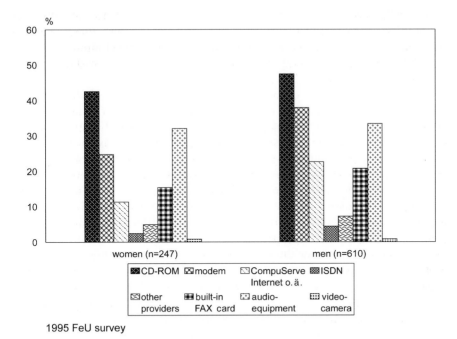

1995 FeU survey

Figure 5.14 Privately owned ICTs by gender

Virtual equality: the place of women in the electronic campus

Recently there has been increased interest, in Germany as in other countries (e.g. Athabasca University 1998), in establishing the virtual university. This development seems to have an extremely close affinity with distance education, although it is by no means confined to this mode as is evidenced by the debate about convergence (see Tait 1997) and by the large number of universities experimenting with the possibilities of the virtual campus (see Simon 1997).

At the German FeU there are many projects, often initiated by individual staff members interested in the possibilities of the new media, for using the world-wide web for course delivery and, especially, for seminars and communication. For instance, the Departments of Computer Science and Electrical Engineering set up a virtual university which:

> ... realises, tests and evaluates the new concept of a virtual university with its new forms of teaching and its flexibility in time and space combined with its individualised and demand-oriented learning provision based on the rigorous use of multimedia and communication technologies

> . . . The teaching concept of this virtual university comprises not only
> components for the transmission of information and knowledge but
> also opportunities for communication, groups and seminars, practical
> applications using computer networks, and access to comprehensive
> information systems.
>
> (FeU 1998a: 5)

Another project originally was stimulated by the federal German government's planning to fund several large-scale projects on the educational use
of ICTs with special emphasis on cooperation between universities and other
providers of continuing education or vocational and professional training.
In a university-wide effort, the FeU as an institution prepared a proposal to
establish a *Lernraum Virtuelle Universität* (LVU), which literally translated
means virtual university learning environment, within the next five years
(FeU 1998b). Although the government ultimately decided to fund a number
of smaller projects, rather than the large projects it had at first encouraged,
work on the proposal is having a long-term effect on the FeU. Since all FeU
departments were involved in the process of formulating the project, it has
provided an impetus for a wide range of activities aimed at using ICTs for
both teaching and administrative purposes. For instance, in developing the
project proposal the university has had to consider the priorities of preparing courses for delivery on the LVU and how to organise every aspect of the
teaching and learning system as part of this virtual learning environment,
including registration, collection of fees, library services, student support,
and assignments and examinations.

It became obvious early on in this process that the issues of equitable
access discussed in this chapter were largely ignored and that the technological challenges of creating the virtual university were predominant. This
neglect of gender issues poses yet another threat for women as once again
'policy and practice for implementing new technologies seems driven more
by ideology and wishful thinking than a sound empirical research basis'
(Kirkup and von Prümmer 1997: 55).

At the same time, it is easy to think of ways in which the women who
work or study at the FeU could use the opportunities offered by the virtual
university and create their own, women-friendly learning environment. It is
encouraging to see that a group of women has formed around the issue of
women and the new educational media and that this group is developing
perspectives for using the 'liberatory potential of information technology'
(Kirkup and von Prümmer 1997: 55) for women in DE.

This will require a lot of effort as resources in general are scarce and
threatening to get scarcer still. There is a general tendency to see gender
issues as marginal to the development of ICTs and to concentrate on the
development of the 'really important' components of the virtual university,
i.e. creating appropriate teaching materials and transmission channels.

Usually evaluation – in itself a marginalised and inadequately funded part of the process of developing the virtual university – is the only area in which attention to gender issues is spelled out.

With respect to the establishment of the virtual university, we find many enthusiasts, for whom 'the development process may be an end in itself' (Thompson, D. 1997: 193) and who do not feel the need to look out for those who might be unable to participate in the final product or process. Yet, as Jennifer O'Rourke argues, 'by examining the impact of new technologies on women distance learners, we may be able to develop some strategies for scrutinizing the effectiveness of new technologies for the whole range of learners we intend to serve' (O'Rourke 1997: 120).

In her article *Canaries in the Mine? Women's Experience and New Learning Technologies*, Jennifer O'Rourke describes how distance education as a whole can benefit from taking gender into account and acting on the warning signals provided through this observation. She concludes:

> This article has touched on some of the issues that new learning technologies raise for women. These technologies will only be a benefit for women if they genuinely accommodate practical needs for flexible learning, allow for the inclusion of women's reality, and support women's preferred approaches to learning to the same extent as current distance education strategies.
>
> (O'Rourke 1997: 125)

While I find the parable of the canaries as early warning system quite compelling, I would not like it to be misunderstood as meaning that women are simply the passive consumers of the virtual air space and that they drop out (as the canaries drop dead) when the air gets unhealthy. In fact, women take an active role in shaping the new and virtual world; they contribute their expert knowledge of both the technologies and the conditions of women's learning realities; also they share their visions of a humane and women-friendly virtual learning environment (see Hauff *et al.* 1999).

Chapter 6

Minority women

Class and gender in distance education

The issue of educationally disadvantaged minorities is relevant to any distance education system because of the potential inherent in this form of education to reach people who do not have the opportunity to study in educational institutions with attendance requirements. Depending on the social and historical context of a DE institution, it has to respond to different kinds of minority group and deal with different parameters of discrimination and compensation. Traditionally, three determinants of minority status have been identified as affecting social chances and educational opportunities in a fundamental way: class or socioeconomic status, gender, and race or ethnicity. Also relevant are factors of health and disability, age, religion and regional distribution.

Which of these determinants is at the centre of attention in any given DE system, depends on its social and historical context. In the early 1970s in West Germany, prior to the establishment of the FeU, there was much concern with the educational discrimination of the working class. In Canada and Australia, to name but two countries, there was growing concern with providing educational opportunities for the aboriginal and native peoples. In South Africa, efforts have been directed toward redressing the educational disadvantages rooted in a profoundly racist regime. World-wide, there is now an increasing concern with the provision of education for refugees from wars, civil unrest, and natural catastrophes.

Within the limits of this book it would be impossible to do justice to all of these contexts and developments. By looking at one country and one DTU in some detail and by placing the research data into a theoretical framework, I am hoping to paint a picture of minority women in distance education which will be meaningful for other distance educators and students. This chapter therefore deals with those inequalities which are rooted in class and gender, looking at women from a working-class background as a group in which both of these factors are present and combine their adverse effects. As a minority, these women have experienced multiple discrimination and have overcome formidable odds in order to study at a university. The empirical data available from a survey at the FeU provide us with evidence which can to some extent be extrapolated to situations in other countries and help contribute to an understanding of the needs of minority women elsewhere.

The following quote from the Speaker of the British House of Commons illustrates the persistent image of the OU UK as an institution providing a previously denied access to tertiary education for working-class people. In her foreword to Patricia W. Lunneborg's book *OU Women. Undoing Educational Obstacles*, Betty Boothroyd writes:

> I have a personal interest in the story of how these mature students obtained their bachelor's degrees. Their story could well have been my own. When I left school the opportunities for higher education were far fewer than they are today. In any case, I came from a working-class family. The lives of my mother and father had been dominated by unemployment and short-time working. There was no talk of sending me to university. The imperative was for me to start contributing to the household – if possible in a job which offered security and even a pension at the end of it.
>
> (Boothroyd 1994: vii)

Many German women from working-class families can relate to these experiences as this chapter amply demonstrates.

Class and gender issues in European distance education

At the time when western European countries such as Britain and West Germany set up their DTUs, concerns with inequality were focused mainly on class or social background, with only secondary interest in gender-related factors, and with no apparent awareness of the role of ethnic or racial background. For instance, the first institution providing tertiary-level education at a distance, the OU UK, was founded with the explicit goal of providing a second chance for all educationally disadvantaged people. This is exemplified in the following sentence from the 1969 Planning Committee report, quoted in the book *A Degree of Difference. The Open University of the United Kingdom*:

> The objects of the Open University were then to be to: 'provide opportunities, at both undergraduate and post-graduate level, of higher education to all those, who for any reason, have been or are being precluded from achieving their aims through an existing institution of higher education'.
>
> (McIntosh *et al.* 1977: 5)

But, as McIntosh and her colleagues observed in their 1977 study of the first stage of the development of this new educational venture, this broad definition of disadvantaged groups tended to be narrowed down to encompass only educational discrimination based on class origin and social background. This narrow view was found unconstructive because: 'Even apart from the problems of definition, it constitutes too limited a view of educational disadvantage. It is only necessary to look at women's education for this to be clear' (McIntosh *et al.* 1977: 6).

Arguing for a broader definition, the authors provide information on gender, age and regional distribution, but their study does not mention other factors which also influence educational opportunities, namely the role of race and ethnicity.

In West Germany, where the second large-scale DTU in Europe was established in 1974, the situation was similar to that in Britain in the late 1960s. There was an urgent concern with educational discrimination due to class inequalities and, to a lesser extent, to gender inequality, and the FeU was set up to help redress this imbalance. It is interesting to note that causes of differential educational opportunities have increasingly been neglected, and that the issue of *how* to provide DE has become more important than the issue of *who* the students are. As an institution, the FeU keeps no statistics on students' social background and only sketchy details on gender patterns regarding enrolments and course choices, or on students with disabilities. There is some concern with regional factors and with disabled or imprisoned students, but not with racial or ethnic minorities who are only a tiny proportion of the student population. It might well be assumed that ethnic groups such as foreign workers and their second or third generation families are among the most educationally disadvantaged people, with a corresponding need for the second chance offered through distance education; yet there is no evidence that the FeU attracts students from these minorities. There is also no evidence that the FeU has played a significant role in the assimilation process following the historic events of the unification of East and West Germany a decade ago.

Class – gender – education: determinants for access to higher education

DTUs provide adults with the chance of entering degree programmes and of gaining academic degrees which previously they did not have the opportunity or inclination to pursue. In this way, tertiary-level distance education is seen to contribute to a more egalitarian society in which earlier educational discrimination can be overcome later in life. Working-class children, especially girls from a working-class background or from the lower social strata, are among the most disadvantaged groups for access to secondary schooling and tertiary education. (The two concepts of working class and lower social strata are often used synonymously; for a discussion of the theoretical and empirical implications see von Prümmer 1997a.) A central question in the analysis of the recruitment of distance students therefore addressed the claim that this form of education helps redress educational discrimination.

Earlier data from other distance teaching institutions had shown that:

> In general, the distant student does not come from the upper social strata, whose members can afford the costs of a traditional university education for their children. Thus the establishment in 1965 of the *Teletechnikum* in Poland raised the percentage of children from working and farming families among the first-year students in technical universities from 41% to 82%. The first intake of students at the Open University [in Britain] already had a percentage of students with working class fathers of 45%.
>
> (Ehmann 1978: 180)

This observation led to the expectation that in comparison with other German universities, students from a working-class background would be over-represented at the FeU. On the basis of her research results, Irene Raehlmann formulated the hypothesis that working class women were especially likely to enrol in degree programmes at a distance:

> Should further research show that the percentage of women students with working-class parents is higher in distance education than in universities with face-to-face teaching, and should this research also show that a sizeable proportion of these women study while in paid work, the results could be interpreted as an additional strengthening of my hypothesis. This hypothesis states that distance education contributes to more equality of educational opportunities.
>
> (Raehlmann 1988: 40)

Following up on Raehlmann's work, the issue of class and gender in relation to access to the FeU was integrated into an evaluation survey on the situation of women and men in distance education in the mid-1980s. In order to do justice to this data, I used it as the starting point for my Ph.D. dissertation which analyses in detail the social mobility of working-class women through distance education (von Prümmer 1996, 1997a). On one level, my dissertation is a contribution to the evaluation of the FeU and draws on the university's statistical databases and research data from a number of evaluation studies. The theoretical framework is based on class analysis and mobility research, educational research, and feminist research and theory. My research question, briefly, was to what extent women from a working-class background strive for upward social mobility and what role their distance studies play in this mobility process.

At another level, my dissertation is a contribution to the recently revived interest in the participation of the daughters of working-class families in higher education and in the study situation of those who had succeeded in becoming university students. This issue had been rediscovered by feminist sociologists in the 1980s when women from working-class backgrounds studying at West German universities realised that their feelings of alienation were structural rather than due to their individual shortcomings in the academic environment. This was first expressed by Hannelore Bublitz (1980) who titled her doctoral dissertation *Somehow I did not really belong . . . : Working class daughters at university*. A few years later Gabriele Theling (1986) speculated on the use her university education would be to her as a graduate of working-class origin in the work entitled: *Maybe I would have been happier as a shop assistant: working class daughters and the university*.

After briefly sketching the methodology used to assign students' class origin the following sections will present some statistical data on the class composition of FeU students and students at other German universities.

Class analysis and the definition of 'class origin'

In order to test the assumption that DE can serve as a second chance for previously denied educational attainment, it was necessary to look at students from disadvantaged social backgrounds and to compare these to students from other social strata. Having chosen women from working-class families for this case study, their class location and class origin had to be defined and analysed in relation to empirical and theoretical findings on the place of women in the class structure and on their social mobility processes within this structure. The focus on women meant that the research became part of the debate on gender and class which is an issue both in sociological and in feminist class analysis and mobility research (for more detail see Chapter 4; and von Prümmer 1997a).

On the practical side, a class schema had to be constructed which paralleled as closely as possible that of the regular government surveys on the student population in Germany, since the argument postulated differences in the enrolment patterns of the FeU and other universities. For this, three indicators of class origin were used, separately and in conjunction:

*   mother's and father's occupational position;
*   mother's and father's educational attainment (highest level of schooling); and
*   mother's and father's vocational or professional training (highest level of formal qualification).

The classification of occupational positions as the major determinant of class position and class origin was based on a catalogue used at the time by the *Deutsches Studentenwerk*, an organisation which carries out national surveys on the social and economic situation of German university students. The data from these surveys is published every two or three years and is the main source of statistical information available for comparative analysis (in this case – BMBW 1983, 1986). Apart from considerations of the comparability of FeU data and data from other universities, there were additional reasons to use a model of the social structure based on occupational positions. These were summarised by Rosemary Crompton who argues the continued validity of this model even if it cannot fully explain all aspects of class and stratification:

> Even if . . . 'class' is losing, or has lost, its capacity to act as a source of collective identity and organisation, the *work* that people do is nevertheless likely to remain as the most important indicator of their 'life chances' and patterns of material advantage and disadvantage more generally. Employment-based class schemes, therefore, will continue to describe the considerable extent of material inequalities, in capitalist societies and these inequalities will, to varying degrees, be reproduced across the generations. Thus those working within the occupational or employment-aggregate approach to class analysis will be able to continue to demonstrate the association between 'class' – as they have defined it – and a range of other factors . . .
>
> (Crompton 1993: 106; emphasis in original)

The data on FeU students are taken partly from the student data banks, partly from a survey which was carried out in 1985/86 and contained a number of questions on students' parental background. The working-class respondents were selected on the basis of premises derived from the theoretical framework mentioned above, drawing on class analysis and mobility research, educational research, and feminist research and theory.

Women, in spite of being approximately half of the population, are either totally ignored by traditional class analysis or else are seen as irrelevant for the explanation of the 'social reality'. Nevertheless, proponents of this sociological approach claim to view society as a whole and to understand social structures and processes without taking the experiences of women into account. By contrast, our own research has tried to avoid this androcentric approach as much as possible and has placed women in the centre of attention by focusing on the women students and on the mothers of both male and female distance students. This allows us to look at women's social background and class position in their own right and to gain a composite picture of the 'working-class family' as a social unit which fundamentally affects people's life chances. Since our concern is with the possibilities offered by distance education to overcome limitations rooted in class origin, the following sections deal not only with the educational and occupational background of working class women at the FeU, but also with processes of social mobility and the value which their distance studies have for these students.

Mobility processes of women

The aim of the analysis was to determine the role which DE plays in the mobility processes of women. Women students of working-class origin are one of the most disadvantaged social groups as far as access to higher education is concerned. The focus on this group provides information about the motivation which leads working-class women, i.e. the adult daughters of working-class families, to enrol in a degree programme at a DTU. Specifically, it is possible to see whether the decision to study at the FeU signifies the beginning or the continuation of a process of upward social mobility. Since we are looking at mature women students it is also possible to see how the women themselves shape this mobility process by gaining further qualifications and how they use their DE as a means for social advancement.

As university students, working-class women enrolled in an FeU degree programme are at a point where their previous or current social position, which is determined by their social background as well as their own occupational qualification and position, intersects with the future class location which requires the degree. In the meantime, students must find a balance between these two directions in order to open up new career chances without endangering their present way of earning a living.

The concept of social mobility is based on a hierarchical view of the social structure and denotes the movement of individuals within this structure in vertical or horizontal directions. *Vertical* social mobility refers to the present class location of a person compared to their class origin, *horizontal* mobility refers to the changes of class position which a person experiences in relation to their own educational and occupational development. Stratification research and class analysis has identified a number of ways in which social mobility happens.

Vertical social mobility

Vertical social mobility is traditionally defined as *inter*generational occupational mobility (Abbott and Sapsford 1987: 62ff), comparing the occupational position of parents, usually the father, with the person's own occupational position. In the case of the working-class distance students in our sample, this means the direct comparison of the educational level and occupational position of both mothers and fathers with the educational and occupational levels which the women themselves have already achieved or are hoping to achieve through their distance studies. A special case of vertical mobility is the so-called *marital* mobility which is usually measured by comparing the occupational position of a woman's father to that of her husband or partner without any regard to her own or her mother's educational and occupational achievement.

The analysis of intergenerational occupational mobility on the basis of a parent–daughter comparison has often been neglected in stratification studies as sociologists have tended to concentrate on father–son comparisons. Yet, as Pamela Abbott and Roger Sapsford observe:

> There have been few studies comparing father's occupation with daughter's (and even fewer have compared daughter's occupation with mother's). Yet there are a number of reasons . . . why an analysis of female mobility in terms of own occupation is essential both for class theory and for understanding sexual stratification.
>
> (Abbott and Sapsford 1987: 62)

The data collected in the FeU survey allows us to analyse mobility processes of women directly rather than resorting to the circumstantial evidence of comparing male heads of household such as the father and husband/ partner. Nevertheless, it is necessary to use the traditional way of measuring mobility in order to judge the situation of women distance students in relation to that of women in general. Combining both approaches we are able to evaluate the claim of conventional class analysis to describe social reality by referring only to men.

The fact that women of working-class origin are enrolled in a degree programme in itself denotes the upward social mobility of this group. Looking at the processes of this intergenerational mobility could lead to an understanding of students' motivation and of the role which DE plays in this process. In the literature we find hypotheses about the influence which the education and occupation of the mother has for the motivation of the daughter to rise above her class of origin. Status discrepancies between parents, especially those where mothers are accorded higher status than fathers, are assumed to be instrumental (see Hoerning and Krais 1987) as is the fact that the mother is not only a homemaker but a participant in the labour market, holding a job or even pursuing a career.

Horizontal social mobility

Horizontal or *intra*generational social mobility happens when individuals change from one point in the social structure to another point in the course of their own educational and occupational history. These mobility processes are no longer measured in terms of parental class location and reflect the individual's career orientation and personal motivations which result from occupational factors and, in the case of distance students, lead to the decision to enrol in a degree programme while continuing one's career.

In addition to occupationally rooted mobility aspirations people may be motivated by personal factors which influence their study goals and course choices. Mobility processes of women are also influenced by structural factors such as the social division of labour. This raises questions as to the possibility of pursuing career ambitions in the first place and of combining a course of studies with family commitments since 'marriage, domestic responsibilities, and childbirth or childrearing influence women's occupational mobility – especially when this involves movement into or out of an occupational class' (Abbott and Sapsford 1987: 75–6).

This is especially relevant in the case of women with children, who do not work outside the home and who have at least temporarily left the labour force:

> The interesting question is what happens to the women who leave the labour market to have children . . . Movement from full- to part-time work or vice versa is an important factor in mobility: women who move from part- to full-time work are likely to move up, while those who move from full- to part-time work are more likely to move down in occupational class terms.
>
> (Abbott and Sapsford 1987: 79–80)

Family of origin

A look at the biographies of women FeU students produces two results which do not support the assumptions of traditional class analysis. First, it shows that the families of origin of working class women students are not the homogeneous units postulated and that the sole use of fathers would not adequately describe class origin. Second, it shows that mothers play an important role for the educational chances and the mobility orientation of their daughters and that their educational attainment, occupational development, and attitude toward higher education must be taken into consideration. This leads to the rejection of the traditional postulate of class and mobility theorists that:

> . . . the class position, and thus the class mobility, of women – as indeed of men also – may best be determined if the family is given priority over the individual as the unit of class composition; or, that is, if individuals living together as a family are regarded as having one and the same class location.
>
> (Erikson and Goldthorpe 1992: 232–3)

In my research I defined working-class women students as those women who reported that their father and/or mother were in working-class (blue-collar, manual) occupations. In a survey with 579 female and 613 male

Table 6.1 Parental background of working-class women studying at the FeU

	abs.	% of working-class women (n = 134)	% of all women students (N = 579)	abs.	% of only father manual (n = 59)	% of working-class women (n = 134)	% of all women students (N = 579)
Father only blue-collar	59	44.0	10.2				
• Mother with own occupation				23	39.0	17.2	4.0
• Mother housewife				35	59.3	26.1	6.0
• No answer for mother				1	1.7	0.7	0.2
Mother only blue-collar	42	31.3	7.3				
Both parents blue-collar/ manual	33	24.6	5.7				
Sum	**134**	**100.0**	**23.1**	**59**	**100.0**	**44.0**	**10.2**

Source: FeU survey data 1985/86.

respondents this definition identified 134 women respondents (23%) and 190 men (31%) as working-class while 445 women and 423 men were from other class backgrounds (see Table 6.1). The two groups of women FeU students provide the basis of the comparisons presented in the following sections.

Educational background of parents

Working-class children are commonly assumed to be educationally deprived, living in an environment which places no value on education and higher degrees. In Germany, this is termed *Bildungsferne* (distance from education). According to this argument, the parents of working-class students are assumed to have no more than the requisite schooling and possibly the vocational qualifications to become skilled workers. Looking at mothers and fathers separately, the data on the educational background of the parents of women distance students show a more complex picture and diverse constellations of educational attainment and occupational positions.

On the most basic level, the data confirm the expectation that the majority of working-class mothers (84%) and fathers (83%) did not attend secondary schools and left school without obtaining intermediate or advanced diplomas (see Table 6.2). In seven out of ten families (72%), both parents had reached only the compulsory educational level, i.e. in three out of ten families at least one parent had more than the legal minimum schooling. Only 13% of the mothers and 12% of the fathers had completed the equivalent of O-level or A-level education, three of the mothers and two of the fathers had even achieved university entrance qualifications.

The picture of homogeneity dissolves when we look at vocational training and occupational qualifications (see Table 6.3). Fathers tend to have higher

Table 6.2 Highest schooling of mother and father

	Mother (n = 134)		Father (n = 134)		Of these: both parents (n = 134)	
	abs.	%	abs.	%	abs.	%
Abitur (A-Levels) High School	3	2.2	5	3.7	1	0.7
Middle School (O-Levels)	14	10.4	11	8.2	3	2.2
Basic schooling	112	83.6	110	82.1	96	71.6
Other qualification	2	1.5	1	0.7	–	–
Not known	3	1.5	7	5.2	–	–
Sum	**134**	**100.0**	**134**	**100.0**	**100**	**74.5**

Source: FeU survey data 1985/86.

Table 6.3 Highest occupational qualification of mother and father

	Mother (n = 134)		Father (n = 134)		Of these: both parents (n = 134)	
	abs.	%	abs.	%	abs.	%
University degree	0	–	2	1.5	0	–
Other degree	0	–	3	2.2	0	–
Master craftsperson	4	3.0	27	20.1	3	2.2
Skilled worker	63	47.0	73	54.5	38	28.4
Sum	**67**	**50.0**	**105**	**78.4**	**41**	**30.6**
plus						
Other vocational qualification	4	3.0	7	5.2	2	1.5
No formal qualification	59	44.0	20	14.9	15	11.2
Not known, no answer	4	3.0	2	1.5	0	–
Sum	**134**	**100.0**	**134**	**100.0**	**58**	**43.3**

Source: FeU survey data 1985/86.

qualifications than mothers, five of the fathers having completed a college or university degree in spite of being considered working class on the basis of their occupational position. The percentage of mothers without any form of vocational or occupational education is very high (44%). This is true for 15% of the fathers, a finding which reflects the historical context. We are dealing with mature students whose parents would have left school and started their training during or after World War Two, a time of upheaval and interrupted biographies and a time in which it often was assumed that women did not need qualifications for a labour market they would not enter permanently. In addition, the daughters were less likely to be informed about their mother's qualifications than about their father's.

Table 6.4 Mother's and father's attitude toward daughter's university studies

| | Working-class women (n = 134) | | | | Other women students (n = 445) | | | |
| | Mother | | Father | | Mother | | Father | |
	abs.	%	abs.	%	abs.	%	abs.	%
Positive	77	57.5	62	46.3	297	66.7	273	61.3
Indifferent/no opinion	23	17.2	24	17.9	58	13.0	60	13.5
Negative	17	12.7	21	15.7	41	9.2	35	7.9
Don't know	8	6.0	11	8.2	14	3.1	19	4.3
Not applicable	8	6.0	14	10.4	18	4.0	39	8.8
No answer	1	0.7	2	1.5	17	3.8	19	4.3
Sum	**134**	**100.0**	**134**	**100.0**	**445**	**100.0**	**445**	**100.0**

Parental attitudes toward higher education

In order to gain an impression of this 'educational distance' of students' families of origin, a number of questions were included in the questionnaire asking respondents to remember how their mothers and fathers felt about university education in general, and about their daughter's intentions to study in particular, and how they reacted to her decision to enrol at the FeU.

Considering the age of the distance students ($\varnothing$ = 28.3 years at the FeU) and the fact that many of them had lived independently of their parents for years before becoming distance students, the response rate to these questions was very high. Nearly all respondents answered closed questions, and half of them added in open-ended comments. Our main interest was in gaining an indication concerning a positive or negative attitude of parents regarding their daughter's higher education and relating this to their chances of entering secondary school and university.

Table 6.4 shows that far more than half of the mothers (58%) and just under half of the fathers (46%) had a positive overall attitude toward an academic education for their daughter. Only 13% of the mothers and 16% of the fathers were explicitly negative. While this demonstrates an unexpectedly favourable educational climate, Table 6.4 also shows that the parents in other social strata were still more positive in their attitudes toward university, two-thirds of these students remembering their mothers as favouring and supporting their interest in advanced education (difference compared to working-class mothers: Δ = 9.2%). The difference in father's attitudes is even more striking as three-fifths of the fathers who are not working-class were in favour of their daughter's attending university (difference compared to working-class fathers: Δ = 15.0%).

Table 6.5 Congruence of mother's and father's attitude toward daughter's studying

	Working-class women (n = 134)		Other women students (n = 445)	
	abs.	*%*	*abs.*	*%*
Both parents positive	50	37.3	245	55.1
Mother only positive	27	20.1	52	11.7
Father only positive	12	9.0	13	2.9
Both parents negative	9	6.7	28	6.3
Other	36	26.9	107	24.0
Sum	**134**	**100.0**	**445**	**100.0**

Overall, students remember their mothers as more positive than their fathers, with their fathers being more inclined than their mothers to react negatively to the idea of the daughter embarking on a degree course. In the case of working-class families, there is less homogeneity in parents' attitudes than in other families (see Table 6.5). Only 37% of working-class parents, as compared to 55% of parents in other social classes agreed in their positive view, a situation which is likely to have been a favourable influence on the daughters' educational aspirations and might explain why nearly half of them (47%) already had some experience with tertiary education. Only few mothers (13%) and fathers (16%) were totally negative in their attitude toward higher education, and very few of the women (6.7%) grew up in a family where both parents were opposed to the idea of their daughter studying.

Students also answered an open-ended question on parents' reactions to their wish to enrol in a university in the first place and to study at a distance. Their answers illuminate the ways in which positive or negative attitudes were experienced by the daughters. The answers vary both in detail and complexity and refer to factors such as the life history of parents, economic considerations, and social norms. A number of students informed us that they had not told their parents of their distance studies and therefore could not provide information about their reaction.

The open-ended answers suggest a variety of reasons for the positive attitude of working-class parents to university education. Some students whose parents reacted positively simply stated that they 'were pleased with their daughter entering a university degree course'; and 'in favour of con-tinuing post-secondary education'; wanting their daughter 'to make use of all educational opportunities offered'. Or, if the parents were negative, this was attributed to a general 'scepticism'; and 'doubts about the daughter's ability to succeed'; or to the fact that the father was 'vehemently opposed to university and did not understand his daughter's wish to study'.

The following quotes are examples of some of the more detailed and thoughtful comments of students regarding their parents' attitudes to university study in general and distance education in particular. The first set of quotes is from women who remember their working-class mothers and fathers as having a *positive* attitude toward their daughter's wish to study for an academic degree:

'*My parents see distance education as very positive because they have great respect for the double load involved in holding a full-time job and studying at the same time.*'

'*My parents have a positive attitude toward distance education but are also doubtful about my continued motivation.*'

'*My parents are hoping that my studies will eventually lead to career advancement. They support us in our household. They are conscious that distance education is the only way in which I can study while keeping my job. They are therefore very positive as regards my studying at the FeU.*'

'*As a young woman my mother was completely exploited by her parents and employer as a domestic. In spite of her good grades in school she was not allowed to enter secondary schooling or to get occupational qualifications. She wants her daughter to have better chances. My father wants his children – regardless of gender – to have a fulfilling occupation based on their inclinations and to keep up with the developments in their field.*'

'*My parents are not opposed to my wish to study for a university degree. Their view is that everyone should choose an occupation according to their preferences and they don't care on what level of qualification this is based.*'

The second set of quotes shows fathers with a traditional point of view who are not in favour of their daughter pursuing a university degree while the mothers have a more positive attitude:

'*My mother encourages my independence. My father is conservative in his thinking. He assumes that marriage will either prevent me from getting the degree in the first place or render it useless.*'

'*My mother almost takes it for granted that I want to study. At the same time she knows about the difficulties women who enter technical or science fields face both during their studies and on the job. My father has misgivings regarding the costs and thinks that a degree will place me under too much of an obligation to support my family later.*'

'*My parents were very worried about the financial burden. They also feared that I would not succeed. Such a failure would have been terrible for them. My mother was more positive and optimistic than my father.*'

'My mother was positive regarding university study because she is very concerned with "image". Since she doesn't view distance education as "proper" studying she would have preferred my enrolling in a conventional university, ignoring previous negative experiences. My father is totally opposed to my studying. As far as he is concerned I already have a "good job" and I'm a woman to boot! In his view distance education is just about acceptable because it does not necessitate too much change in present life-style. For him it is not "real" university study, more a continuing education course.'

Other women were supported by their fathers in their decision to study while their mothers were indifferent or opposed to it:

'My mother feels that studying will be too demanding and that I won't be able to cope. With regard to studying at a distance she is afraid that I won't have the stamina and determination to complete the degree. My father sees the possible use of the degree in the labour market. He is of the opinion anyway that everyone should learn as much as possible and do something worthwhile with their "free time". Concerning the distance mode of studying my father is taking a wait-and-see attitude, but nevertheless expects me to be able to study a few semesters even under these difficult conditions (e.g. studying through written materials only, no contact with other students).'

'My mother has always made sure that I wouldn't take on more than I can handle. With regard to my studying at a distance she is very concerned that I will make myself ill through overworking. This is the reason for her negative attitude. When I first enrolled in a (conventional) university my father would have liked for me to study medicine. He is proud of my student status which he uses to impress people. He doesn't know that I am studying at the FeU.'

'My mother is afraid that I am taking on too much work. My father is greatly in favour of studying through night school since he himself went this route.'

'My mother: a waste of time! My father: the gate to prosperity.'

Finally, there are those women whose decision to study was not supported by either parent and who had to find the motivation to pursue a university education outside their family of origin. These women are the group traditionally considered 'working-class daughters' in the sense of being *bildungsfern*, i.e. from a social background distanced from higher education:

'Both parents: women don't need university education!.'

'My mother is dead. My father says: "You are crazy. You ought to stay at home and take care of your husband and child. Cook, clean ..."'

'My mother is amused. She thinks distance education is a joke. My father is opposed to my studying. In his opinion there are already too many unemployed academics.'

'My mother wishes me success but does not believe I will manage to get the degree. When she was still a housewife she herself had tried to do a distance education course and failed. This was a very unsatisfactory experience for her. My father is totally disinterested.'

'My mother is opposed to my studying. She can impress her friends with a daughter who is a civil servant on the upper-middle level of the hierarchy. But nobody is impressed with a daughter who is a student. Distance education is not prestigious. My father cannot understand that I want to give up the security and status which being a civil servant confers. Distance education is not "respectable" work (but maybe he is secretly impressed?).'

'My mother thinks that my marriage, my household and my job suffer because of my studies. She strongly discourages me from continuing after the arrival of our baby in the autumn. My father considers continuing education a good thing in general.'

'My mother died while I was still in school. My father thinks that there are already too many unemployed graduates and that I would do better to get a job. In his view I could find employment if I really wanted to work. But he only was afraid that he would be asked to pay for my university education. I did not tell him that I am studying at a distance rather than at a conventional university. If he did know about it he would be convinced that I have no chance to succeed since this is what happened to him when he tried to do distance courses. In reality, he simply did not want to put any effort into his studies and was too lazy to learn.'

Data on working-class women at the FernUniversität

Highest level of previous education

The very fact of matriculation at the FeU marks the working class students as upwardly mobile. Since admission to a degree programme is dependent on formal entrance qualifications, these students have already had a higher level of schooling than is to be expected on the basis of their class origin:

No other social group in the Federal Republic [of Germany] has so few chances of achieving an education and occupational training in keeping with their potential as do the daughters of manual workers. If the 'man from another planet', who is so popular in light fiction, were to come to West Germany, and if he were to draw conclusions about the social structure from observing the circumstances in institutions of higher education, he would have to believe that working class families only bring sons into the world.

(Pross 1969: 56)

In accordance with other German universities registration for the M.A. level degree programmes at the FeU requires the university entrance qualifications which are usually conferred with the *Abitur* upon the successful completion of secondary school. As a comprehensive university, the FeU offers integrated degree programmes in computer science, electrical engineering, economics/business studies and mathematics, which lead to either the *Diplom I* after three years to the *Diplom II*, after four years of full-time study. The *Diplom I* requires a lower level entrance qualification than does the 'proper' university *Diplom II* degree. The successful completion of the *Diplom I* entitles students to continue studying for the *Diplom II* (see FeU 1999a: 13).

Approximately 15% of FeU degree students enter the university with qualifications below the *Abitur*, the highest school leaving certificate. The percentage of FeU women with this qualification is nearly as high among working-class women as it is among women from other social backgrounds (83% versus 86%). The difference lies in the less direct way in which the former have achieved this qualification since only 65% of them have had a straightforward school career, while the rest have gained their *Abitur* later in life. By contrast, 83% of the women students from other class backgrounds completed the full 9 years of secondary schooling achieving the regular university entrance qualification in the most direct way.

In keeping with the character of the FeU as an institution of tertiary education for mature people, most students have already attained a formal qualification before enrolling in a degree programme at a distance. While 85% of women students in other universities have no previous occupational qualification, the same is true of only 27% of women studying at the FeU. Similarly, as Figure 6.1 shows, seven out of ten women from a working-class background (71%) already had formal qualifications upon entering their FeU degree programme. In most cases these qualifications were on the vocational level (65%), but also on higher levels (20% lower tertiary degree and 15% university degree).

With respect to the existence of previous qualifications our data show no difference between FeU women from divergent social backgrounds, but differences do exist with respect to the type of qualification students had

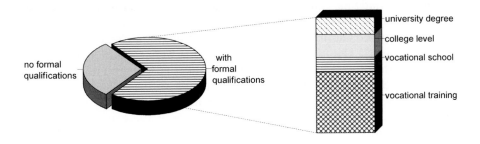

no formal
qualifications

with
formal
qualifications

university degree

college level

vocational school

vocational training

working-class women 1985/86 (n = 134)

Figure 6.1 Highest occupational qualification of women FeU students

already earned. Women from other social backgrounds are more likely to possess a university degree already since nearly one quarter of these women (24%), as compared to one sixth of the women of working-class origin (15%), have already completed an M.A. or university *Diplom.*

Of the students with formal qualifications, more than half of the working-class women (53%) have completed a three-year vocational training course, another 13% have done advanced vocational training. The reasons for choosing this type of practical qualification were either due to external circumstances or to personal inclination, for instance a strong desire to earn one's own living and have a secure and independent existence. The latter wish may also be the deciding factor to pursue university education at a distance as the following quotes illustrate:

> '*I would never have dared to give up the security my job offers That's why I study at a distance.*'

> '*Now that I have achieved security and a certain standard of living (including financial aspects) I can pursue further educational aspirations only through distance education. Otherwise I would have to start over, at the very beginning (e.g. no money, small bedsit).*'

> '*I get no financial aid whatsoever so I have to continue working to earn my living. A drastic reduction of my working hours would have meant the loss of my present job responsibility. I could not have continued working on the same level as no adequate position (senior post in personnel) exists in my firm for part-time workers.*'

> '*I do not want to give up my relatively secure job, which I enjoy, in favour of a degree programme with uncertain career perspectives.*'

Many FeU students had begun or completed a university degree before registering at the FeU. In 1987 a total of 13% of the newly matriculated students in other German universities had already completed a degree on the tertiary level. The majority of these students were registering for a doctorate, and the official statistics showed no gender differences (BMBW 1989: 161–2). At the FeU the percentage of students with previous degrees in 1985/86 was 36%, and most of these students were enrolling in 'normal' degree programmes leading to a Master's degree or the equivalent *Diplom II*. Also in contrast to the other universities, the FeU registrations did show gender effects as the men (43%) were much more likely than the women (29%) to pursue a second degree course.

The question arises why these students embark on a DE degree course in order to gain additional or higher qualifications than they already have obtained. Some answers are provided in response to open-ended questions on students' reasons for studying in the first place and for registering as distance students.

Reasons for wanting additional qualifications

A number of working-class women enrolling at the FeU have negative feelings about their previous training or hope to lay the foundation for better career prospects through the degree they aim to get from the FeU. Among these are women who have not yet completed another training and plan to study parallel to their other programme in order to make certain of a regular income regardless of the progress of their distance studies.

> '*Keeping and extending the ability to think for myself and to increase my knowledge through independent learning.*
>
> *Filling the gaps in the incomplete and "predigested" knowledge gained through my occupational training programme.*'

> '*The course I am studying at the College [for administrators] is of a very low quality and in no way can serve as the basis for a career in the private sector. Since I want to enter such a career and do not want to work in a mindless administrative job as a civil servant I need to get an additional qualification.*'

The open-ended comments of women respondents also suggest that working-class women are likely to develop a discontent with their educational and occupational situation which in turn leads them to seek alternatives in studying for a degree. This often happens when the chosen occupation does not satisfy the person on an intellectual level as the following quote illustrates:

'A decisive factor in choosing to study for a degree was the fact that my employment before enrolling did not satisfy me intellectually.'

Women distance students from a working-class background are more likely than other women to have gone through a practical training programme, even in tertiary education, while women from other backgrounds are more likely to have completed a more theoretical qualification. For these women, registering for a degree programme at the FeU may mean a keen desire to achieve career advancement or an acute discontent with the career possibilities open to them without a degree:

'I did complete a university degree as a teacher in a middle school but this was a special kind of examination which is considered a lower level degree, not really academic. Since I am looking for a career in the school system or in the adult education sector I want to achieve the status conferred by a "proper" university degree.'

'Having successfully completed night school it was only natural that I wanted to put my new university entrance qualification to use and enrol in a degree programme. It was only afterwards that I realised that this did not satisfy me. I wanted to relate my studies to practice and I wanted to have a job while pursuing the degree. I'm studying at the FeU because it offers me the opportunity to get the degree while holding down a job and at the same time opens up career prospects.'

In addition to working-class women students who have already obtained a degree, there are a number of women who wish to complete a previously interrupted course of academic study. This is one of the most prominent reasons for entering a distance education course, and the percentage of women with previous experience of colleges and universities is generally high among women FeU students (55%).

Occupation and extent of paid work

Research on the situation of women and men in DE has shown the effect the students' work situation has on their distance studies. These are influenced by the extent and type of paid work, the congruence of qualification levels and career prospects, and the work-related motives of students to enrol in a degree programme at the FeU.

The research on which the present analysis is based included 95 women of working-class origin who had completed a formal qualification. Most of these had always (45%) or sometimes worked in a job for which their qualification was a prerequisite. In this respect they do not differ from women of other class origins. The majority of the 52 students who had never worked in the profession which they had trained for did so because they decided to begin another educational programme instead of entering a job (39%). One-third of these women could not find an adequate job (33%) and one quarter had personal reasons such as having a baby or moving house (26%). In some cases, students mention more than one reason making it impossible for them to enter the profession they had originally chosen.

The majority of women students from all class backgrounds are in full-time or part-time paid work, with a noticeable reduction in the extent of employment after the start of their distance studies. As far as working-class women are concerned, there was a reduction of full-time paid work with three-quarters of the 58 women previously in full-time jobs maintaining this extent of paid work. After enrolling at the FeU, half of the women from the working class (49%) and from other backgrounds (48%) were employed full-time, one-tenth part-time (10% in each group).

After enrolling in distance education, 55 working-class women were unemployed or earned a little money doing hourly or occasional jobs. Approximately one quarter of these women (24%) were engaged in additional training programmes and 15% were officially registered as unemployed. With 38%, the largest group were women who worked exclusively at home doing unpaid household and family work. Most of these 21 women had completed some form of occupational qualification (n = 15, i.e. 73%), some had worked in the job for which they were qualified (n = 11, i.e. 53%). Those housewives who had not held a job for which they were qualified attribute this to the circumstances of their personal life, such as marriage or motherhood and tend to see their status as transient, intending to re-enter the workforce at a later stage.

A total of 105 out of 134 working-class women (78%) gave detailed information on their employment history and present work situation. Compared to students from other class backgrounds there were no significant differences in employment status, although there was a slight tendency for them to hold less secure and lower-level positions.

Personal data

The FeU, in keeping with other DTUs, attracts people who want to pursue academic studies at a later stage in their lives. This means that newly registered distance students are older than their colleagues at other universities and that their private situations differ in many respects from that of full-time students entering conventional universities more or less directly after graduating from secondary school. This has implications for their learning environments and the way in which they can study:

> In essence, people . . . appear to be largely unaware of the domestic circumstances and the social and physical environment of home-based

learners. A recognition of the diverse contexts within which much distance learning takes place is essential, not only for those directly involved in the development of distance learning materials, but also for the policy-makers responsible for the introduction and maintenance of the teaching system.

(Kirkwood 1995: 130)

Age and household composition

Age distribution

Statistical data from other German universities shows that the age distribution of their students is directly opposite to that of the students enrolled in degree programmes at the FeU. Only one-fifth of the FeU women are under 24 years of age (19%) and more than one-third are thirty years of age (35%). At other universities, far more than half the women students are in the younger age group (56%) and only 6% in the older age group. Altogether, five out of ten FeU women (48%) and nine out of ten women students elsewhere (88%) were under 28 years of age. These differences are even more pronounced than the statistics suggest since the FeU survey only includes beginners and the data from other universities includes students in all stages of study. In addition to being older, FeU students are more heterogeneous than the age composition of students at conventional universities (see Figure 3.8).

The other side of the coin is the fact that half of the women studying at the FeU are older than the age at which students have normally finished their university studies. This means that most of the distance students had life histories which, as has been shown for working-class women, were diverse in their educational and occupational development. The following sections show a similar diversity in their personal lives and learning environments.

The average age of working-class women at the FeU was 28 years and four months at the time of the survey which was carried out at the end of their first semester. More than half of them (55%) were between 25 and 31 years of age, the others were younger (23%) and older (22%). The span between the oldest and youngest woman was 29 years, the oldest respondents being 49 years of age. Women from a working-class background were younger than the other women students at the FeU, some of whom (2.2%) were 50 years and older.

Marital status and household composition

With respect to their official marital status, more than half of the working-class women in the survey were single (54%), four out of ten were married (40%), only a few were separated/divorced (5.2%) or widowed (1.5%).

Compared to other women distance students, the proportion of single women was higher, that of married women lower among students from working-class origin. As was to be expected, marital status is closely related to age. A comparison of the women from different class backgrounds yields some striking differences showing that working-class women marry at a later age or perhaps not at all. By the time they reached the age of 28, one third of the other women (33%) and just over one quarter of the working-class women (27%) were married.

Even in the mid-1980s, the official marital status did not adequately represent the household composition of mature people. We identified five types of household in our analysis of women distance students:

- SINGLES: unmarried, single women living on their own;
- COUPLES: women living in the same household with a husband or partner, but without children;
- NUCLEAR FAMILY, FAMILY: women living in the same household with a husband or partner and with one or more children;
- WITH PARENTS: unmarried women living in the same household as their parents; plus
- OTHERS: a residual category of household types not covered by the previous four categories.

This last category includes diverse households such as communal households, single parents, extended families, institutional situations of various kinds. A total of 23 working-class women (17%) belong to this category.

Approximately one-fifth of the working-class women are singles living alone (19%). One third live as childless couples with their partner (31%), a smaller group (27%) as family with partner and children. This is the household composition which shows the greatest divergence between women distance students from working-class and other social backgrounds with just over one-third of the latter being family women (34%).

Working-class women students with children

Working-class women are less likely to be mothers and to live with children than are women from other social origins. This confirms the impression that this group of distance students is inclined to postpone the start of their own family, probably for reasons connected to their educational biographies and their desire to establish themselves in an occupation as a way of earning their own income.

Children and childcare responsibilities

Fewer than one-third of the 134 working-class women students in the FeU survey had children (31%). Of these 42 mothers, 36 lived in the same

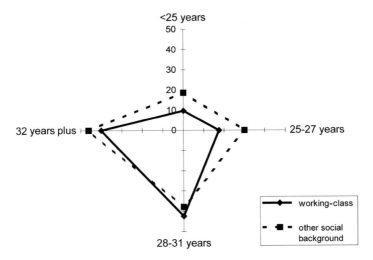

Figure 6.2 Women with partner and children by age

household as their partners and children. The others were single mothers or shared their living quarters with other people (3 women each). Most of the mothers had just one child (48%) or two children (38%). Six mothers had three children (14%). The average number of children per woman was 1.4.

Considering the tendency of these women to start their families at a later stage in their lives, it is not surprising to find that the children were young and in most cases under the school age of six years. Seven out of ten mothers had one (33%) or more (36%) children under three years of age.

As mentioned before, women from other class backgrounds are more inclined to start families at an earlier age and therefore the percentage of mothers in this group of distance students is higher (40%) than among the women from a working-class background (31%; $\Delta = -9.1\%$; see Figure 6.2).

The research does not provide information on the reasons for this class differentiation, but two explanations are plausible, even though they are contradictory to some extent:

1 Working-class women studying at the FeU reflect the general patterns of this social group: they postpone their childbearing in order to obtain job qualifications and enter the workforce at an early age. For these women, distance education is primarily a means of achieving further occupational qualifications and securing or furthering their career or occupational position. Because of their personal circumstances, these women have less need of entering or re-entering the labour market after a childrearing phase of unpaid work.

Table 6.6 Childcare responsibilities of mothers studying at a distance and of their partners

| | Working-class women with partner and child(ren)* | | | | Women with partner and child(ren) from other backgrounds* | | | |
| | respondents | | their partners | | respondents | | their partners | |
	abs.	%	abs.	%	abs.	%	abs.	%
Always, exclusively responsible	11	30.6	1	2.8	44	29.5	1	0.7
Often, high level of responsibility	23	63.9	2	5.6	96	64.4	21	14.1
Sometimes	2	5.6	21	58.3	3	2.0	67	45.0
Rarely, low level of responsibility	0	–	10	27.8	3	2.0	55	36.9
Never	0	–	1	2.8	–	–	3	2.0
No answer	0	–	1	2.8	3	2.0	2	1.3
Sum	**36**	**100.0**	**36**	**100.0**	**149**	**100.0**	**149**	**100.0**

* including women in full-time and part-time paid work (7 working-class women, 31 other women).

2   Working-class women studying at the FeU are a self-selected group of women not representative of their group of origin. As family women in the lower social strata, the mothers have fewer resources and are more in need of working outside the home to contribute to the family income. Studying is seen as incompatible with these other commitments, which take up too much time and energy already.

Chapter 3 presented evidence regarding the problems which women face in trying to reconcile DE with their household and family commitments. These are almost always and exclusively the woman's responsibility and an additional burden for a woman who wants to study. This situation is basically the same for women in full-time or part-time paid work whether they are childless or whether they are mothers of small children. We must assume that the situation of those working-class women who have children and enrol at the FeU is characterised by the same structural patterns and is no different from that of other mothers.

Childcare is the responsibility of the mothers, regardless of social background. One-third (33%) of the 42 working-class women with children said that childcare was exclusively their responsibility or always done by themselves (see Table 6.6). A further 26 women (62%) said that they spent a large amount of time on childcare or did it often. Only two of the mothers (4.8%) left the care of their children mostly to other people.

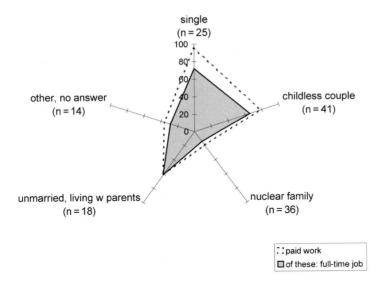

single
(n = 25)

other, no answer
(n = 14)

childless couple
(n = 41)

unmarried, living w parents
(n = 18)

nuclear family
(n = 36)

```
┆┆ paid work
☐ of these: full-time job
```

Figure 6.3 Extent of paid employment by household composition

Work situation

If we look at the 36 working class (W_1) and 149 other women (W_2) in nuclear families we find that in both groups they carry the burden of childcare alone (W_1 31%; W_2 30%) or mostly (W_1 64%; W_2 64%). This is true even for women in paid work outside the home. They have only marginally more help from their partners in taking care of their children than do those women without paid work. In the light of these patterns of gendered division of labour in the family it is not surprising to find that the existence of children drastically curtails the employment of mothers (see Figure 6.3). While nearly all single women (96%) and more than three-quarters of the childless women living with a partner (78%) are in paid work, this is true for only one-fifth of the working-class women with children (19%). The majority of family women who answered a question on their work situation are engaged full-time in unpaid domestic and childcare work.

Data on husbands and partners

Irrespective of class origin, four-fifths of the women studying at the FeU had a husband or partner (W_1 81%; W_2 80%), and three-fifths lived with their partner (W_1 58%; W_2 60%). All couples in the survey were heterosexual, i.e. the partners of women were men and vice versa. Class differences show only with regard to childless couples and nuclear families. The former have a higher percentage of working-class women (W$_1$ 31%; W$_2$ 27%), the latter a higher percentage of other women (W$_1$ 26%; W$_2$ 34%).

Most partners of working-class women had a high-level educational qualification. Two-thirds of them had completed secondary school and university entrance qualifications (68%). At the time of the survey, only one in ten partners had not completed an occupational or professional qualification. One third of the partners had a university (32%) degree compared to 40% of the partners of women from other social backgrounds.

Four out of five partners of working-class women were in full-time (78%) or part-time (3%) paid work. Some of the partners were employed occasionally or did odd jobs, 15 men were in full-time education. Of the partners with jobs, the largest group (42%) worked in an office (white-collar employment), followed by manual or blue-collar workers (19%) and civil servants (15%). A small group of the men were self-employed (8%).

Comments on the class and gender of FernUniversität students

This chapter has looked at women from a working-class background as an example of multiple discrimination in accessing higher education, and has examined their representation in DE. The data from the FeU confirms the expectation that the DT mode does offer opportunities which do not seem to exist in the regular, on-campus university system. This is documented by the fact that the percentages of women and men with working-class parents are higher among distance students than among students at conventional German universities, although they are still extremely under-represented when compared to their share of the population in general.

The analysis has also revealed that the institution is not as concerned with increasing the proportion of students from educationally disadvantaged social strata. This is evident in the lack of data since the FeU has not collected and kept continuous statistical data on the class background of its students. In addition, the information which does exist on the parents is only partially comparable to the statistical data of the government surveys to which it could be compared in order to see the extent of the differences in enrolment rates of working-class students in the university system in general and in the FeU in particular. Specific surveys, designed to parallel the regular government surveys on the social structure of the student population, would have to be carried out to gain reliable answers to the questions concerning the special role of distance education for adults, especially women with multiple discrimination experiences, who want to obtain a degree which was denied them earlier because of their class origin.

As far as the women distance students are concerned, there is another question which remains unanswered on the basis of the data we could use in this analysis. We do not know whether the working-class women studying at the FeU are representative of this whole social group, or even of those women from a working class background who study at university level anywhere in Germany. It is possible that the FeU attracts a special type of working-class woman whose parents are atypical in having more educational and better occupational qualifications than is usual for this social class in general. We can thus present information on the working-class women studying at the FeU, but at present the mechanisms of self-selection remain as unclear as the similarities or differences between distance students and women studying at other universities.

Chapter 7 therefore looks at the motivations and goals of these women, to find out what role they themselves assign to their distance studies with regard to any ambitions for social advancement and occupational mobility.

Chapter 7

Distance education and the social mobility of women

The starting point for looking at the role of distance education for the social mobility of women and especially of students from a working-class background was the following quote from an early study of OU UK students:

> This report . . . shows that Open University students are not only not typical of conventional university students, but are also not typical of their contemporaries in the community at large. From whatever background they come, they have already displayed a propensity to learn which is remarkable. They have in addition displayed a degree of social mobility both inter-generational and intra-generational which is unusually high.
>
> (McIntosh *et al.* 1977: i)

Naomi McIntosh and her colleagues concluded that distance students are exceptionally career-oriented and use their DE to continue a process of upward social mobility. This statement implies that it is an inherent characteristic of DE to attract such individuals and to offer them the opportunity for progress on a journey they are already embarked on. Some questions arising from this are still relevant today:

- Is this an isolated finding in the historic context of the newly founded OU UK or a more general phenomenon found in all DTUs? Does it confirm the claim that DE as a form of teaching and learning is especially suited to provide educational chances otherwise not available?
- Are we dealing with individual motivations and efforts or are there social forces which influence the decision to study at a distance? Is it a prerequisite of distance studying that students have previously exhibited upwardly mobile tendencies or can DE provide an initial impetus for such ambitions?

In order to find answers to these questions it is useful to look at distance students who, as a group, epitomise social inequality and lack of educational and career opportunities, namely women of working-class origin as described in previous chapters of this book. Specifically, we ask:

- Why do women from working-class families, i.e. from a social background which is usually characterised as having no affinity to higher education, decide to study for a university degree in the first place?
- What makes them pursue this degree in the form of DE?
- What do these women hope to achieve through their studying at a distance and what are their personal and professional goals?

When we designed our research project on the situation of women and men in distance education in the mid-1980s, we included a battery of questions on students' family background with a view to testing some hypotheses derived from a small-scale interview study. By chance, this study had turned up evidence to suggest that the FeU offered itself as a special opportunity to women from a working-class background who found themselves in dead-end or uninteresting jobs. These women all wanted to open up new career options through gaining a degree, but were not able or willing to give up the financial security these jobs provided (Raehlmann 1984). The data gathered in the 1986 survey of FeU students allows us to look in detail at the connection between class and gender and at the role of distance education for women's social mobility. It can also contribute to the ongoing class and gender debate in class analysis and mobility research.

Mobility patterns of working-class women

This section deals with processes of social mobility of women who have already demonstrated upward mobility in relation to their working class parents. Many of the FeU women whose mothers and/or fathers were in lower-level jobs had achieved a higher level of education and a higher occupational position than their parents. The fact of their registration in a university degree programme documents their wish to enter a career for which an academic qualification is required and which is usually located higher up in the social hierarchy. The group of working-class women students therefore serves as a case study for looking into processes of *inter*generational or *vertical* mobility as well as highlighting aspects of *intra*generational or *horizontal* mobility in the students' own biographies.

Vertical mobility: comparisons with parents

Comparing educational attainment

In Germany, admission to university degree programmes is based on the formal entrance qualifications usually conferred by secondary schools with the successful *Abitur* examination after a total of thirteen years of schooling. Unlike many other DTUs, the FernUniversität does not have an open admission policy but requires the same formal entrance qualfications as do other German state universities. This means that the majority of the daughters of working-class parents studying at the FeU had achieved a higher level of schooling than their working-class mothers and fathers. This is borne out by the data from our survey of FeU students: only two of the 134 fathers and three of the mothers had attained the *Abitur*, and there was only one family where both parents had achieved this highest level of schooling. Overall, only 16 fathers and 17 mothers had attended middle or secondary school, with five sets of parents having the same educational level.

Compared to women from other social backgrounds, a significantly higher proportion of working-class women had some previous experience with night-school and weekend courses, as they had achieved their A-levels through adult education. Here, it is interesting to note that women whose parents had at least some more advanced schooling were more likely than others from this class background to take the direct route of attending secondary school and taking the school-leaving examination qualifying them for university studies. This is true for all of the five women who grew up in families where both parents had gained more than the basic school leaving certificate.

As far as vocational or professional education is concerned, the data show that the qualification of the mother seems to have a more positive effect on the kind of qualification the daughter gets, while the effect of the father's qualification is not as pronounced. On the whole, the very fact of parents having completed a vocational training programme or professional qualification seems to correlate with an interest in education on the part of the daughter. Figure 7.1 documents that women whose mothers and/or fathers had formal occupational qualifications were much more likely to have completed a college diploma or university degree even before enrolling in a DE degree programme.

It follows from the empirical data that working-class women studying for a degree at the FeU are upwardly mobile with respect to the educational level and occupational qualifications of their mothers, none of whom has completed a university degree programme, and most of the fathers. Two of the fathers have a university degree and three have completed a lower-level (college, polytechnic) degree. Students whose fathers also hold appropriate occupational positions would not have been considered working class if the criterion had been the occupation of the (male) head of household.

Comparing occupational status

As we have seen earlier (in Chapter 6), most of the working-class women studying at the FeU are in full-time or part-time employment and thus have earned their own position in the class structure. It is an *a priori* effect of the

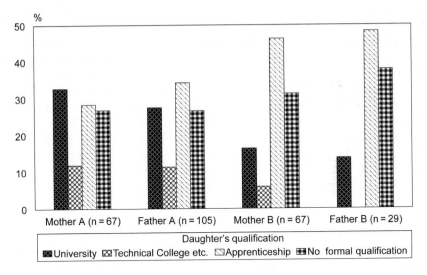

%

Daughter's qualification
■ University ▨ Technical College etc. ▤ Apprenticeship ▦ No formal qualification

Vocational/professional qualification of parents:
A = formally qualified / B = no formal qualification

Figure 7.1 Highest level of occupational education and formal qualifications of parents

sample definition that they are also considered to be upwardly mobile both in relation to their parents and to their own occupational position. This is due to the fact that the university degree for which they are studying opens new career options or directions and is the foundation on which higher occupational positions as well as social prestige are built.

In the government surveys on students in Germany, working class families are generally defined as lower class regardless of the educational levels of fathers and, less often, mothers. Statistical analyses of the class composition of families of origin then shows that lower-class students are severely under-represented considering they are the largest segment of the adult population in general (BMBW 1986: 106). They are therefore the least likely social class to gain access to the higher social strata on the basis of a career which requires university level qualifications.

Half of the 134 working-class women students in our survey said they were employed in middle-class jobs as white-collar workers (n = 65) or civil servants (n = 9), twelve of them having achieved higher level positions. Only six of the women placed themselves into a working-class job, doing unskilled or semi-skilled manual work. This represents 4.5% of the total group or 6.3% of those women of working class origin who answered questions on their paid work. Strictly speaking, only these six women had 'inherited' their family class position and had not been upwardly mobile in their own occupation.

In addition, there were 16 women who worked in 'routine non-manual' jobs which are usually placed on the same level as the manual work traditionally done by working-class people. This is the case, for instance, in the hierarchical class structure used in the government surveys and constructed specifically to represent the stratification of university student populations in Germany (see BMBW 1986: 106ff). Using a similar class model, we can identify 22 FeU women students as belonging to the lower social class on the merit of their own occupational position. These women represent 16% of the total group of women from working-class origins and comprise one quarter of those members of the group who are in paid work. For these 22 women the completion of their FeU degree would mean upward social mobility.

Marital mobility: comparisons with husband or partner

The concept of marital mobility usually refers to a process of intergenerational social mobility comparing the position of a person's family of origin with that of their own family (Abbott and Sapsford 1987: 54ff). Since traditional stratification research uses the occupational position of the head of household, in most cases the male breadwinner, in order to determine the whole family's class location, intergenerational mobility is measured by comparing the father to the husband or partner. In other words, instead of looking at the woman's own occupational position and comparing this to the positions of her father and her mother, the married woman's class location and social mobility is determined indirectly by comparing her father to his son-in-law (Erikson and Goldthorpe 1992: 323ff). This has been a contentious issue in class analysis and stratification research since the early 1980s, a debate which I have discussed extensively in my Ph.D. dissertation (von Prümmer 1996, 1997a).

Another way of looking at marital mobility is that of comparing the woman's own class position to that of her partner or husband. In the case of the distance students in the FeU survey we cross-tabulated the occupational positions of the women respondents with those of their partners.

Comparing the women and their partners

The term marital mobility suggests that individuals may change their class position by marrying a person in a different class position, whose status affects their own favourably or unfavourably, or by establishing a joint household with such a person. Usually it is the woman who takes on the class position of her husband/partner, as in the romantic cliché of the secretary who marries the tycoon or the nurse who marries the doctor, or in the reverse cliché of the rich girl who marries 'beneath her'. In both cases of cross-class couples, the woman is generally seen as losing her own class

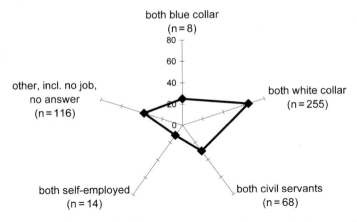

Figure 7.2 Congruence of occupational class of women distance education students and their husbands/partners

identity – or the class identity conferred by her father's class location – while the man keeps his.

A total of 461 women respondents answered questions about their partner and his education and occupation. Three-quarters of these women have an occupational position of their own (n = 345; 75%), and nearly half of these (n = 161; 47%) place their husband or partner on the same level in the occupational hierarchy. This congruence between the women and their partners is most pronounced with regard to the white-collar jobs which half of the women in paid work hold (51%). Two-thirds of these women have partners in similar posts (65%; see Figure 7.2).

Using the class schema of the German university surveys which is constructed of educational and occupational levels, we can show marital mobility in terms of differences in the positioning of the women and their partners in this hierarchical structure. Overall, one-third of the women have partners who are on the same level, 42% have partners on a higher level, and 20% have partners on a lower level of the class structure. This means that the marital mobility of women is twice as high in an upward than in a downward direction. In a symmetrical, non-androcentric reference system this would be complementary to the marital mobility of men, with two-fifths of the partners moving down (42%) and one-fifth moving up (20%). By definition, women and men on the lowest level of the hierarchy cannot be downwardly mobile.

Disregarding the issue of whether the class location of the partner denotes a woman's social mobility, we can still see whether they are likely to form partnerships within their own social class. Taking the class position of the woman as the starting point, Figure 7.3 shows that upper-class women are

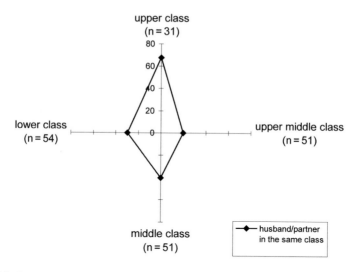

upper class
(n = 31)

lower class
(n = 54)

upper middle class
(n = 51)

middle class
(n = 51)

husband/partner
in the same class

Figure 7.3 Congruence of class position of women and their husbands/partners

most likely to choose partners in the same status group, followed by middle-class, lower-class, and lastly upper-middle-class women.

Comparing fathers and partners

The traditional analysis of marital mobility bypasses the occupational position of the woman and looks only at her father and her husband or partner. This is possible because the family is seen as the unit of analysis (see Abbott and Sapsford 1987: 54ff) and all family members are assigned the class position of the head of household. For various reasons, unless they are single parents or live on their own, women are seldom considered the head of the household they live in. The data on women distance students shows that this approach does not contribute to the understanding of women's class location and mobility processes. In the first place, we have to ignore the information about mothers which has already been shown to have a bearing on daughters' attitude to education and upward mobility. In order to test the question of whether social mobility can be described by movements 'from man to man' we concentrate on the fathers of the women respondents and compare their occupational position with that of their sons-in-law. In addition we also show the occupational position of the women themselves in relation to their fathers. Figure 7.4 documents the different mobility patterns emerging from the two comparisons.

If it were true that the class position of married women – or women living permanently with a partner – can be derived from their husband's or partner's class location, the mobility of working-class women studying at the FeU

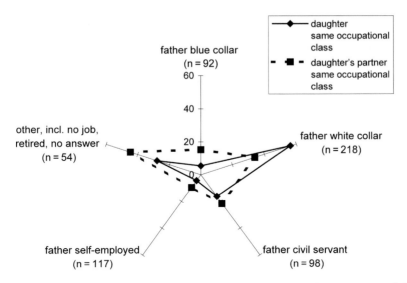

Figure 7.4 Congruence of class position by father's occupational class: women and their husbands/partners

could be determined by comparing the two men. The data on FeU students shows that, with the exception of white-collar employees, the degree of congruence between daughters and fathers is lower than the degree of congruence between the partners and the fathers of the women. This means that we find a different rate of social mobility if we ignore the occupational position of the women whose place in the social structure we want to determine. The concept of intergenerational marital mobility would be misleading about the factual mobility processes of women.

Social mobility and occupational goals of housewives

If it is not possible to judge a woman's social mobility adequately by referring to her husband's rather than to her own occupational position, how do we determine the class location and mobility of those women who do not hold a job by which they could be judged? The data used in the present analysis contains information about women in the family phase who have postponed or interrupted their employment in order to bring up their children. This has profound consequences for their life chances and for their personal circumstances since 'marriage, domestic responsibility, and childbirth or childrearing influence women's occupational mobility' (Abbott and Sapsford 1987: 75–6).

The housewives in this situation who are enrolled in a degree course at the FeU show by the very fact of studying for a university qualification that

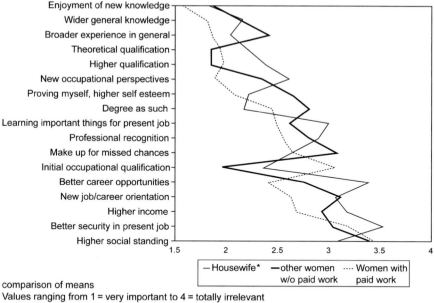

comparison of means
Values ranging from 1 = very important to 4 = totally irrelevant
* Woman with family and no paid work

Figure 7.5 Study goals of working-class women with and without paid work

they have ambitions for the future. Their answers indicate that these ambitions are directed toward a career and that these women have plans for a new beginning after the phase in which they give priority to their families. DE, which is the only option these women have for pursuing their qualification, is intended as the basis for this new start and in this sense is a means for achieving upward mobility *in their own right*. If they are successful in completing a degree these women will have the qualification necessary for (re-)entering a professional career which, in itself, will be of higher social standing than their working-class origin.

This interpretation of the data is supported by the answers which the housewives from a working-class background give concerning the goals of their distance studies. Although the most important motives for enrolling at the FeU were connected to personal development, the data analysis does show an interest in occupational study goals. The goal of 'initial occupational qualification' is the one which the highest percentage – 45% – of the housewives considered 'very important'. The job-orientation of this group of women is necessarily directed toward those goals which are expected to help them get a new start (after the childrearing phase), but the working-class women in this group are more inclined to refer to a previous job and to an interest in building on the experience and qualifications gained in this employment than the other women in the survey (see Figure 7.5).

The fact that they are currently without paid work is seen by these women as a passing condition which they do not want to waste but put to use as the following quotes concerning the goals associated with distance studying illustrate:

'To keep up with theoretical developments in my field while I'm on a leave of absence from my job.'

'[It is] the only possibility to get a professional qualification since there is no waiting list. I have already waited for two years to be admitted to the degree programme in journalism which is my real interest.'

'Distance education makes it possible for me to gain both theoretical (through studying) and practical (through my training programme) qualifications.'

'I don't want to lose time because I'm also doing a training programme.'

'Originally I wanted to complete a training programme and enrol in a university afterwards. But since the job training does not come up to my expectations I want to enter a university degree programme right away. Still, I don't want to drop out of the training programme since this would have negative effects on my formal qualifications and my employment prospects. Because of the time constraints I can only pursue distance studies, and I hope to be able to transfer credits to a face-to-face university course once I complete my training.'

'After completing my apprenticeship (which will be in a year's time) I plan to enrol in a face-to-face university, having already gained some credits studying at a distance.'

Women in the childrearing phase tend to have mixed motives for their decision to study for a degree, placing equal emphasis on personal and occupational goals. This is the case, for instance, when a woman has not found an adequate job after finishing her vocational or occupational education but has become pregnant and is staying at home in order to take care of her child. For this woman, the decision to enrol at the FeU is multifaceted: She wants the intellectual challenge as much as the occupational qualification, a meaningful way to pass the time as much as an improved chance for re-entering the labour market. The decision to pursue these goals at a distance also is complex and may be due to a lack of time, to geographical and organisational conditions or to health problems:

'The most attractive feature of distance education is the opportunity to structure your own time and work patterns and to study at home using

written materials. This seemed to be much more effective than studying at a university with attendance requirements.'

'I can study at home and save time as well as spare myself long and tedious travel to a university.

I have registered as a part-time student at the FeU and am taking very few courses. This would not be possible at a conventional university.'

'It is impossible to study at a conventional university when you have a school-age child and a baby which you are breastfeeding.'

Major subject choice and its role in women's social mobility

Class origin, choice of major subject, and gender

With the choice of their major subject students also make a decision about the occupational opportunities their degree will open up for them. The major subject they study does not only affect their options concerning the areas of their future career, it also affects the level of the occupational hierarchies which they can reach and the income they will be able to realise. Considering university education in general, gender inequality is more prevalent with respect to course choice than with respect to access:

> It is sufficiently known that gender plays a dominant role in students' course choices. The exclusion of women from degree programmes in the natural sciences and in technical subjects has already been well-researched, making it unnecessary for us to discuss this further . . . Irrespective of students' social background, gender relations become visible in the field of tertiary education through the fact that women students are over-represented in those subject areas which are connected to uncertain professional prospects and which are likely to confer lower incomes and less prestige than is associated with other professional careers for which a university degree is a prerequisite.
>
> (Engler and von Prümmer 1993: 109–10)

While it is clear that gender is a dominant factor in students' course choice, the relation between choice of major subject, gender, and class origin is very complex and difficult to unravel. The question is: what can the inclusion of class origin contribute to the explanation of gendered course choices? (Engler and von Prümmer 1993: 110).

It was possible to look at the matriculation data of distance students in the academic year 1985/86 and use these data to pursue the questions outlined above. This year was chosen for two reasons: first, it was one of the

Table 7.1 Class origin and choice of major subject by gender

University departments	Education, social sciences and humanities		Economics		Mathematics, computer science, electrical engineering		All departments	
	abs.	%	abs.	%	abs.	%	abs.	%
All (N =) of these: father manual	1,001	20.1	3,239	19.2	2,645	26.8	6,885	22.2
Women (n =) of these: father manual	538	17.3	878	17.2	400	18.8	1,816	17.6
Men (n =) of these: father manual	463	23.3	2,361	19.9	2,245	28.2	5,069	23.9

Source: FeU databanks 1985/86.

few years when statistical data on the parental background of FeU students was collected upon registration and made available for secondary analysis. Second, this survey, which provides more detailed information, was conducted in the same year and the empirical findings from the sample can be related to the statistical data on the total student population. In 1985/86 a total of 11,179 FeU students had filled in background information about their parents, among them 6,885 new students enrolled in degree programmes. Three groups of students were identified according to the academic department to which they belonged on the basis of their degree programme:

1   The Department of Education, Social Sciences and Humanities with M.A. programmes in the two major subjects Education and Social Sciences.
2   The Department of Economics with the two diploma options of political economy and business administration.
3   A combination of the Departments of Mathematics, Computer Science, and Electrical Engineering, each offering degrees in one major subject.

Looking at major subjects, we see that working-class women tend to enroll equally in all three areas while working-class men are more likely to choose economics and are over-represented in the mathematical and technical areas (see Table 7.1).

The nature of the data available for the FeU and for other universities does not allow direct comparisons since official statistics are always cross-tabulated on the basis of one or the other variable but never with both gender and social class simultaneously (BMBW 1986: 368ff). Another difficulty lies in the different ways in which the subject areas are presented in the general

Table 7.2 University students in selected subject areas by class background –
all students

	All students n	Education, social sciences, row %	Economics, row %	Mathematics, sciences, row %	All, row %
*Students at West German universities:**					
Lower-class	2,686	17	18	23	58
Middle-class	4,621	16	20	22	58
Upper-middle class	3,825	12	22	20	54
Upper-class	3,667	8	21	19	48
Students at the FernUniversität:[†]					
Lower-class	161	25	47	29	101
Middle-class	584	22	53	25	100
Upper-middle class	285	35	41	24	100
Upper-class	151	36	29	35	100

* Government survey 1985, students in their 1st through 4th semester (BMBW 1986).
[†] FeU databanks 1985/86, newly matriculated degree students.

university statistics and in the FeU statistics. The latter refer to fewer subject areas which means that the percentages of students in each subject are much higher than is the case in other statistics where enrolments are more widely spread throughout a large range of subject areas. Still, a rough comparison is possible and shows the enrolment patterns at both the FeU and other universities.

Table 7.2 indicates that students from a lower-class position enrol in economics at the FeU and in mathematics and science-oriented degree programmes at other universities. Since the FeU figures in this table are taken from a research project rather than the student database, the sample definition must be taken into account when interpreting the data: the men in this survey did not represent a random sample but a stratified sample of the male student population. Students of economics are under-represented, students of mathematics, computer science and electrical engineering are over-represented.

As reflected in Table 7.2, the government survey of universities in 1985 shows that in the degree programmes in the social sciences, psychology, and education:

> ... the percentage of children from the lower levels of the social continuum ... is twice as high as from the highest social stratum. The opposite is true in the subject area of 'medicine' ... In all other subject areas there is no noticeable correlation between choice of subject and social class origin. At most there is a slight tendency for Economics and Business Studies and for Law to attract more students from social strata with an affinity to higher education while Engineering programmes and

Table 7.3 University students in selected subject areas by class background –
women students

	All students n	Education, social sciences, row %	Economics, row %	Mathematics, sciences, row %	All, row %
*Students at West German universities:**					
Lower-class	312	23	16	18	57
Middle-class	569	19	19	19	57
Upper-middle class	557	14	22	18	54
Upper-class	561	11	20	19	50
Students at the FernUniversität:†					
Lower-class	66	36	47	17	100
Middle-class	404	31	48	21	100
Upper-middle class	66	35	39	26	100
Upper-class	39	13	33	54	100

*   Government survey 1985, students in their 1st through 4th semester (BMBW 1986).
†   FeU databanks 1985/86, newly matriculated degree students.

the natural sciences attract more students who are distanced from
education.

(BMBW 1986: 368)

At the FeU a similar trend of increased enrolments in the Department of
Education, Social Sciences and Humanities could not be identified. Considering the nature of the sample with its under-representation of economics students the data suggest that there are indeed different recruitment patterns to
the major subjects offered at the FeU. This assumption is further strengthened
by the data presented in Table 7.2. This shows that the percentage of all
working-class students is higher in the mathematical–technical subjects (27%)
than it is in economics (19%) or in education, social sciences and humanities.

As far as the course choice of women at German universities is concerned,
they are over-represented in the social sciences and humanities and under-
represented in science and in technology (see Table 7.3). Although gender
patterns in students' choice of degree programmes at the FeU exist, a comparison of women students only shows that the FeU patterns are different
from those found in other universities. Again, these differences must not be
over-interpreted since the statistical basis is different in the different types of
universities. At the FeU all subject areas offered have been included in the
analysis while the comparable subject areas at other universities comprise
only 50–57% of the female student population.

As for working-class women at the FeU, Figure 7.6 shows that they tend
to differ from the other female distance students who are more inclined to
enrol in economics, in computer science, and in the social sciences.

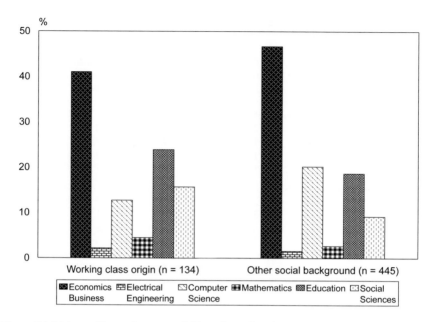

Figure 7.6 Major subject of women FeU students by class origin

Reasons for course choices of women distance students

The statistical analysis on the enrolment patterns does not provide reasons for students' course choices. In order to get some understanding of the relevance of their chosen subject area for the students themselves and for their career plans, we look at the open-ended comments on the questions relating to course choice, especially to the choice of a non-traditional subject area. Many students were willing to share their reasons with us. For instance, only 21 of the 134 working-class women students did not avail themselves of this opportunity to explain their motives, often in detail and sometimes mixing their reasons for choosing a particular subject with their reasons for the decision to study this subject at a distance.

Work-related reasons for course choice

The reasons for enrolling in a particular degree programme may be complex and may refer to external factors, career considerations, and personal interests in varying combinations. Women studying computer science and economics are most likely to have work-related reasons such as getting their first professional qualification, consolidating their occupational position, or opening up new career prospects. Frequently, students choose a subject because they already work in a related field rather than for the opposite reason of wanting to discover a suitable occupational area. The following quotes are examples for this phenomenon:

> '*I find studying economics/business studies useful because this subject provides the theoretical underpinnings for that part of my job which has to do with business administration. This did not feature in my training programme.*' (Economics/Business major)

> '*This subject area offers the opportunity to acquire theoretical background knowledge for my present occupation. If I complete the degree course successfully, I will have a basis for promotion and improve my career prospects.*' (Economics/Business major)

This fits in with results from research on mature women in continuing and adult education programmes who were motivated to undertake vocational or professional courses because of their job situation (Pusbak 1984: 140). Many working-class women want to use their degree programme in order to qualify for an occupation in the first place or to improve their career prospects. On the whole, the value of their studies for their paid work is the most powerful motivating factor for this group of distance students:

> '*Enrolling in economics/business studies seemed to be the most sensible choice since I like working with numbers. I also believe that the knowledge I gain through majoring in business or economics will open many diverse opportunities in the labour market.*' (Economics/Business major)

> '*I chose the subject area because of my occupational field; I'm counting on having better job chances when I enter the labour market after completing my degree.*' (Economics/Business major)

> '*It was important to me to choose a subject with long-term career perspectives offering more chances to me as a woman than the "typically female" subject areas. Also, I am very interested in computer science.*' (Computer Science major)

> '*The subject complements my job (only chance for advancement); my interest in mathematical problem-solving; good chances on the labour market, career prospects.*' (Computer Science major)

Frequently, the women stress the fact that their course choice was based on previous knowledge of the subject matter which they had gained through a vocational education, an earlier university course, or their job. This previous knowledge could affect students in different ways. Some see their course choice as continuing education, for some it serves to complete a degree they

dropped out of; and others hope to reduce the time needed for the degree by
building on credits given for previous work:

> '*Being a qualified (kindergarten) teacher I felt I had a good basis for
> studying education, especially since I have seven years of professional
> experience.*' (Education/pedagogy major)

> '*Through my previous occupational qualification and the fact that my
> university entrance qualification already specialised in economics I had
> already spent six years "learning" economics. Studying it seemed to be
> the logical continuation.*' (Economics/Business major)

> '*My previous occupational qualification provided me with some knowledge
> in the field of social sciences and I want to build on this by studying this
> subject on the degree level.*' (Social Sciences major)

> '*I want to build on my previous qualification as social education worker,
> partly as continuing education but also in order to keep up with develop-
> ments in my field.*' (Education/Pedagogy major)

> '*I have experience working with computers in my job and enjoy this a lot!
> Studying computer science will give me the opportunity to see what's below
> the surface.*' (Computer Science major)

> '*Continuing a previous course of studies – interest in the subject matter – very
> flexible opportunities in the labour market.*' (Economics/Business major)

Interest in the subject matter

It may seem obvious to say that many distance students are interested in the
subject matter for which they enrol. At the FeU with its limited range of
major subjects it is not always possible for students to follow their own
inclinations. Also, working-class women place a special emphasis on this
aspect which is not found to the same extent in the comments of women
from other social backgrounds. It seems that these women have finally found
a way to pursue interests which were denied to them before and which they
could not risk taking up, other than through distance education (i.e. without risking their jobs and their income). In this way, the opportunity to
study at a distance can be said to provide the chance to follow their interests
which had not been available in the regular educational system:

> '*The wish to understand economic interrelations and different standpoints
> on various economic issues, partly in order to have convincing arguments
> in political debates.*' (Economics/Business major)

'I'm very interested and have some previous knowledge in the humanities. Therefore I see the greatest possible chance to complete my degree in education.' (Education major)

'Interest in the subject, mostly because I move in the social circles of sociologists, political scientists, psychologists and other professional people. I also work in this field (in a social education institute).' (Education major)

'My interest in sociology was first awakened in school and at work. I also needed a subject with little mathematical content. In addition, the degree programme in sociology is very varied because it has two minor subjects in addition to the major.' (Sociology major)

'I have a personal interest in sociology: I like people and strive for ever-increasing knowledge and for an understanding of the internal and external workings of society. I am also engaged in politics.' (Sociology major)

'For years I have had a passionate interest in sociology – for instance, what are the reasons for the suicidal behaviour of humans in the political sphere?' (Sociology major)

'I chose computer science because:

I wanted to increase my knowledge of computers;

I want to increase my ability to program computers (programming languages, technologies);

I want to learn about the inner workings of computers as well as about operating systems, data transmission etc.' (Computer Science major)

'I decided to study electrical engineering because I am very interested in mathematics. Since pure mathematics is too theoretical for me I chose a subject which uses a great deal of applied mathematics.

I am also fascinated with the way technical things relate to each other. Hence, electrical engineering.' (Electrical Engineering major)

Other reasons for course choice

The limited range of subject areas at the FeU at the time of the survey has already been mentioned. This led students who wanted a degree and could not attend a conventional university to enrol in subjects which were of only secondary interest to them. This happened especially for those students who wanted to study law. Although the FeU has a Department of Law, it does not offer a degree programme, concentrating on offering minor subjects for other degree courses and some continuing education packages. Some years ago a joint degree programme with Düsseldorf University was established, but this degree is only partly in the distance education mode and students have to be prepared to attend courses in Düsseldorf for part of this law degree. Some students had entrance qualifications which only entitled them to study certain subject areas and therefore an even more limited choice.

> '*I would have liked to study law but the FeU does not offer the degree programme. The choice of economics is second-best for me.*' (Economics/ Business major)

> '*I wanted to gain some basic knowledge in the field of mechanical engineering, and the first phase of the degree programmes of electrical engineering, which is offered at the FeU, and mechanical engineering are nearly identical.*' (Electrical Engineering major)

> '*The type of university entrance qualification which I have restricts my course choices so I had to choose Economics.*' (Economics/Business major)

> '*Unfortunately I could only study law in combination with social sciences as my major subject.*' (Sociology major)

Some students chose a major subject as a test, feeling uncertain about their ability to study their preferred subject successfully:

> '*I first tried out mathematics as my major subject combined with economics, but did not manage the huge course load. Now I am hoping that economics will provide a chance to combine the degree with a course in journalism.*' (Economics/Business major)

> '*When I first enrolled in the M.A. in Education I did it in order to gain the self-confidence which will allow me to enrol in the subject I had wanted to study all along, namely electrical engineering. In the coming semester I will change my major to electrical engineering.*' (Education major)

> '*Originally I had enrolled in economics but soon realised that this subject was too "dry" for me. I therefore chose a more interesting subject area, namely social sciences.*' (Sociology major)

Reasons for non-traditional course choice

Women who studied electrical engineering, computer science, or mathematics at the FeU were asked to tell us the reasons for their non-traditional course choice. Some of them told us in no uncertain terms that they considered

Table 7.4 Reasons for choosing electrical engineering, computer science or
mathematics — FeU women students from a working-class background

	Corresponds to my reason exactly			Corresponds to my reason exactly or mostly		
	n	% of answers (n = 39)	% of women (n = 134)	n	% of answers (n = 39)	% of women (n = 134)
Enjoy maths, theory	15	38.5	11.2	21	31.3	15.7
Study with my partner	2	5.1	1.5	2	3.0	1.5
Self-confidence as a woman	5	12.8	3.7	9	13.4	6.7
My partner helps me	3	7.7	2.2	4	6.0	3.0
Interest in technology	9	23.1	6.7	18	26.9	13.4
Opportunities in the labour market	5	12.8	3.7	13	19.4	9.7
Sum	**39**	**100.0**	**29.0**	**134**	**100.0**	**50.0**

Source: FeU survey data 1986.

this a sexist question based on the assumption that women should or could
not enter such subject areas. The parallel survey in England, which was carried out a few months after the FeU study, therefore phrased this question
differently and asked all respondents in these subject areas for their reasons
for enrolling in these fields.

In spite of these reservations, most of the women answered both closed
and open-ended questions (see Table 7.4), showing that many of them
simply 'enjoy mathematical problem-solving and working with theoretical
models' or have a 'keen interest in technical matters'. The women enrolling
in a distance course in these subject areas had previously not been able to
pursue these interests or else they had developed such an interest in the course
of their training or through their work. In some cases women wanted to
overcome the traditional gender roles in the workplace by getting a degree
in an atypical subject. The following quotes illustrate the type of reasons
women had for their course choice:

*'I don't believe in the traditional role models where men study mathem-
atics and women study social education, if they study at all. After they get
their degrees, the men get jobs, the women are unemployed. On top of
that, those jobs which are traditionally female are usually underpaid.'*
(Computer Science major)

*'I believe that the degree in Computer Science will provide me with the com-
petence to participate in the systems analysis and to share in the decision-
making process concerning the choice of computers in my place of work. I
will have gained enough technological know-how in the course of my studies.*

Professionally I am interested in research as well as work in a software engineering firm or a computer hardware manufacturer.' (Computer Science major)

'*I enrolled in electrical engineering because the sciences, mathematics, and technology were subject areas which were always strongly encouraged by my father. I could enter these fields without a "humanistic education" and without speaking proper "high" German.*

I never conformed fully to the traditional image of girls and women, and I never wanted to. During the last three years in school I studied the roles of women and men and the women's movement.' (Electrical Engineering major)

'*I enrolled in electrical engineering because I have always been interested in so-called men's jobs. But in spite of good grades I never had a chance. I do not want to end up in the typing pool again but want to do something which is more visible and more prestigious – especially in the eyes of the men.'* (Electrical Engineering major)

Family-orientation and the course choice of women

With regard to the issue of social mobility it is interesting to note that working-class women mention their personal interest in the subject matter and work-related reasons, but do not refer to their children or other family-related factors. This is different in the case of women from other social backgrounds who stress the role which their studying a given subject will play in their private lives. A few years ago we did a gender analysis of the course choices of male and female distance students and concluded that women with partners and children saw their course choice as serving their families, especially their children. The men, by contrast, never mentioned their children and rarely referred to their wife or partner (see von Prümmer and Rossié 1987). The difference between the comments of the men and the women were so striking that we formulated a hypothesis concerning the need of women distance students to justify their studying as supporting their families rather than detracting from their duties as wives and mothers. We summed this up in the phrase 'family-orientation as a strategy for the justification of distance education' and identified three ways in which this strategy was employed by women (see von Prümmer and Rossié 1990b):

- The woman originally had planned to do a university degree but was prevented from doing so by marriage or pregnancy. Her enrolment in a DE degree programme is her chance to begin or to complete her studies.

- The woman may or may not have started or completed a previous degree course, but she now feels that she needs (another) degree in order to better her chances for (re-)entry into the labour market. Her distance studying serves the purpose of gaining better occupational qualifications.
- The woman wants to use the knowledge gained in her DE programme directly for her own family, possibly because she needs it to help her children with their homework or because she feels it would contribute to her understanding of child development.

A closer look at the arguments put forward by the women showed that it was necessary to differentiate between family-related reasons based on fact and those which covered up the student's own wish to study a given subject. The first of these occurs in situations where a woman has postponed a career because of her children and now studies in order to qualify for (re-)entry into the labour market, enrolling in a 'family-friendly' DE programme. She sees her enrolment at the FeU as a way of catching up on an education without neglecting her family. In other situations, such as an interest in computer science, the reason put forward may be the wish to be able to help a child with her or his schoolwork, but in reality the woman might have a keen interest in computers and mathematics which she feels unable to admit because it is not typical for women. Other women argue that they study pedagogy to help them fulfil their role as a mother, an argument which preempts charges that a degree in education will not be of use in finding a job and provides a legitimate reason for the course choice.

In twenty years of research, our statistical analyses, surveys and interviews with students have all shown that women, especially those without their own income and those responsible for bringing up children, do indeed find it necessary to justify their embarking on a course of studies, even in cases when they do it at a distance and without neglecting their family duties. Interestingly, this phenomenon would not have been uncovered, if we had only looked at the women from working-class backgrounds. In telling us their reasons for choosing a given degree programme, this group of women gives arguments more similar to those of the men than to those of the other women. They never mention their children in this context and refer mostly to work-related and personal factors. This cannot be explained in terms of any higher percentage of working-class women who are in paid work, since both groups of women have similar employment patterns. The explanation may partly be found in the household composition, since fewer of the working-class women were living in a nuclear family situation with a husband or partner and children (47%; other women 57%). It is also plausible that these students, who have often achieved their formal education as mature women, have less need to subject their course choice to the approval of their families and to find an 'acceptable' reason for their enrolment.

The study goals of women distance students

Registering for a degree programme: formal qualifications and continuing education

It is characteristic for distance and open learning that this form of education serves more than one purpose. As a DTU, the FeU provides a means to achieve a formal university degree. It also allows adults to enrol as continuing students to further their professional qualifications or personal interests or to supplement the degree programmes at another German university. An expression of this diversity of study purpose is the fact that there are five enrolment categories from which students can choose their matriculation status. The first three categories denote regular student status and are meant for students who wish to pursue a degree full-time or part-time, or study for a minor subject in conjunction with a degree programme somewhere else. These students need formal entrance requirements in order to enrol. In addition, there are two categories of course students who subscribe to individual courses or course packages and do not study for a FeU degree. One of these groups comprises 'visiting students' enrolled at another university and therefore in possession of the formal entrance qualifications. The other group are the associate students who take individual courses out of personal interest and are not required to have any university entrance qualifications. This last group cannot get a degree, but in some instances may get a certificate for having passed a continuing education package.

It is generally accepted that those students who enrol as regular students are degree oriented and, by virtue of their matriculation status, study seriously for their M.A. or diploma while course students by definition do not pursue a degree goal. In reality, not all students enrolled as full-time or part-time regular students are seriously studying for a degree as the following quote shows:

> 'In no way do I see my studies as something I "have to" do. I don't even need the degree. Maybe I will switch from one subject area to another in the course of my studies, depending on what I enjoy doing at the time.
>
> The study material is very good. It is comprehensive and can serve as an encyclopedia.'

This phenomenon was the subject of an evaluation survey some twelve years ago which focused on the 'subjective study goals' of distance students. Although the sample included only regular students who were expected to be degree oriented, this was the case for only 52% of the women and 43% of the men (Bartels *et al.* 1988: Table 9). It was patently obvious that matriculation status alone was no sure indicator of a student's serious interest in a degree.

In order to gain more information about the relevance distance students accord their studies, the questionnaire included a catalogue of statements on the goals of academic study, as well as an open-ended question about the reasons for becoming a student.

The goals of academic study

With regard to their general study goals, students were asked to answer a catalogue of 18 items, which had been constructed to parallel other research instruments used in the context of evaluation at the FeU, and an open-ended question on their motives for pursuing an academic degree. This set of questions referred to the *first* time the students had entered a university, and not necessarily their time at the FeU. For each of the 18 items students were asked to mark whether it had been '1 = very important'; '2 = fairly important'; '3 = not important'; or '4 = totally irrelevant'. To begin with, the answers, which were analysed individually, and are graphically presented as polarity profiles of means: values less than the arithmetic mean (Ø) of 2.5 on the scale from 1 to 4 denote a higher importance, values of more than 2.5 a lower importance of the given item. In addition, the statement catalogue was subjected to a factor analysis, the resulting factors providing the basis for further statistical analyses.

The data show that the most important reasons cited for academic study were related to general knowledge and better qualifications, the opening of new career perspectives, but also to gaining experience and self-assurance.

In the following paragraphs we look at women of working-class origin as a group which we expected to be more interested in using academic study as a vehicle of upward social mobility. Working-class women are slightly more inclined than others to look for occupational gains, but they place the same high value on studying because they enjoy expanding their knowledge and want to have a broader understanding of all areas of knowledge. They place the highest value on the 'enjoyment in opening up new areas of knowledge' (Ø = 1.67); followed by the wish for a 'wider general knowledge/being better informed' (Ø = 1.96), 'broadening my experience of life' (Ø = 2.01), 'acquiring a comprehensive theoretical background' (Ø = 2.01); 'higher professional qualification' (Ø = 2.05); and 'opening up new professional perspectives' (Ø = 2.14). Not very important are 'security in my present job' (Ø = 3.26); and a 'higher social standing as an academic' (Ø = 3.35). The issue of 'taking over the parental firm' is totally irrelevant (Ø = 3.98) for the distance students in the survey.

The comparison of means within the group of working-class women studying at the FeU shows the expected variations in study goals depending on students' family and work situation (see Figure 7.7; for clarity, the items have been sorted in order of relevance.). With respect to the extent of paid employment, it is clear that work-related study goals are consistently more

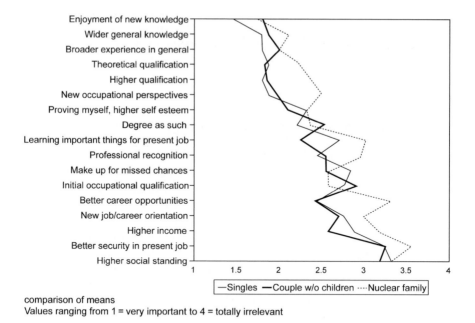

comparison of means
Values ranging from 1 = very important to 4 = totally irrelevant

Figure 7.7 Study goals of working-class women in different family situations

important for women who have a job. The only exception, not surprisingly, is the item 'basic job-related/professional qualification', which is more relevant for women not (yet) in the workforce who need to obtain qualifications for entering or re-entering the labour market.

In order to simplify the analysis of the data and the presentation of the results, the items were subjected to a factor analysis using the SPSS factor analysis procedure (SPSS 1997: 253–62). This yielded four factors of study motivation, two of which are related to paid work and career aspects:

Work-related study goals: Factor 1 (*F1*) job security and promotion
         Factor 4 (*F4*) new career perspectives

Personal study goals: Factor 2 (*F2*) general knowledge
         Factor 3 (*F3*) social mobility and self-image

The answering patterns of the women from working-class families show that they place a higher priority on personal development than on job and career. On average, the work-related study goals *F1* 'Job security and promotion' and *F4* 'New career perspectives' were named 'very important' by 28 respondents. The personal study goals, *F2* 'General knowledge' and *F3* 'Social mobility and self-image' were cited as 'very important' by 40 respondents. For

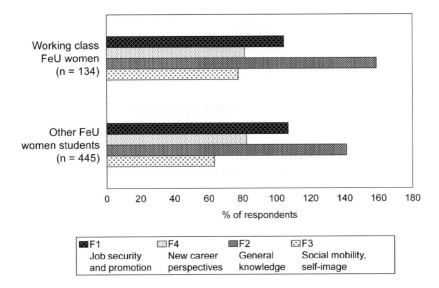

Figure 7.8 Very important goals of academic study by class origin

this group, the value of studying at the FeU clearly lies in the opportunity for personal development and indicates their need to make up for educational chances previously missed. The one item which is most important for these women is the 'enjoyment of discovering new areas of knowledge'.

It must be noted that the results of the factor analysis for working-class women are different from those emerging from a factor analysis run on the answers of the other women in the survey. The differences between the two groups of respondents can be demonstrated by using the four factors identified in the analysis of working-class women and comparing the percentages of women in the two status groups. We do this simply by adding the percentages of those women who mark the items of each factor as '1 = very important'. The results are shown in Figure 7.8.

The results of this comparison confirm our expectations that working-class women are more in need of redressing educational disadvantages by pursuing a university degree later in life. Specifically, they place more emphasis on those study goals which would lead to their gaining broader general knowledge and they hope to become more self-assured as people through gaining a degree.

In addition to the quantitative data provided by the catalogue of statements, we were also able to refer to many detailed and thoughtful open-ended comments in which students put forward their reasons for wanting to do a university degree programme. These comments illustrate the meaning of the answers given in the closed questions and are often tied in with the reasons for choosing a particular degree course or subject area.

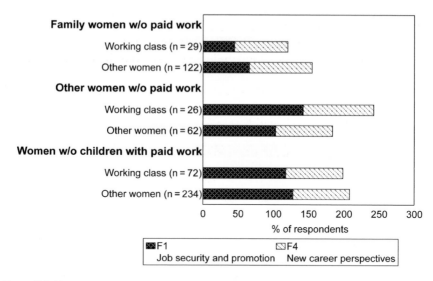

Figure 7.9 Very important job/career-related study goals

Occupational study goals

Since we were interested in processes of social mobility and the role which university distance education could play in these processes we looked specifically at those study goals which referred to work and career-related aspects. The factor analysis had identified the two factors of occupational study goals *F1* 'Job security and promotion' and *F4* 'New career perspectives'. Our original assumption was that both of these factors must be closely connected to students' work situations and to the extent of their paid employment. This was found not to be the case, although both factors bundle work-related items (see Figure 7.9). Only *F1* shows the expected differences between women who have jobs outside the home and those who exclusively perform unpaid family and domestic work. The items under *F1*, relating to job security and occupational advancement, were irrelevant for housewives, in their current situation, but very important for single women who did have a job.

The situation of housewives, who are defined as women with domestic and childcare responsibilities and without paid employment, is quite different from that of women without family and without paid work. The latter group is more inclined to value the work-related items in *F1*, a sign that they view their unemployment as a passing phase and their degree studies as spanning their previous job and their future career. The percentage of working-class women who consider these items 'very important' is higher than that of the other women. These differences suggest that working-class women distance students do have a higher stake in the labour market than their colleagues from other social backgrounds. As far as *F4* is concerned, there are no noticeable differences between women with and without paid work. At most, there is a slight tendency for women with jobs to consolidate their current occupational position and job security and be less interested in new beginnings.

The open-ended comments show nuances in the meaning of occupational goals, having for instance an interest in a professional field or wanting to improve their professional qualifications:

> '*Further job qualifications.*
>
> *Enjoyment of the learning process and acquiring knowledge.*
>
> *Interest in the subject matter.*'

> '*I want to keep up with theoretical developments in my field while I'm on leave of absence from my job.*'

Other women want to get a degree because they hope it will confer professional recognition and respect which they obviously lack at present:

> '*In my firm they have a system of only employing university graduates in responsible positions in the personnel department. It follows for me that I have new bosses frequently (every two to three years). Fresh from the university, they have no experience but they are given the authority as my superiors.*'

Students may also be motivated by considerations relating to the situation on the labour market and their chances of keeping or finding a job:

> '*I decided to enrol in an FeU degree programme in case I become unemployed. In that case, I can switch from part-time to full-time study and won't be out on the street.*'

> '*The labour market is very competitive and requires constantly increasing qualifications. For women it is necessary to be much better qualified than the competition for a given post in middle and higher management.*'

According to the open-ended comments, women who are not currently in paid work are more likely to value the items under *F4*, 'New career perspectives' because they hope that a degree will help them to (re-)enter the labour market after a childrearing phase:

> '*I would like to utilise the time when my children are still small and I am housebound to get a qualification for the labour market. I cannot enter a*

training programme which requires my presence in a firm. Private evening classes are too expensive. Studying at the FeU is therefore the only way to pursue a qualification. In addition it is very good to work with your brain for a change.'

Some of the women, especially those of working-class backgrounds, who do have a job express dissatisfaction with their previous occupational education or with their work situation or career prospects:

'I gave up my job for one year while attending a secondary school. But because of the dismal job prospects I decided to go back to the kind of job I had before. I enrolled at the FeU because I wanted to make use of the university entrance qualification I had gained during that year.'

'Autonomy. I want to be independent of the orders others might give me.'

'I would like to have a job I enjoy and which is varied and interesting. Also I want to break out of the role cliché.'

Those women from a working-class background who are manual workers or routine non-manual workers themselves are especially unsatisfied with their present job. Two of the three women who characterise their own occupation as working class want to re-orient their employment:

'I am afraid of ending up as an unskilled labourer and I am hoping to complete a journalism degree as well as the FeU degree.'

'After my divorce: economic independence.

No future in my original job.

To realise my abilities and interests through studying.'

On the whole, the open-ended comments show more clearly than the answers to the closed question that working-class women have a greater need than other women to enrol in a degree programme at the FeU in order to overcome the restrictions they experienced in their educational and occupational biographies. Many comments refer to an urgent desire to obtain better qualifications as a basis for finding more meaningful work and securing or obtaining material security. It seems that these women do not rely on others, such as husbands or partners, to provide new perspectives for them. Rather, they work toward creating their own options for a better future through better career prospects. In this sense it can truly be said that women of working-class origin use their DE as a means for achieving upward occupational and social mobility.

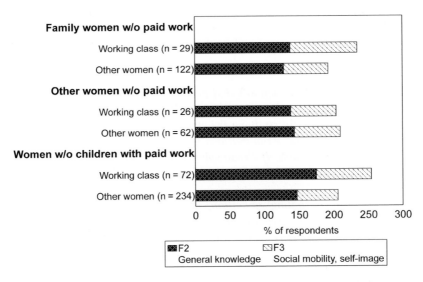

Figure 7.10 Very important study goals related to personal development

Personal development

Apart from study goals related to their occupation and career aspirations working-class women placed a high value on personal study goals promising to provide a broader general knowledge (*F2*) and upward social mobility (*F3*). Figure 7.10 shows that these students value the items combined in these two factors much more highly than the work-related items. The open-ended comments illustrate just which aspects of personal development the working-class women connect with their goals as distance students.

On a very general level the following reasons for studying may be seen as referring to personal development:

> '*To prove that it is possible to make something of yourself in spite of the family work.*'

> '*My parents pressured me into taking up studying;*
>
> *There is an opportunity for meeting others;*
>
> *Autonomy as a woman; independence as a woman.*'

> '*I wanted to free my husband from the enormous pressure of being the sole provider for our family because this leads to the worry about our future if anything should happen to him.*'

The following comments of working-class women refer to study goals grouped in *F2* 'general knowledge', and show how mixed some of the motivation may be. Some of the women simply enjoy the process of learning and continuing their education:

> *'Compared to private schools and colleges studying at the FeU is an inexpensive form of continuing education. The course choices meet my areas of interest. Successful studying is acknowledged through the credits given for passing tests and examinations which creates some pressure toward being an active student. If I read specialist literature in my subject I put it down even more quickly than I do the course materials.'*

> *'A thirst for continuing education, for learning more and more. Partly idealistic visions of what it means to study at a university, even though I knew that studying normally is quite different from DE and that the most important thing is to get the credits.'*

> *'I am interested in so many questions to which I cannot find the answer. These I hope to find through my studies, both answers which are given and answers which I work out for myself on the basis of my learning.'*

Some women stress work-related aspects even in this context:

> *'To make good use of my free time.*
>
> *To demonstrate to myself that I am qualified to meet the highest standards in my work.*
>
> *To acquire a theoretical basis for the practical knowledge gained in my job.'*

> *'Theoretical information for the practice of my present job which is computer organisation/organisational programming.'*

> *'Firstly, I enjoy learning. Secondly, in order to start my own firm or become self-employed, I have to pass an examination. Only people with ten years of experience on the job or a university degree are allowed to take this exam.'*

> *'I want to make use of educational opportunities which are offered. I have a vague hope of finding work which will be fun and fulfilling.'*

> *'My study goals:*
>
> *I need additional information to supplement my studies at Münster University.*

I am thinking of switching to a degree programme at the FeU and am using my present enrolment as a chance to see what kind of study situation a distance student has.'

Other women instrumentalise their studying as a means to escape from frustrating personal circumstances or from intellectual boredom. This mostly happens in the case of non-employed housewives who have given up their education or reduced their paid work when they started their families and became mothers:

'To make good use of the time during which I raise my child (one son of $3\frac{1}{2}$ years).'

'Fear of dullness.

Contrast to housework and childcare.

The need to experience success.

Don't want to unlearn learning.

Not to stagnate, keep up with current developments.'

'Not to fall into an intellectual stupor.

To "use" my head, otherwise 13 years of school would have been in vain.

To offset the effects of being under-taxed in my job (secretarial work).'

Few women wrote in open comments on the theme of *F3* 'social mobility and self-image'. The answers do not clarify whether this goal really was relatively unimportant or whether the students found it difficult to put in writing. It is possible that considerations of 'socially acceptable' behaviour led them to play down the role which a university degree could play in gaining higher social standing.

'I first took up studying because at that time university students as a group were very privileged compared to my own situation as employee. I have now taken up DE in order to gain further qualifications or, rather, to obtain the academic degree which seems to be essential in the workplace today.'

Conclusion: working-class women using the opportunities in distance education

Chapter 7 has dealt with the goals which women distance students themselves associate with their studying for a university degree, and with the value they place on the distance learning mode in helping them to advance in their careers or in their social position. The findings from our research suggest that this group of women differs from other women distance students in two respects, and that their answering patterns are seemingly contradictory.

On the one hand, working-class women place a slightly higher value on study goals which can contribute to wider general knowledge and access to new areas of knowledge (*F2*). The value they place on those goals which promise an increase in self-esteem based on successful studying (*F3*) is noticeably higher than is shown for other women distance students. This could be explained in terms of the educational chances which these women missed out on in the course of their lives, and which they want to take now that they are adults in charge of their own lives. On average, percentages of women from working-class backgrounds (W_1) and of other women studying at the FeU (W_2) who saw the individual goals in each factor as 'very important' were as follows: *F2* 'general knowledge': 40% (W_1) and 35% (W_2); *F3* 'social mobility and self-image': 19% (W_1) and 28% (W_2).

On the other hand, there seems to be little difference between the working-class women and the other women studying at the FeU with respect to the value they place on the study goals combined in the work-related factors. Both groups place a higher value on goals referring to a new career direction and beginning (*F4*) and less on those goals which could guarantee job security and the consolidation of an existing occupational position (*F1*). On average the percentages of women from different social backgrounds who saw the individual goals in each factor as 'very important' were as follows: *F1* 'job security and promotion': 17% (W_1) and 18% (W_2); *F4* 'new career perspectives': 27% (W_1) and 28% (W_2).

This picture of similarity changes when we look at the open-ended comments on the reasons students had for choosing a given subject area or degree programme. In this respect the working-class women, who almost exclusively refer to their interest in the subject matter or to the usefulness of this degree for their career plans, are distinct from the other women studying at the FeU and their answers more closely resemble those of the men in the survey.

By contrast, women from other social backgrounds display a tendency to refer to their family responsibilities when explaining why they decided to study a given major subject. This answering pattern was so strong that it caused us to assume the reason given by the women respondents for their choice of subject area might be a justification strategy for the very fact of studying rather than the real explanation of their choice of degree programme. It seems fair to assume that these women are subtly subversive in using their mothering and homemaking roles as the unassailable reason for a course of action which reduces their domestic commitments and accessibility.

A look at the study goals shows that here, too, working-class women mainly refer to the workplace. In their open-ended answers they express a wish to gain the formal qualifications necessary for a better-paying job with more responsibilities, and to become economically independent and secure. This suggests that these women enrol as distance students in order to improve their life chances, which for them can be achieved through improving their career chances. This in turn, can be achieved through getting the university degree. In this sense we can legitimately conclude that women of working-class origin consciously use their distance studies as a vehicle for upward occupational and social mobility.

Chapter 8

Challenges, chances, changes
Distance education for women

This book is concerned with the opportunities and the challenges associated with the DE mode of teaching and learning. These exist both at the institutional level and at a personal level, as do the changes which accompany the process of studying.

In looking at the role of distance education for women I draw on my work as an institutional researcher at the German FeU which is a single-mode DTU with approximately 56,000 students. I also can draw on international contacts which began with a study leave at Athabasca University in 1983 and led to my involvement in WIN, in which I have been active since 1985. For many years I have also done comparative research, mostly with Gill Kirkup of the OU UK.

Being part of an evaluation of the distance teaching system, my research has addressed the teaching system as well as the situation and the learning environment of men and women studying at a distance. The aim of the research was to identify factors which facilitate successful studying and factors which make it more difficult for the students to pursue their educational goals. The identification of these positive and negative aspects is the prerequisite for pointing out the need and direction of institutional changes in order to improve the open and distance learning provision.

As far as women distance students were concerned, the research brought to light some patterns in their personal circumstances and their learning styles as well as in their use of the institutional provision of support services which differed systematically from those of the male distance students. Examples of this have been presented throughout the chapters of this book.

The under-representation of women in tertiary DE in Germany could at least in part be directly attributed to the fact that the FeU did not recognise these gender patterns and therefore failed to accommodate the needs of women distance students to the extent necessary to guarantee equal access and study conditions for both men and women.

In the face of these findings which, moreover, are replicated year after year in new evaluation studies it may seem strange that I talk about the chances which distance education offers to women. Am I whistling in the dark trying to convince myself that all is well? Do I just want to believe that my work has meaning and that distance education can indeed serve the needs of women? Or can we really challenge the existing distance teaching system to become less androcentric and more women-friendly?

Challenges

Distance education is about challenges. On the institutional level, concern with women students and gender issues challenges a distance teaching university to review the study materials, the course contents and presentation, the teaching system, and even the composition of its staff and course authors. Once it is discovered that the seeming neutrality is in fact biased and unfavourable circumstances are created for women, the university is faced with the challenge of developing measures which will ensure equal opportunities in all areas. It will need to overcome resistance to these changes based partly on a natural inertia favouring the *status quo* and partly on deep-seated attitudes concerning the status of men and women. Some may even question the legitimacy of gender as a category in ODL.

The starting point for looking at gender issues at the FeU was the observation that women were extremely under-represented as compared to other German universities, and to DTUs in countries such as Britain and Canada. The reasons for this low rate of participation were usually sought in limited course choices coupled with the continued existence of traditional gendered subject preferences. Both of these factors were assumed to be outside the influence of the university and therefore demanded no action.

From the beginning, our research showed that this was not a sufficient explanation and that other factors were at work hindering women's access to university level DE. In parallel surveys at the OU UK and the FeU empirical evidence was collected which demonstrated a relation between certain characteristics of the distance teaching systems on the one hand and the personal circumstances and learning styles of male and female distance students on the other hand. The data suggested specific areas in which institutional action could reduce the male bias and contribute to a more equitable representation of women. At the FeU, for instance, all of the areas mentioned above did not take gender into account. This included not only the teaching system and organisation of local support, but also the contents and presentation of courses and the overwhelmingly male academic staff. The question is how to overcome the male bias and implement women-friendly perspectives without, as is often feared, compromising high standards of quality and academic standing.

Whether the challenge of creating an equitable distance education system is taken up and how vigorously it is pursued depends in part on whether the decision-makers see this as a problem which needs to be addressed, or whether they perceive it as an irrelevant side issue, or even an irritant brought up by a few incorrigible feminists. In part, too, outside pressures could build up and create a more urgent need for the university to be seen as an equal opportunities institution. This is the case when part of the government funding is paid out only on the condition of an increased proportion of women enrolling and completing degrees or being promoted to higher staff levels and tenured posts.

At the personal level, becoming a distance student presents more than one challenge. For instance, there is the question of how to fit the distance course into an already busy day, coping with a household and children, possibly a job and other responsibilities. What priorities with regard to family, work and distance studying must be set and what limitations are necessary and acceptable? How can the wish to pursue a course of studies be justified when it threatens to detract from the woman's duties as mother and from her domestic and partnership role?

Our research has shown time and again the multiple pressures on women due to their domestic and mothering responsibilities, which often have to be fulfilled in addition to outside paid work and other commitments. There are many studies which show that the social division of labour has basically remained unchanged along traditional gender lines according to which the full responsibility for the private sphere is assigned to women, with the men occasionally helping with some of the domestic chores and childcare. Even though in countries such as Germany, a socially acceptable attitude of partnership has evolved in the past few decades, in practice this leads to an increase in women's workforce participation, but not to a corresponding increase in men's participation in domestic labour. Distance students, as part of the larger society, *a priori* are no exception.

To mention only some of the consequences, this means that women enrolling in a degree course have to fit it in not only with paid work, but also with family work, thus carrying a double or triple load. An additional challenge results from the fact that the domestic work, especially childcare, is extremely fragmented and difficult to plan, thus making it hard to schedule contiguous blocks of study time and to find the time and space for uninterrupted and concentrated work. On top of that, as research also has shown, the demands made by their families on women distance students increase rather than decrease as is the case with men who enrol in a degree course. It follows that women face a formidable challenge in having to set priorities and negotiate with family and friends their right to 'do their own thing'.

Chances

Distance education is about chances. Opportunities of obtaining an education and formal qualifications which were denied earlier in life. Opportunities to pursue a degree without giving up one's job and one's livelihood or disrupting one's career or one's family. Chances of studying while being in a situation which prevents attendance at 'regular' universities, be it a tour in the army, a stay in hospital, a job abroad or without regular hours, a family to take care of, or any other of numerous circumstances which preclude participation in classroom education.

On the face of it, these opportunities are no different for women than they are for men. In some countries, where girls and women are largely excluded from education at all levels, DE may be the only option, as has been reported by colleagues in India, for instance. In reality, as we have seen, the opportunities are not equal since women have to overcome greater odds in order to access a degree programme and face more obstacles in reconciling their distance studies with the other areas of their lives. They have fewer resources but more responsibilities, less support from their family and more scruples about the legitimacy of getting an education for themselves. In the face of this, are we even justified in assuming that the DE mode offers special opportunities for women in any situation and, especially, for the housebound mothers of small children which the early literature was so fond of? I believe we are.

For one thing, women do take the opportunities offered by DE. In spite of all the difficulties and obstacles confronting women in DE, there are many successful students who either complete a degree or gain personal development through studying. Many of these women would not have been able to do this if they could not have done it at a distance.

The expression 'taking a chance' indicates that a certain element of risk is involved in an undertaking. It is part of the DE philosophy that students can enrol in a degree programme without incurring the existential risk entailed in giving up one's job and income in order to attend university. This is true for women who study without risking their jobs, thus maintaining what may be their only source of income or a necessary supplement to the family income. At another level, women are taking a chance when they risk upsetting the balance of power in their own homes. Since it is not possible to study without at least partially changing the routines and taking time out, the family will feel somewhat neglected – and will let the student know what her priorities ought to be. This, in turn, reinforces her own feelings of guilt which often lead her to try and be an even better housewife and mother than before enrolment. In set-ups like this, with their totally unrealistic expectations, there is a real danger of the woman giving up her education before she has achieved her goals, be they the completion of a formal degree or her personal development.

Another problem concerns the question of whether the woman, who often has no recent experience with formal education, feels she is capable of studying successfully or that she will be able to 'learn how to learn'. How will she cope if she decides to pursue a university degree and does not complete the course or does badly in her exams? Where does she find motivation and energy needed to continue? Again, our research shows gender-specific patterns, since women are more likely to feel that 'failure' in their distance studies obliges them to discontinue and return to devoting their full time and attention to their families.

The answers to these questions seem to lie in the support and connection with other students in similar circumstances. This is where the gender differences in learning styles, brought to light through research by and with women, play an important role. For one thing, finding a group of women to study with can be a tremendous help in the learning process, fulfilling the need for social contact and connectedness. Also, due to the women's movement it has long been known that the sharing and exchanging of individual experiences often leads to the discovery of common patterns and structural discrimination where the isolated woman has felt personally responsible for not being able to cope or for her 'failure' as a mother, a wife, and as it were a distance student. In taking the opportunity to seek out other women and sharing her experience of the difficulties, the lack of study progress, the fights with her partner, the 'bad' mothering, and the neglected household, with other women, a distance student can find out that this is not her individual shortcoming but an almost automatic and universal pattern. She can also find out how other women deal with this situation. Together, the women can help each other to develop coping strategies as well as provide more tangible support, such as taking turns babysitting, forming car-pools, joining up on the computer, explaining some of the course-material.

Another aspect of the opportunities arising in DE concerns the institution. Our research has not only brought us insights into the way in which women deal with the problems, but also provided information on the measures the institutions of open and distance learning can take in order to facilitate access and success. This may be of benefit not only to the women but also to the men studying at a distance. For instance, the research on communication preferences and patterns showed an unexpectedly high interest in personal interaction and communication amongst all students. Until then it had often been taken for granted that the typical distance student was not only content to study in the privacy and isolation of the single, unconnected learner, but was actually happy doing this. There are other instances of how a supposedly more women-friendly approach could benefit *all* students, and in this lies a chance for DTUs to improve their systems for both men and women which surely must be a goal of distance education everywhere.

Changes

Distance education is about change. By virtue of their very existence, DTUs change the previously clear structure of the educational system in a given society. If schooling and vocational or professional qualifications are no longer confined to the traditional places of learning, schools and universities lose their monopoly, and restrictions in access to education can no longer be as rigidly enforced. In addition, as access to educational opportunities becomes more fluid, there must also be changes in the social structure, at least in those areas where status and position are conferred on the basis of formal qualifications.

My own research on women from working-class backgrounds confirms that changes of this kind are taking place. In the 1960s race and ethnicity were not yet relevant sociological categories for the analysis of inequality in West German society and in the West German educational system. Rather, 'Roman Catholic working-class girls living in rural areas' had been identified as the educationally most disadvantaged social group, with extremely low chances of getting secondary schooling and entering university. In the FeU survey which I used for my analysis, many of the working-class women students had obtained their university entrance qualifications – a prerequisite for enrolling in a degree course – via evening classes and 'second-chance' schools. They were employed in dead-end, boring jobs which provided a basic income and a certain degree of highly valued security, but did not offer career prospects or intellectual challenges. In choosing to study for a degree at a distance these women could pursue a dream of upward occupational and social mobility and of personal development which would not have been possible in any other university setting. As far as these women are concerned, I have no way of knowing how their plans progressed and whether their hopes were eventually realised. Conducting an earlier small-scale interview study of three randomly chosen women graduates, Irene Raehlmann (1984) found that all three women happened to be of working-class origin. Her analysis of the in-depth interviews led her to conclude that all had been highly motivated to break out of their 'inherited' class position and on the basis of their studying and gaining their M.A. had brought about changes in their personal and professional lives.

DE has other important functions for women which obviously makes it worth their while. They use their newly acquired formal qualification to enter or re-enter the labour market after a period of raising children, they break out of a dead-end job, or they get started on a new career or promoted to a higher position. Sometimes, of course, their expectations are not met and the hoped-for changes do not materialise in the labour-market for which they may be considered too old by the time they finish their studies or not experienced enough in the field they want to enter.

One of the most profound changes which can happen through DE is connected to the challenges mentioned above with respect to the domestic and family situation. There is, rightly, some concern over the possibility that DE could reinforce the traditional role of women being responsible for household and childcare and relegated to the private sphere. Home study, which can be pursued without entering the public sphere, could serve to 'keep women in their place' and to 'domesticate' them even further in accordance with traditional cultural values and social norms.

While we have to keep this possibility in mind and make sure counter-measures are taken to prevent it happening, it is likely that the liberating potential will be the stronger of the two forces inherent in ODL. For one thing, it has been noted that education as such serves to empower women. This may be on the most basic level through literacy programmes, or on more advanced levels through university study and even Ph.D. programmes. As recently as March 1998, for instance, a UNICEF study on violence against women in south-east Asia concluded that compulsory schooling for all girls would be a long-term measure to reduce violence against women by providing them with qualifications as the basis for getting a job which in turn would enable them to earn their own income and improve their status. Simultaneously, they propagate a campaign to educate the general populace about human rights and the need for attitude changes toward women.

Returning to the family situation of women distance students, we find that many more or less far-reaching changes take place. Not all of these were probably intended from the start, and some may not be welcome.

Taking up a course of studies invariably affects the private arrangements and domestic division of labour and the way in which the woman sees her role and sets her priorities. In order to study successfully, the woman has to try and organise her time differently; she must find a space in which she can study without being disturbed; and she must spread at least some of her household chores and childcare responsibilities around. This means getting her partner, older children, parents and friends to take over chores such as doing the dishes, the laundry and the shopping, or dropping the kids off at nursery school, to mention just a few. Even in cases where the student tries to change as little of her routine as possible, there will be times when she has to prepare for exams or attend a seminar, or when she is simply too tired and exhausted or too frustrated to be as patient as she might wish to be or as her family expects her to be. There is some evidence that it might be better to become aware of these kinds of things early on and negotiate demands and support with one's family, including the use of family resources such as the car for visits to the study centre and the PC for communication and course work.

Another change which has been observed relates to aspects of personal development. Many women enter DE unsure of their ability to study at university level or uncertain whether they could master their chosen subject. Their success in doing it increases their self-esteem and their study progress provides them with a broader knowledge and more self-confidence. Family women who do not also have a job outside the home can profit from joining self-help study groups as has been shown in a project providing a support infrastructure for mothers of young children. The participants, who started out as isolated housewives with little self-esteem and not much control over their domestic situation, eventually became self-confident emancipated women who claimed their own study space and time and their right to pursue their chosen course.

Finally, there are those changes which occur on the institutional level. Some of those are apparent, such as the shift in emphasis from distance teaching to open and distance learning and the increase in flexibility and learner-centredness this implies. In the 1990s there has been an increasing concern with quality assurance in distance education which is part of this shift, but also must be seen in the context of fiscal and administrative control over the use of resources.

Some changes are very rapid and seemingly inevitable, such as the increased use of ICTs, which transform not only the organisation of the DE systems but also have an impact on the design of teaching materials and media and on the target groups. The use of the internet and the electronic highway is envisioned to lead to the establishment of the electronic campus and the virtual university which, via the world-wide web, has global connections.

Other changes are more gradual and less automatic. They depend on attitude shifts and new policy decisions. Among these is the change from androcentric to women-friendly distance education, i.e. from gender-blind DE systems and pedagogy to an awareness of gender as an important category. Let us continue to whistle in the dark! Not in order to pretend all is well, but because others will hear us and take notice.

Bibliography

Abbott, P. and Sapsford, R. (1987) *Women and Social Class*, London: Tavistock.

Abbott, P. and Wallace, C. (1990) *An Introduction to Sociology: Feminist Perspectives*, London: Routledge.

Acker, J. (1973) 'Women and Social Stratification: A Case of Intellectual Sexism', *American Journal of Sociology* 78, 4: 936–45.

—— (1989) 'Making Gender Visible' in R.A. Wallace (ed.) *Feminism and Sociological Theory*, Newbury Park: Sage.

AK Wiss (ed.) (1996) Memorandum III: Vorwärts – Auf der Stelle!, Dortmund: Arbeitskreis Wissenschaftlerinnen von NRW.

AMTEC (1998) 'Programme of the joint conference of AMTEC, CNNML and the Edmonton New Media Association', June 3–6 1998, Edmonton: Association for Media and Technology in Education.

Athabasca University (1998) 'Strategic University Plan', Online. HTTP: http://www.athabascau.ca/html/info/sup/sup.htm (4 August 1998).

Bandlow, U., Begander, E., Eckert, S. and Niederdrenk-Felgner, C. (1994) 'Fernstudium und Fernunterricht – ein attraktives Angebot für Frauen?!' in DIFF (ed.) *Report – Literatur- und Forschungsreport Weiterbildung*, Tübingen: Deutsches Institut für Fernstudienforschung.

Bartels, J. (1989) 'Methods and Experience with Course Evaluation at the FernUniversität', paper presented to 3er Encuentro Iberoamericano de Educacion a Distancia. La Planificacion, la Produccion y la Evaluacion del Material Didactico en un Sistema de Educacion a Distancia, April 1989, San José, Costa Rica.

Bartels, J. and Helms, F. (1995) 'Formen der Kursevaluation an der FernUniversität 1975–1995' in Rektor der FernUniversität (ed.) *20 Jahre FernUniversität. Daten, Fakten, Hintergründe*, Hagen: FernUniversität.

Bartels, J. and Nogales Arroyo, E. (1996) 'How did Economics Graduates Benefit from Studying at a Distance in Germany and Spain?' in G. Fandel, R. Bartz and F. Nickolmann (eds) *University Level Distance Education in Europe. Assessment and Perspectives*, Weinheim: Deutscher Studien Verlag.

Bartels, J., von Prümmer, C. and Rossié, U. (1988) *Subjektive Studienziele*, Hagen: FernUniversität.

Becker-Schmidt, R., Brandes-Erlhoff, U., Karrer, M., Knapp, G.-A., Rumpf, M. and Schmidt, B. (1982) *Nicht wir haben die Minuten, die Minuten haben uns. Zeitprobleme und Zeiterfahrungen von Arbeitermüttern in Fabrik und Familie*, Bonn: Verlag Neue Gesellschaft.

Becker-Schmidt, R., Knapp, G.-A. and Schmidt, B. (1984) *Eines ist zuwenig – beides ist zuviel. Erfahrungen von Arbeiterfrauen zwischen Familie und Fabrik*, Bonn: Verlag Neue Gesellschaft.

Belenky, M.F., Clinchy, B.M., Goldberger, N.R. and Tarule, J.M. (1986) *Women's Ways of Knowing. The Development of Self, Voice, and Mind*, New York: Basic Books.

BMFJ (ed.) (1992) *Frauen in der Bundesrepublik Deutschland*, Bonn: Bundesministerium für Frauen und Jugend.

BMBF (ed.) (1998) *Grund- und Strukturdaten 1998/99*, Bonn: Bundesministerium für Bildung und Forschung.

BMBW (ed.) (1981) *Arbeiterkinder im Bildungssystem*, Bad Honnef: Bundesminister für Bildung und Wissenschaft.

——— (ed.) (1983) *Das soziale Bild der Studentenschaft in der Bundesrepublik Deutschland. 10. Sozialerhebung des Deutschen Studentenwerks*, Bonn: Bundesminister für Bildung und Wissenschaft.

——— (ed.) (1986) *Das soziale Bild der Studentenschaft in der Bundesrepublik Deutschland. 11. Sozialerhebung des Deutschen Studentenwerks*, Bonn: Bundesminister für Bildung und Wissenschaft.

——— (ed.) (1989) *Das soziale Bild der Studentenschaft in der Bundesrepublik Deutschland. 12. Sozialerhebung des Deutschen Studentenwerks*, Bonn: Bundesminister für Bildung und Wissenschaft.

Boothroyd, B. (1994) 'Foreword' in P.W. Lunneborg (ed.) *OU Women. Undoing Educational Obstacles*. New York: Cassell.

Bröhl, G.R. (1981) 'Eine provozierende Frage: Ist das Fernstudium "frauenfeindlich"? Einige statistische Daten geben Aufschlüsse', con-tacte. *Zeitschrift für Studenten der FernUniversität* 1981, 1: 25–8.

Bublitz, H. (1980) *Ich gehörte irgendwie so nirgends hin . . . : Arbeitertöchter an der Hochschule*, Gießen: Focus Verlag.

Burge, E.J. (1988) 'Foreword' in K. Faith (ed.) *Toward New Horizons for Women in Distance Education. International Perspectives*, London: Routledge.

——— (1990) 'Women as Learners: Issues for Visual and Virtual Classrooms', *The Canadian Journal for the Study of Adult Education*, 4, 2: 1–24.

——— (1995) 'Electronic Highway or weaving loom? Thinking about conferencing technologies for learning' in F. Lockwood (ed.) *Open and Distance Learning Today*, London: Routledge.

——— (1997) 'Gender in distance education'. Manuscript for publication in a book edited by Chère Campbell Gibson. Madison: University of Wisconsin.

Burge, E.J. and Lenskyj, H. (1990) 'Women Studying in Distance Education: Issues and Principles', *Journal of Distance Education* 5, 1: 20–37.

Crompton, R. (1993) *Class and Stratification. An Introduction to Current Debates*, Cambridge: Polity Press.

Davoust, M. (1996) 'The same but different – a study of the differences in interaction among participants in three distance courses'. Unpublished M.A. Thesis. English summary on-line: e-mail: Marie.Davoust@mailbox.swipnet.se (17 August 1997).

Dickenhorst, C., Fürstenberg, A., Metzger, S., Rauch, A., Rosigkeit, V. and Theobald, H. (1992) *Kommen Sie auch aus der BILDUNGSFERNE? Reader zum Projekttutorium 'Studiensituation von ArbeiterInnentöchtern an der Hochschule'*, Berlin: Freie Universität.

Easlea, B. (1973) *Liberation and the Aims of Science. An Essay on Obstacles to the Building of a Beautiful World*, London: Chatto & Windus/Sussex University Press.

Ehmann, C. (1978) *Fernstudium in Deutschland*, Köln: Verlagsgesellschaft Schulfernsehen.

Engler, S. and von Prümmer, C. (1993) 'Studienfach, Geschlecht, "soziale Herkunft". Zum Verhältnis von Geschlecht und Klasse an der Hochschule' in A. Schlüter (ed.) *Bildungsmobilität. Studien zur Individualisierung von Arbeitertöchtern in der Moderne*, Weinheim: Deutscher Studien Verlag.

Erikson, R. and Goldthorpe, J.H. (1992) *The Constant Flux: A Study of Class Mobility in Industrial Societies*, Oxford: Clarendon Press.

Faith, K. (1988a) 'Naming the Problem' in K. Faith (ed.) *Toward New Horizons for Women in Distance Education. International Perspectives*, London: Routledge.

—— (ed.) (1988b) *Toward New Horizons for Women in Distance Education. International Perspectives*, London: Routledge.

Faith, K. and Coulter, R. (1988) 'Home study; keeping women in their place?' in D. Sewart and J.S. Daniel (eds) *Developing Distance Education*, Oslo: ICDE.

Farnes, N. (1993) 'Open University community education: emancipation or domestication?' in A. Tait (ed.) *Key issues in open learning – a reader. An anthology from the journal Open Learning 1986–1992*, Harlow: Longman.

FeU (1979) *Studentenstatistik 1975–1980. Ausgewählte Daten zur Entwicklung der Studentenschaft*, Hagen: FernUniversität.

—— (1980 ff) *Studentinnen- und Studentenstatistik. Ausgewählte Daten zur Struktur der Studentenschaft*, Hagen: FernUniversität.

—— (1993) *Abschlußbericht des Projektes zur Förderung von Frauen in mathematisch-ingenieurwissenschaftlichen und wirtschaftswissenschaftlichen Studiengängen an der FernUniversität–Gesamthochschule– in Hagen*, Hagen: FernUniversität.

—— (1998a) *Das Studium an der FernUniversität. Informationen zum Studium*, Hagen: FernUniversität.

—— (1998b) *LVU. Lernraum Virtuelle Universität. Antrag der FernUniversität auf Förderung des Leitprojekts 'Lernraum virtuelle Universität' im Rahmen des BMBF-Wettbewerbs 'Nutzung des weltweit verfügbaren Wissens für Aus- und Weiterbildung und Innovationsprozesse'*, Hagen: FernUniversität.

—— (1999a) *General Prospectus. Study Opportunities*, Hagen: FernUniversität.

—— (1999b) *Studentinnen- und Studentenstatistik. Entwicklung der Studierenden vom WS 1975/76–WS 1998/99*, Hagen: FernUniversität.

Geiersbach, F.-W. (1981) 'Öffnung der Fernuniversität – Bedingungen und hochschulinterne Diskussion einer bildungspolitischen Innovation', *Zeitschrift für Hochschuldidaktik* 5, 3–4: 501–10.

Gilligan, C. (1982) *In a Different Voice. Psychological Theory and Women's Development*, Cambridge, MA: Harvard University Press.

Groten, H. (1992) 'The role of Study Centres at the FernUniversität', *Open Learning* 7, 1: 50–6.

Hauff, M., Kirkup, G. and von Prümmer, C. (1999) *Frauen und neue Medien. Nutzen des Internets am Arbeitsplatz Hochschule und im Studium*, Hagen: FernUniversität.

Heiler, P. and Richards, W. (1988) 'By Print and Post: Vocational Training for Isolated Women (Australia)' in K. Faith (ed.) *Toward New Horizons for Women in Distance Education. International Perspectives*, London: Routledge.

Heinze, I. (1980) 'Probleme einer studierenden Hausfrau', *Mentor* 1980, 8: 10–12.

Herbst, I.M. (1992) 'Distance learning for women in the family period', *INBJUDAN – Distansundervisning*, June: 2–4.

—— (1993) 'Bericht über bisherigen Verlauf und Programmatik des Forschungs-projektes "Weiterbildung für Familienfrauen durch Fernunterricht" der Bergischen Universität GHS Wuppertal zur Vorlage beim BIBB', unpublished manuscript.

Herbst, I.M., Müller, H.J. and Voelker, S. (1994) *'Mütter lernen anders!' Eine Studie zur Weiterbildung für Familienfrauen durch Fernunterricht*, Wuppertal: Bergische Universität-Gesamthochschule Wuppertal.

Heron, M. (1997) *In my own skin. Dialogues with women students, tutors and counsellors. Researching reality, meaning, change and growth in the Open University*, Milton Keynes: Regional Academic Services of the Open University.

Hoerning, E.M. and Krais, B. (1987) 'Der Ausbruch aus der Normalbiographie. Milieu-untypische Lebensläufe von Arbeitertöchtern' in A. Bolder and K. Rodax (eds) *Das Prinzip der aufge(sc)hobenen Belohnung. Die Sozialisation von Arbeiterkindern für den Beruf*, Bonn: Verlag Neue Gesellschaft.

HRK (1995) *Rundschreiben* No. 3/95, Bonn: Hochschulrektorenkonferenz.

Humm, M. (1989) *The dictionary of feminist theory*, New York: Harvester Wheatsheaf.

Jenkins, J. (1995) 'Past Distance' in D. Sewart (ed.) *One World Many Voices: Quality in Open and Distance Learning*, Milton Keynes: ICDE and The Open University.

Kirkup, G. (1988) 'Sowing Seeds: Initiatives for Improving the Representation of Women (United Kingdom)', in K. Faith (ed.) *Toward New Horizons for Women in Distance Education. International Perspectives*, London: Routledge.

—— (1995) 'The Importance of Gender as a Category in Open and Distance Learning' Keynote paper given to the Cambridge International Conference on Open and Distance Learning 3–5 July 1995, Cambridge. Published version: Kirkup, G. (1996) 'The Importance of Gender' in R. Mills and A. Tait (eds) *Supporting the Learner in Open and Distance Learning*, London: Pitman.

—— (1997) 'Telematics and Gender in Distance Education'. Paper given at Sheffield Hallam University 23 April 1997.

Kirkup, G. and Keller, L.S. (1992) *Inventing Women. Science, Technology and Gender*, Cambridge: Polity Press.

Kirkup, G. and von Prümmer, C. (1990) 'Support and Connectedness: The Needs of Women Distance Education Students', *Journal of Distance Education* 5, 2: 9–31.

—— (1992) *Value of Study Centres and Support Services for Women and Men in a Comparative Perspective. Selective Results from a Research Project at the FernUniversität and the Open University*, Hagen: FernUniversität.

—— (1996) 'How Can Distance Education Address the Particular Needs of European Women?' in G. Fandel, R. Bartz and F. Nickolmann (eds) *University Level Distance Education in Europe. Assessment and Perspectives*, Weinheim: Deutscher Studien Verlag.

—— (1997) 'Distance Education for European Women. The Threats and Opportunities of New Educational Forms and Media', *European Journal of Women's Studies* 4, 1: 39–62.

Kirkup, G. and Abbott, J. (1997) *The Gender Gap. A Gender Analysis of the 1996 Computing Access Survey*, Milton Keynes: The Open University.

Kirkup, G., Jones, A., Jelfs, A., Kirkwood, A. and Taylor, J. (1995) 'Diversity, openness and domestic information and communication technologies' in D. Sewart (ed.) *One World Many Voices: Quality in Open and Distance Learning*, Milton Keynes: ICDE and The Open University.

Kirkwood, A. (1995) 'Over the threshold. Media technologies for home learning' in F. Lockwood (ed.) *Open and Distance Learning Today*, London: Routledge.

Körnig, H. (1979) *Bildungsexpansion und Fernstudium als bildungs- und gesellschafts-politische Aufgaben*, München: Minerva Publikation.

—— (1985) 'Distance Education as a Social Chance for Women' Paper presented to the ICDE Conference, August 1985: Melbourne.

Kuhn, T.S. (1970) *The Structure of Scientific Revolutions*, (2nd edn, first published 1964) Chicago: The University of Chicago Press.

Laurillard, D. (1995) *Multimedia and the changing experience of the learner*, Milton Keynes: The Open University.

Lunneborg, P.W. (1994) *OU Women. Undoing Educational Obstacles*, New York: Cassell.

MacArthur, B. (1974) 'An interim history of the Open University' in J. Tunstall (ed.) *The Open University Opens*, London: Routledge & Kegan Paul.

McIntosh, N., Calder, J.A. and Swift, B. (1977) *A Degree of Difference. The Open University of the United Kingdom*, New York: Praeger.

Martin, B.S. (1988) 'Women and distance education in Papua New Guinea' in E. Wormald and A. Crossley (eds) *Women and education in Papua New Guinea and the South Pacific*, Waigani: University of Papua New Guinea Press.

mentor. Zeitschrift für Erwachsenenstudium. December 1980.

Menzies, H. (1994) 'Hyping the Highway. Is the Information Highway the road to a common future or just another trip to the mall?', *The Canadian Forum* June: 3–8.

Metz-Göckel, S. and Müller, U. (1985) *Der Mann. Brigitte-Untersuchung 85*, Hamburg: Verlag Gruner+Jahr.

Morgan, A. (1995) 'Adult change and development: learning and people's lives' in D. Sewart (ed.) *One World Many Voices: Quality in Open and Distance Learning*, Milton Keynes: ICDE and The Open University.

Oakley, A. (1974) *The Sociology of Housework*, Bath: Martin Robertson.

O'Rourke, J. (1997) 'Canaries in the Mine? Women's Experience and New Learning Technologies', in A. Tait (ed.) *The Convergence of Distance and Conventional Education: Patterns of Flexibility for the Individual Learner*, Cambridge: The Open University, East Anglia.

Park, E. and Nooriafshar, M. (1997) 'Student's Perceptions of the Most Suitable Methods of Contacting the University' in *The New Learning Environment: A Global Perspective*, University Park, PA: International Council for Distance Education and Pennsylvania State University (on CD-ROM).

Peisert, H. and Framhein, G. (1980) *Das Hochschulsystem in der Bundesrepublik Deutschland. Funktionsweise und Leistungsfähigkeit.* (2nd expanded edn), Stuttgart: Klett-Cotta.

Peters, O. (1976) *Die FernUniversität. Das erste Jahr. Aufbau, Aufgaben, Ausblicke. Bericht des Gründungsrektors*, Hagen: v.d.Linnepe Verlagsgesellschaft.

—— (1981) *Die FernUniversität im fünften Jahr. Bildungspolitische und fernstudien-didaktische Aspekte. Bericht des Gründungsrektors*, Köln: Verlagsgesellschaft Schulfernsehen.

—— (1997) *Die Didaktik des Fernstudiums. Erfahrungen und Diskussionsstand in nationaler und internationaler Sicht*, Neuwied: Luchterhard.

—— (1998) *Learning and Teaching in Distance Education. Pedagogical Analyses and Interpretations in an International Perspective*, Hagen: FernUniversität.

Picht, G. (1965) *Die deutsche Bildungskatastrophe*, (originally 1964) München: Deutscher Taschenbuch Verlag.

Pravda, G. (1994) 'Regeln für den nicht-sexistischen Gebrauch der deutschen Sprache oder: Wie alle Menschen Schwestern und Brüder werden!', *DGB Gewerkschaftliche Bildungspolitik* 5: 126–9.

—— (1997) 'Frauenzentriertes Denken. Ansätze einer feministischen Analyse zu einem Ausbilderhandbuch', unpublished manuscript.

Pross, H. (1969) *Über die Bildungschancen von Mädchen in der Bundesrepublik*, Frankfurt/Main: Suhrkamp.

Pusbak, B. (1984) 'Chancengleichheit für Frauen auf dem Zweiten Bildungsweg? Eine Untersuchung über die Studentinnen an der Hochschule für Wirtschaft und Politik' in *Karriere oder Kochtopf? Frauen zwischen Beruf und Familie*, Opladen: Westdeutscher Verlag.

Raehlmann, I. (1984) *Arbeitertöchter im Fernstudium: Studieren neben dem Beruf. Ergebnisse einer Voruntersuchung*, Hagen: FernUniversität.

—— (1988) 'Arbeitertöchter im Fernstudium: Studieren neben dem Beruf. Ergebnisse einer Voruntersuchung', *Hochschulausbildung. Zeitschrift für Hochschuldidaktik und Hochschulforschung* 6, 1: 29–40.

Rau, J. (1974) Die neue Fernuniversität. Ihre Zielsetzung, ihr Aufbau und ihre geplante Arbeitsweise, Düsseldorf: Econ Verlag.

Rimbach, G. (1992) *Vom Reformmodell zur modernen Universität. 20 Jahre Gesamthochschulen in Nordrhein-Westfalen*, Düsseldorf: Ministerium für Wissenschaft und Forschung NRW.

Sadik, N. (1994) 'Kairo und die Folgen', *Emma* 6: 36–8.

Schuemer, R. (ed.) (1991) *Evaluation Concepts and Practice in selected Distance Education Institutions*, Hagen: FernUniversität.

Schultz, U. (1989) 'Frauen im Recht – Frauenrecht', *Jahrbuch 1989 der Gesellschaft der Freunde der FernUniversität*, Hagen: FernUniversität.

—— (1992) 'Das Projekt "Frauen im Recht"' in O. Peters (ed.) *Grundlagen der Weiterbildung–Praxishilfe*, GdW-Ph June 1992: 9.20.20.9.

Sewart, D. (ed.) (1995) *One World Many Voices: Quality in Open and Distance Learning*, Milton Keynes: ICDE and The Open University.

Simon, H. (ed.) (1997) *Virtueller Campus. Forschung und Entwicklung für neues Lehren und Lernen*. Waxmann, Münster.

Smith, J.M. (1998): 'A Place of Her Own', *Smith Alumnae Quarterly* 84, 3: 20–23, 31.

SPSS (1997) SPSS Base 7.5 for Windows. User's Guide, Chicago: SPSS Inc.

Tait, A. (1993a) 'Systems, values and dissent: Quality Assurance for Open and Distance Learning' in A. Tait (ed.) *Quality Assurance in Open and Distance Learning: European and International Perspectives*, Cambridge: The Open University, East Anglian Region.

—— (ed.) (1993b) *Quality Assurance in Open and Distance Learning: European and International Perspectives*, Cambridge: The Open University, East Anglian Region.

—— (ed.) (1993c) *Key issues in open learning – a reader. An anthology from the journal Open Learning 1986–1992*, Harlow: Longman.

—— (1995) 'Student Support in Open and Distance Learning' in F. Lockwood (ed.) *Open and Distance Learning Today*, London: Routledge.

—— (ed.) (1997) *The Convergence of Distance and Conventional Education: Patterns of Flexibility for the Individual Learner*, Cambridge: The Open University.

Taylor, J. and Jelfs, A. (1995) *Access to New Technologies Survey (ANTS) 1995*, Milton Keynes: The Open University.

The Women's Studies Center of Umeå (1993) *Feminist Pedagogy and Women-Friendly Perspectives in Distance Education*, Umeå: Umeå universitet.

Theling, G. (1986) *Vielleicht wäre ich als Verkäuferin glücklicher geworden. Arbeitertöchter & Hochschule*, Münster: Verlag Westfälisches Dampfboot.

Thompson, J. (1983) *Learning Liberation. Women's Response to Men's Education*, London: Croom Helm.

Thompson, D. (1997) 'From Marginal to Mainstream: Critical Issues in the Adoption of Information Technology (IT) for Tertiary Teaching and Learning', in A. Tait (ed.) *The Convergence of Distance and Conventional Education: Patterns of Flexibility for the Individual Learner*, Cambridge: The Open University.

Thorpe, M. and Grugeon, D. (1987) 'Moving into open learning', in M. Thorpe and D. Grugeon (eds) *Open Learning for Adults*, Harlow: Longman.

Tunstall, J. (ed.) (1974) *The Open University Opens*, London: Routledge & Kegan Paul.

von Prümmer, C. (1983) 'Report on a study leave spent at Athabasca University, Edmonton, Canada', unpublished paper.

—— (1985) *Gender-Related Differences in the Choice of Degree Programs at the FernUniversität Hagen*, Hagen: FernUniversität.

—— (1992) 'Women in Education in Papua New Guinea and the South Pacific. Book Review', *Open Learning* 7, 1: 71–2.

—— (1993a) 'Women-friendly Perspectives in Distance Education. Keynote 1', in *Feminist Pedagogy and Women-Friendly Perspectives in Distance Education*, Umeå universitet.

—— (1993b) 'Women in Distance Education. A Researcher's View', in *Research in distance education. Present situation and forecasts*, Umeå: Umeå universitet.

—— (1994) 'Women-friendly perspectives in distance education', *Open Learning*, 9, 1: 3–12.

—— (1995a) 'Communication Preferences and Practice: Not always a good fit for German distance students', in D. Sewart (ed.) *One World Many Voices: Quality in Open and Distance Learning*, Milton Keynes: ICDE and The Open University UK.

—— (1995b) 'Frauen an der FernUniversität. Entwicklungen und Trends der Frauenanteile unter den Studierenden und Beschäftigten', in Rektor der FernUniversität (ed.) *20 Jahre FernUniversität. Daten, Fakten, Hintergründe*, Hagen: FernUniversität.

—— (1996) 'Frauen im Fernstudium. Bildungsaufstieg für ArbeiterInnentöchter', unpublished Ph.D. Thesis, Universität Dortmund.

—— (1997a) *Frauen im Fernstudium. Bildungsaufstieg für Töchter aus Arbeiterfamilien*, Frankfurt/Main: Campus.

—— (1997b) *Nutzung und Stellenwert der Studienzentren und des mentoriellen Angebotes an der FernUniversität. Ergebnisse einer Befragung im Wintersemester 1996/97*, Hagen: FernUniversität.

von Prümmer, C. and Rossié, U. (1987) *Gender-Related Patterns in Students' Choice of Major Subject. Selected Research Findings*, Hagen: FernUniversität.

—— (1990a) *Einschreibungen und Fachwahlverhalten von Studentinnen und Studenten der FernUniversität in den 80-er Jahren*. Hagen: FernUniversität.

—— (1990b) 'Familienorientierung als Erfordenis und als Strategie', in A. Schlüter and I. Stahr (eds) *Wohin geht die Frauenforschung?*, Köln: Böhlau Verlag.

—— (1990c) *Value of Study Centres and Support Services. Selected Research Findings*, Hagen: FernUniversität.

—— (1994) *Kommunikation im Fernstudium. Ausgewählte Ergebnisse einer Befragung im Wintersemester 1992/93*, Hagen: FernUniversität.

von Prümmer, C. and Stein, R.H. (1991) *Zur Situation von Fernstudentinnen in der DDR*, Hagen: FernUniversität.

Wellendorf, F. (1980) 'Das Fernstudium in der psycho-sozialen Dynamik der Familie', *mentor* 8: 35–9.

Wormald, E. and Crossley, A. (eds) (1988) *Women and Education in Papua New Guinea and the South Pacific*, Waigani: University of Papua New Guinea Press.

Index

Abbott, J. 127
Abbott, P. 47, 145, 146
Abitur 31, 75, 154, 168
academic reputation: and open access 28–9, *see also* evaluation
academic study goals 188–91, *see also* career-orientation; subject areas
Acker, J. 48
admissions policy 30, 168, *see also* enrolment patterns
Adult Change and Development: Learning and People's Lives (Morgan) 73–4
age 159; FernUniversität students 60–1
androcentrism 41; overcoming 46–8, *see also* gender
ArbeiterInnentöchter 39
Australia, distances 25–6
autonomous learner, perception of distance learner 111

Bachelor of Arts degree 6, 29
Becker-Schmidt, R. 46
Belenky, Mary F. 82, 83
Bildungsferne 147
Boothroyd, B. 139
Brandes-Erlhoff, U. 46
Bublitz, H. 142
Burge, E.J. 83, 84
business studies 7

career-orientation 166–7; choice of course 180–2, *see also* course; study; subject areas
childcare responsibilities 57–8, 60–7, 160–3; attendance at study centres 98–100, 102, *see also* domestic responsibilities; household chores; mothers; Mothers' Centres
children, educational opportunities in Germany 31
class: access to computers 126; access to higher education 31–2; and choice of

subject 176–87; family of origin 146–53; FernUniversität 142–4, 153–65; and gender 138–53; inequality in higher education 35–8; occupation 142–3, 168–70, *see also* social equity; social mobility; working-class women
class origin, definition 142–4
Clinchy, B.M. 82
collaboration *see* communication; connectedness; learning styles
commitments *see* childcare responsibilities; domestic responsibilities; employment; mothers
communication 109–11; preferences forms of 111–17; reasons for contacting FernUniversität 117–19; students experience with ICTs 120–34; virtual university 135–7, *see also* information and communication technologies
comprehensive schools, Germany 32–3
comprehensive universities 29; FernUniversität as 33
computers: access to 126–9; differences in women's and men's attitude to 129–32; and electronic communication 132–4; purchase of 128–9, *see also* information and communication technologies
con-tacte 4
connectedness: collaboration 45; learning style 8–9, 82, 84, 110–11, *see also* communication; learning styles
consultation, flexibility 2
contact *see* communication; connectedness; learning styles
cottage industry, distance education as 55, 68
Coulter, R. 67, 68, 70
course: choice of 180–7; content male-dominated 10–11; material sexist 11, *see also* career-orientation; subject areas
course load, problem of reconciling multiple commitments 55–9